Study Guide to Accompany

Sociology
SECOND EDITION

David B. Brinkerhoff
University of Nebraska-Lincoln

Lynn K. White
University of Nebraska-Lincoln

Prepared by
Charles L. Mulford
Iowa State University

Charles K. O'Connor
Bemidji State University

West Publishing Company
St. Paul   New York   Los Angeles   San Francisco

COPYRIGHT © 1988 by   WEST PUBLISHING CO.
      50 W. Kellogg Boulevard
      P.O. Box 64526
      St. Paul, MN 55164-1003

ISBN 0-314-80572-9

CONTENTS

STUDY GUIDE PREFACE

Welcome to your study guide that accompanies SOCIOLOGY by Brinkerhoff and White. Brinkerhoff and White have written an outstanding text that is interesting, well organized, and very readable. This study guide has been carefully designed in consultation with them to help you in your efforts to successfully comprehend the course material. Each chapter is keyed directly to the corresponding chapter in the text, and contains a series of exercises that will allow you to actively participate in the learning process.

To achieve the greatest success in the course, we suggest you first carefully read the whole chapter paying very close attention to the key terms printed in boldface type. Your ability to master these concepts and to apply them to a variety of situations will be an important factor in doing well in the course. Also, don't forget to include in your studies the "Focus on" and "Issues" section of each chapter.

Once you are reasonably satisfied that you have a solid grasp of the chapter, turn to the study guide and carefully examine each of the learning objectives. The learning objectives are the key to success because they are the concepts that have been singled out as the most important in each chapter. Failure to master these most basic learning objectives will undoubtedly lead to poor performance on examinations. Keeping this in mind, thoroughly and completely answer each learning objective. If you have a difficult time understanding a particular objective, return to the text and review the appropriate portion of the chapter. If you still have difficulty understanding what is important in the text, you may wish to turn to the chapter outline in the study guide for a brief overview of the topic. If you have truly mastered the material in the chapter you should be able to successfully complete each objective.

Next, begin the process of self-testing. Start with the matching and fill-in-the-blank questions. Answer each and turn to the key at the back of the study guide to correct your answers. If any of the answers are wrong, review the applicable learning objective and turn to the page indicated and find the correct response in the text. Now try the multiple choice questions, again checking the key and looking up the correct answer in the text. Finally, you should try writing out detailed answers to the essay questions and comparing your answer to the text.

If you have diligently done all that has been suggested, then you should have mastered the chapter. You are ready to move on to the next chapter and, ultimately, the examination.

Good luck and best wishes,

Charles L. Mulford
Charles K. O'Connor

Chapter 1
The Study of Society

LEARNING OBJECTIVES

1. Define sociology and differentiate between sociology and the other social sciences in terms of the patterned social regularities each focuses upon.

2. Discuss what is meant by the term "sociological imagination."

3. Describe the impact of the industrial revolution on traditional values and beliefs.

4. Explain how the concepts of role and social structure lend insight into the "human drama."

5. Identify the major contributions and key concepts associated with each of the following individuals: Comte, Spencer, Marx, Durkheim, and Weber.

6. Discuss how integration into society can be both confining and rewarding to the individual.

7. Recount the historical development of sociology in America focusing upon the role played by Albion Small, W. I. Thomas, Jane Addams, and the University of Chicago.

8. List the assumptions underlying structural-functional theory and note the criteria used to assess the consequences for the operation of social structures.

9. Define the following: function, dysfunction, manifest function and latent function.

10. Note the assumptions underlying conflict theory and identify the two major questions asked by conflict theorists.

11. Describe the basic premise and guiding concern of symbolic interaction theory.

12. Discuss the strengths and weaknesses of structural-functional, conflict and symbolic interaction theory.

13. Analyze the practice of prostitution using each of the three major theories.

14. Differentiate between macrosociology and microsociology.

15. Contrast basic or pure sociology with applied sociology and note the different contexts where each is practiced.

16. Explain what is meant by the term dramaturgical approach.

17. Discuss what is meant by the method of scientific inquiry.

CHAPTER OUTLINE

   I. What is Sociology?

   A. <u>Sociology</u> is the systematic study of human social interaction.
       1. Using the analogy of the theater allows the sociologist to observe <u>social roles</u> within the context of a broader <u>social structure</u>.

   B. The <u>sociological imagination</u> is the quality of mind that promises an understanding of the intimate realities of ourselves in connection with larger social realities (<u>Mills</u>).
       1. The sociological imagination allows us to see our personal troubles within a broader social and historical context.
           (a) Problems of this nature are often beyond the control of individuals and may require changing the structure of society to affect a solution.
           (b) Social structure and roles thus become important determinants of human behavior.

   C. Sociology is one of the social sciences, and as such, shares an emphasis on the <u>scientific method</u> as the best approach to knowledge. This means relying upon critical and systematic examination of evidence utilizing moral neutrality.
       1. The subject of scientific sociological inquiry is <u>patterned social regularities</u>. Specifically, the systematic study of social interaction.

(a) All the social sciences are interested in some-
what differing patterned social regularities.

II. The Emergence of Sociology

   A. The emergence of sociology coincided with the rise of
the industrial revolution in western Europe during the
18th and 19th centuries.
      1. The industrial revolution produced radical changes
in the basic structures of society.
      (a) The newly discovered methods of science were
now turned upon society in order to understand
and possibly control the tumultuous changes
that occurred.

   B. The founders of sociology were philosophers, econo-
mists, and preachers.
      1. August Comte (1798-1857) was considered the founder
of sociology. In fact, he even coined the term
sociology.
      (a) He urged the application of science to human
affairs and called the process positivism.
Scientists could thus learn the laws of social
behavior and eventually predict and control
that same behavior.
         (1) Comte stressed that the study of society
requires a concern for both the sources of
order (statics) and continuity and the
sources of change (dynamics).
      2. Herbert Spencer (1820-1903) advanced the thesis
that social, as well as natural, life had arisen by
progressive evolution.
      (a) Society was analogous to a giant organism with
the parts interacting to help the whole
survive. This view is still important in
structural functionalism.

   C. The founders of modern sociological theory include
Marx, Durkheim, and Weber.
      1. Karl Marx (1818-1883) was a philosopher, econo-
mist, social activist, and the highly influential
originator of contemporary conflict theory.
      (a) Marx viewed poverty, inequality, and aliena-
tion as the products of capitalism and private
property. Thus he sought to eliminate
capitalism.
      (b) Social institutions such as the family, law,
etc., all develop after and adapt to the economic structure. The idea is called economic
determinism.
      (c) The dialectic is a three step process of social
change in which every idea fosters a counter
idea which conflicts with it. Over time they

            blend to produce a new idea. The steps are
called the thesis, antithesis, and synthesis.

       (d) Applying the dialectic to capitalism shows the ruling class (thesis) in conflict with the working class (antithesis). Marx predicted that communism would emerge as the new economic system (synthesis).

2.   <u>Emile Durkheim</u> (1857-1917) was a French scholar who was devoted to understanding the stability of society and the importance of social participation for individual happiness.

      (a) Durkheim stressed the study of patterned social regularities as being the subject matter of sociology. He called them social facts.

      (b) Positivism should be used to investigate social facts. This included an emphasis on clarifying concepts, objectivity, and discovering cause and effect relationships.

      (c) The social integration arising out of participation in society is constraining for the individual while at the same time providing a sense of satisfaction.

      (d) An individual who is either too constrained or is too unrestrained by society may be prone to suicide.

3.   <u>Max Weber</u> (1864-1920) was a German economist, historian and philosopher whose work provides the theoretical base for half a dozen areas of sociological inquiry.

      (a) In order to understand the behavior of the individual it is necessary to understand the meanings the individual attributes to that behavior. This approach is called <u>verstehen sociology</u>.

      (b) Weber rejected Marx's theme of economic determinism and instead stressed the interplay between social and economic factors. In The Protestant Ethic and the Spirit of Capitalism, Weber argued that Protestant religious values were necessary for the rise of the economic system of capitalism.

      (c) Sociology for Weber must be practiced so as to be <u>value free</u>.

D.   Sociology in the United States shared the same intellectual roots as European sociology and featured a concern with social problems, a reforming rather than a radical approach and an emphasis on the scientific approach.

1.   The pioneers included <u>William Graham Sumner</u>, an evolutionary theorist who studied folkways and <u>Albion Small</u> who founded the first department of sociology, wrote the first sociology textbook and founded the American Journal of Sociology.

2. The <u>University of Chicago</u> dominated American sociology until the middle of this century. It is re-
nowned for its interest in social problems and an
emphasis on the subjective meanings of social
action.
   (a) Early sociologists of note who were at the
       "Chicago School" included Robert Park, Charles
       Horton Cooley, George Herbert Mead, and W. I.
       Thomas.
       (1) <u>W. I. Thomas</u> pioneered an innovative
           research methodology for verstehen sociol-
           ogy called participant observation. He
           also originated the concept of the <u>defini-
           tion of the situation</u>.
       (2) <u>Jane Addams</u> was typical of early activists
           in sociology.
3. American sociologists grew in number from approximately 100 at the turn of the century to over
12,000 today.
   (a) Today America leads the world in the number of
       sociologists and nearly every college in the
       country features a program in sociology.
   (b) The professional association representing most
       sociologists is the American Sociological
       Association.

III. Current Perspectives in Sociology

   A. <u>Structural-functional</u> theory has its roots in natural
      sciences and in the analogy between society and an
      organism. This perspective directs attention to iden-
      tifying the structures of society and how they
      function.
      1. The assumptions of structural functionalism.
         (a) Stability -- whether or not a structure or
             social pattern contributes to the mainten-
             ance of society.
         (b) Harmony -- as the parts of an organism work
             together for the good of the whole so do the
             parts of society contribute to the good of
             the society.
         (c) Evolution -- social structures evolve and adapt
             to new needs and demands
      2. Structural-functional analysis involves two import-
         ant steps.
         (a) The first step is to identify social structures
             or patterned regularities and the roles and
             rules that make them up.
         (b) The second step is to assess the consequences
             for the operation of the social structure in
             terms of stability, harmony, etc. This in-
             cludes looking for positive consequences called

<u>functions</u> and for negative consequences called <u>dysfunctions</u>.

3. An evaluation of structural-functional theory shows that in practice a strong emphasis is placed upon judging structures primarily by the degree to which they contribute to the maintenance or status quo of society.

  (a) Structural-functional theory tends to produce a static and conservative analysis of social systems that appeal to those who wish to preserve society and not to those who seek to change it.

B. <u>Conflict theory</u> sees the world in terms of conflict and change. Conflict theory critically examines the role of competition and conflict in society and emphasizes the processes by which some people are winners and others losers.

1. The assumptions of conflict theory.

  (a) The dialectic - that change occurs through (a three step process of) conflict rather than through evolution.

  (b) Economic determinism - economic competition is at the root of all social relationships.

  (c) Social activism - that the first task of social analysis is social criticism.

2. Analyzing conflict theory.

  (a) Conflict theorists ask two basic questions: How is access to scarce resources built into social structure? How do tensions arising from this inequality affect change and stability?

  (b) Concerns focus upon identifying the way social structures give people unequal access to scarce resources and the processes through which those with advantages manage to protect them.

  (c) Conflict is seen as the ultimate source of social change with the tensions producing conflict arising from the consequences of inequality and competition.

3. Evaluating conflict theory shows that it produces a critical picture of society that focuses on conflict while ignoring important issues related to stability, order, and predictability in society.

  (a) A critical view evaluating what is good and bad for society runs counter to the value free position of most sociologists.

C. <u>Symbolic interaction theory</u> addresses the subjective meanings of human acts and the processes through which people come to develop and communicate shared meanings. Consequently, this perspective focuses on the everyday aspects of social life.

1. Guiding assumptions of symbolic interaction theory.
   (a) Interaction is made possible by the development of shared symbolic meanings.
       (1) The acquisition of language allows us to understand both simple and subtle symbolic meanings.
   (b) Symbolic interactionists are concerned with the process through which people learn the symbolic frameworks of their culture.
   (c) Mechanisms for learning include what we learn from our family and friends as well as the roles set for us by society.
2. Role theory and the dramaturgical perspective.
   (a) Role playing is the foundation of the dramaturgical perspective.
   (b) This perspective was developed by Erving Goffman (1922–1982) and uses the analogy of the theater to focus on the minor dramas of everyday life.
   (c) Through role playing the individual actor is able to manage a particular type of impression. Terms utilized include: role, script, performance, front stage performance, backstage performance, and props.
   (d) A key dimension centers upon the personal identity shifts that occur with the playing of different roles.
3. An evaluation of symbolic interaction theory shows that its focus is on small groups and daily face to face interaction. It explains how roles and social structure become an inseparable or natural part of human existence.
   (a) The major weakness stems from a lack of emphasis on larger social structures.

D. Each theoretical perspective can be used as a photographer uses interchangeable lenses, i.e., to accentuate some aspect of the social scene.
   1. Conflict theory and functional theory are better suited for the study of larger social structures, or macrosciology, while symbolic interaction theory is better suited to the study of interactions among individuals or microsociology.

IV. Sociologists at Work

A. Four out of five sociologists are employed in college
and university settings where they teach and do
research.
1. <u>Basic or pure sociology</u> seeks to understand some
aspect of human behavior.
2. <u>Applied sociology</u> seeks to provide immediate
answers to problems.
(a) Sociologists employed to do applied research
may be employed in government, business, or
nonprofit organizations.

MATCHING

A. Comte

B. Spencer

C. Marx

D. Durkheim

E. Weber

F. Goffman

G. W. I. Thomas

H. Structural-Functional
Theory

I. Conflict Theory

J. Symbolic Interaction
Theory

K. Pure Sociology

L. Jane Addams

M. Microsociology

N. Applied Sociology

O. Albion Small

_____ 1. Has its roots in natural
sciences and the analogy
between society and an
organism.

_____ 2. Definition of the
situation.

_____ 3. How do tensions arising
from inequality affect
change and stability.

_____ 4. Society both constrains
and rewards the
individual.

_____ 5. Interaction is made possible by shared symbolic
meanings.

_____ 6. Applied Hegel's dialectic to economic change.

_____ 7. Analogies to the
theater.

_____ 8. Early female American
activist.

_____ 9. Value free sociology.

_____ 10. Originated the term
sociology.

FILL IN THE BLANK QUESTIONS

1. _____ is the philosophy arguing that
   the social world can be studied with the same scientific
   accuracy and assurance as the natural world.

2. The dialectic consists of three steps called _____,
   _____, and _____.

3. _____ _____ empha-
   sizes the subjective meanings of human actions.

4. Providing a sexual outlet for the kinky is a _____
   function of prostitution.

5. Urban life during the early years of industrialization was
   characterized by _____,
   _____, and dynamic change.

6. Marx regarded private property and capitalism as the causes
   of _____ and _____.

7. _____ rejected _____
   idea that economic factors were the determinants of all
   other social relationships.

8. The first department of sociology was established at
   _____ under
   _____.

9. "If men define situations as real, they are real in their
   consequences" is called _____.

10. _____, _____,
    and evolution are the three assumptions behind structural-
    functionalism.

11. Positive consequences are called _____
    and negative consequences are called _____.

12. Structural-functional and conflict theories emphasize the
    _____ sociological level of analysis while symbolic
    interaction theory emphasizes the _____ sociological
    level of analysis.

13. A major weakness of _____ theory
    is that it ignores the larger social relationships.

14. Making the connection between personal troubles and the
    larger social and historical forces in society requires one
    to use the _____ _____.

15. Science requires the _____ and
     _____ examination of evidence before
     reaching any conclusion.

MULTIPLE CHOICE

1. The expected performance of someone:

    a. role.
    b. social structure.
    c. work.
    d. behavior.

2. Public issues are different from personal troubles in that:

    a. issues affect a few people and require personal
        adjustments.
    b. issues affect a few people and require structural
        adjustments.
    c. issues affect a large number of people and require
        structural adjustments.
    d. issues affect a large number of people and require
        personal adjustments.

3. He coined the term "sociology" and was the first major
    figure concerned with the science of society:

    a. C. Wright Mills.
    b. August Comte.
    c. Herbert Spencer.
    d. Emile Durkheim.

4. Karl Marx saw all human relationships stemming ultimately
    from the:

    a. family.
    b. education.
    c. religion.
    d. economy.

5. A characteristic of the subject matter of most concern to
    all social scientists:

    a. patterned social regularities.
    b. unique and rare social behavior.
    c. psychological functioning.
    d. historical analysis.

6. The statement that sociology should be value-free means that sociologists should be concerned with:

   a. what is rather than what ought to be.
   b. identifying the major values of a free society.
   c. analyzing how values affect individual behavior.
   d. making recommendations about how to make a better society.

7. When members of an athletic team do what is expected of them during a contest, a sociologist would say that they are:

   a. well coached.
   b. playing their roles well.
   c. talented.
   d. motivated.

8. An example of a public issue:

   a. John can't find a part-time job to help pay his tuition.
   b. John's girlfriend is angry.
   c. John received a grade of F.
   d. many students find it difficult to pay for their tuition.

9. If parents wished to use Durkheim's perspective on regulation and freedom when bringing up their children, they would:

   a. balance regulation and freedom.
   b. provide maximum freedom.
   c. always be strict and when in doubt overregulate.
   d. be noncommittal with regard to expectations.

10. If one's purpose is not only to study society but to reform it, this would be consistent with:

    a. Max Weber's view of a value-free sociology.
    b. the early Chicago school sociologists.
    c. Emile Durkheim's concern for appropriate methods.
    d. Herbert Spencer's concept of progressive evolution.

11. As a supervisor John knows that what counts is how fairly workers think that they are treated. John's orientation toward his fellow workers is consistent with:

   a. W. I. Thomas' definition of the situation.
   b. Karl Marx's economic determinism.
   c. August Comte's positivism.
   d. Emile Durkheim's concept of anomie.

12. A structural-functional analysis of a college would tend to focus on:

   a. the roles that pattern the behavior of students, faculty, and administrators.
   b. how symbols influence student-teacher interaction.
   c. factors that alienate students from college.
   d. the mechanisms of learning that cause some students to succeed and others to fail.

13. A major concern of symbolic interaction:

   a. development and communication of shared meanings.
   b. competing interest groups.
   c. social order.
   d. integrated wholes.

14. The theory most likely used by a sociologist whose analysis of athletics is guided by the question, Who is receiving benefits; who is being hurt by athletics?

   a. structural functionalism.
   b. conflict.
   c. symbolic interactionism.
   d. macrosociology.

15. A guiding assumption of conflict theory:

   a. the dialectic.
   b. stability.
   c. harmony.
   d. evolution.

16. The theory that can be most directly linked to the ideas of Emile Durkheim and Herbert Spencer:

   a. conflict.
   b. symbolic interaction.
   c. structural functional.
   d. dramaturgy.

17. When Weber emphasized the subjective meanings of human
    actions he was providing a foundation for:

    a. positivism.
    b. value-free sociology.
    c. applied sociology.
    d. verstehen sociology.

18. Which theoretical perspective emphasizes the analysis of
    social organization and how it is maintained?

    a. conflict theory.
    b. exchange theory.
    c. structural-functional theory.
    d. symbolic interaction theory.

19. Of particular importance for the emergence of sociology in
    western Europe:

    a. industrial revolution.
    b. wars.
    c. decline of morality.
    d. government scandal.

20. This school dominated sociology in the U.S. during the first
    years of this century:

    a. Harvard.
    b. Michigan.
    c. Berkeley.
    d. Chicago.

21. Early sociology at the University of Chicago was character-
    ized by an interest in:

    a. social problems.
    b. theoretical issues.
    c. revolution.
    d. preserving rural society.

22. The majority of sociologists in the U.S. are employed in
    this sector:

    a. government.
    b. business.
    c. higher education.
    d. nonprofit organizations.

23. The "founding fathers" of sociology all came from this part
    of the world:

    a. South America.
    b. Europe.
    c. Africa.
    d. Asia.

24. The idea that the religious values of early Protestantism
    (self-discipline, thrift, and individualism) were the
    foundation for capitalism is attributed to:

    a. Durkheim.
    b. Goffman.
    c. Marx.
    d. Weber.

25. Students who gain the ability to see even the intimate real-
    ities of their own lives in the context of social structures
    can be said to:

    a. have a sociological imagination.
    b. have verstehen.
    c. be experiencing anomie.
    d. be aware of latent functions.

26. If the trend continues for more and more sociologists to
    take jobs in business or in government, increasingly they
    will emphasize:

    a. pure research.
    b. a disregard for prediction and trend analysis.
    c. work that breaks with the traditions of American
        sociology.
    d. applied research.

27. Compared to other social sciences, the unique province
    (emphasis) of sociology is a concern for:

    a. scientific method.
    b. human social interaction.
    c. patterned social regularities.
    d. human behavior.

28. Generalizing from the factors that encouraged the development of sociology in the 19th century and sociology in the U.S. in the 1900's, which condition would lead to the further development of sociology?

    a. rapid social change.
    b. stability.
    c. disregard for social problems.
    d. disillusion with science.

29. The two founding fathers of sociology who played key roles in the debate over the primacy of economic forces versus social and religious values:

    a. Karl Marx and Max Weber.
    b. Karl Marx and Emile Durkheim.
    c. Max Weber and Herbert Spencer.
    d. August Comte and Herbert Spencer

30. Durkheim's study of suicide focused on:

    a. the loss to society.
    b. patterned regularities in suicide rates.
    c. the personal troubles of suicide victims.
    d. the condition of social disorganization.

ESSAY QUESTIONS

1. Discuss how the industrial revolution helped to break down traditional values, beliefs, and behavior.

2. Discuss what is meant by the concept of the "sociological imagination."

3. Explain how conflict theory appeals to the "have nots" in society and how structural-functional theory appeals to the "haves" in society.

4. Describe the process used by the structural-functionalist in assessing the consequences for the operation of a given social structure.

5. Describe the assumptions underlying the scientific approach and discuss how we use these same assumptions in solving everyday problems.

Chapter 2
Doing Sociology

LEARNING OBJECTIVES

1. Define what is meant by the concept science and contrast it to common sense.

2. Use the following terms to discuss the relationship between observation and theory: induction, deduction, theory, hypotheses, and correlation.

3. Outline the steps of the research process.

4. Differentiate between the following concepts: variable, independent variable, dependent variable, and control variable.

5. Explain the role played by operational definitions in the research process.

6. Discuss what a sample is and note the criteria involved in sample selection.

7. Explain how sociologists conceptualize causation.

8. Outline the procedures, advantages and disadvantages of the controlled experiment, the sample survey, and participant observation.

9. Compare and contrast the longitudinal and cross sectional research designs.

10. What is replication and how is it used in the pursuit of scientific knowledge?

11.   Note some alternative research strategies to experiments, surveys, and participant observation studies.

12.   Outline the research methodology and results for each of the three studies noted as examples of sociological research.

13.   Discuss the ethical issues associated with the experiment, the survey, and participant observation research.

CHAPTER OUTLINE

  I.   The Application of Science to Sociology

     A.   Sociology is an academic discipline that uses the procedures of science to critically examine common sense explanations of human behavior. Science can thus be considered an extension of common sense.
          1.   Science is a way of knowing based upon systematic empirical evidence.

     B.   In science there is a close relationship between observation and theory.
          1.   The goals of science are an accurate description and explanation of reality.
          2.   Building and testing explanations requires the following:
               (a)   Data collected must be systematically and critically evaluated.
               (b)   Generalizations are made when a correlation is found to exist between two variables.
               (c)   Theories are interrelated sets of assumptions that explain why correlations exist.
                     (1)   Science requires the testing of theories to see if the explanations offered are consistent with the empirical data.
               (d)   Hypotheses are derived from theories and then tested.
                     (1)   Hypothesis testing leads to a further testing and revision of a given theory.
               (e)   The process of science is analogous to that of a turning wheel moving from data to theory (induction) and from theory to data (deduction).

 II.   General Principles of Research

     A.   Four important principles underlying most research are variables, operational definitions, sampling, and causality.
          1.   Variables are measured characteristics that vary from one individual or group to the next.

(a) When variables are stated in a causal order as in a hypothesis, the cause is called the <u>independent variable</u> and the effect is the <u>dependent variable</u>.

2. <u>Operational definitions</u> describe the exact procedures by which a variable is to be measured.

3. <u>Sampling</u> involves the systematic selection of representative cases from a larger population.

(a) Accurate empirical data can be obtained by sampling if one acquires a good list of the population and enough individual cases are selected from it in an unbiased manner.

(1) Random selection of sample cases is preferred.

4. Sociologists assume that behavior is not random; behavior has causes.

(a) Sociology relies on a probabilistic notion of causality where the presence of the independent variable increases the probability of the dependent variable occurring.

(1) Sociology uses a model of multiple causation.

5. The research process involves a series of steps where the researcher chooses a topic, reviews the literature, defines the specific research problem, chooses a research design, gathers the data, and analyzes the data.

(a) Finally the conclusions from research are presented to other scientists for critical review and possible publication in professional journals.

III. Three Strategies for Gathering Data

A. An <u>experiment</u> is a method in which independent variables are manipulated in order to test theories of cause and effect explicitly.

1. A controlled experiment requires that the researcher create two equivalent groups, impose the independent variable on one group (<u>the experimental</u> group) and not in the second group (<u>the control</u> group). If the dependent variable appears only in the experimental group, a cause and effect relationship can be assumed between the independent and dependent variable.

(a) Serious limitations arise with experiments due to the appearance of the <u>guinea-pig effect</u> and the influence exercised by the highly artificial setting used in most experiments.

(1) Experiments can occur in the field or every day setting or in laboratories.

(2) No experimentor can ethically expose subjects to any potential harm.

B. <u>Survey</u> <u>research</u> involves asking a relatively large number of people the same set of standardized questions.

   1. Because large samples are used, survey research is an ideal methodology for providing evidence on <u>incidence</u>, <u>trends</u>, <u>and</u> <u>differentials</u>.

   2. Most surveys use a <u>cross-sectional</u> <u>design</u> which takes a sample or cross-section of the population at one point in time.

     (a) <u>Control</u> <u>variables</u> can be utilized to eliminate background factors in order to better understand the relationship between the study variables.

   3. <u>Longitudinal</u> <u>designs</u> follow a sample over a period of time during which some portion of the sample experiences the independent variable.

     (a) Longitudinal designs are more expensive and time consuming.

   4. Despite the use of control variables, longitudinal and cross-sectional designs are less efficient than experiments in demonstrating causation.

     (a) Another problem of survey designs is the misrepresentation of data known as <u>social</u> <u>desirability</u> <u>bias</u>.

C. <u>Participant</u> <u>observation</u> is a method that seeks to examine the contexts of human interaction and their meanings for the individuals involved.

   1. Participant observation has its roots in verstehen sociology and the work of W. I. Thomas.

   2. The major elements of this method are interviewing, participating, and observing.

     (a) The data produced is usually unrepresentative and unsystematic as a sample; conversely it is very rich data on the few individuals involved.

     (b) Examining real behavior, uncooperative populations, and deviant behavior is best suited to participant observation techniques.

     (c) In order to validate the findings of a study other scientists may engage in <u>replication</u> and repeat the study with another investigator.

D. Alternative strategies exist, many of which focus upon the analysis of social artifacts rather than people.

IV. Examples of Sociological Research

A. <u>Kantner</u> <u>and</u> <u>Zelnick</u> studied teenage sexual activity. Specifically, they sought to describe its incidence, trends, and differentials among women 15-19 years old.

   1. The sample was a representative selection of 5,000 young women selected randomly through a complex national sample of households.

2. The interview itself was developed from 24
   informal interview sessions and further
   sharpened by pretesting 406 young women.
   (a) The final version of the instrument was
       administered by white middle-class middle-
       aged women and had an 80% response rate.
3. The research was repeated three times in eight
   years from 1971 to 1979, during which sexual
   experience increased at every social class
   level, at all levels of religious commitment,
   and at all ages.
   (a) A key result was to document the extremely
       sporadic and episodic nature of teenage
       sexuality.

B. <u>Elliot Liebow</u> conducted a participant observation
   study of street corner men in a slum in Washington,
   D.C.
   1. Liebow sought to uncover the relationship between
      the social structure of their community and what
      meanings the street corner men attached to their
      behavior.
      (a) A key relationship for these men was work which
          usually consisted of low-paying, unskilled,
          dead-end jobs that robbed men of self-esteem
          and self-respect.
   2. The typical response was to reject work and hang
      out on the street corner where a set of shadow
      values permitted fictional accommodations that
      permitted them to be men again.
      (a) The shadow values included the theory of manly
          flaws that rationalized their behavior by
          saying that they were too manly to fill a man's
          role, hold a job, or submit to authority.
          (1) This explanation required neither social
              activism or self-hate.

C. <u>Schwartz</u> and <u>Gottlieb</u> conducted an experiment on the
   bystander effect where the research question centered
   upon the circumstances under which bystanders will
   intervene to help a stranger.
   1. A laboratory setting was chosen to carefully con-
      trol the circumstances of the investigation and
      to avoid ethical problems. Two experimental con-
      ditions were created.
      (a) Group one consisted of students who believed
          that they were the lone bystander and that
          the victim knew of their presence.
      (b) Group two consisted of students who believed
          there were other bystanders in the area who
          could help and that the victim was unaware of
          their presence.

2. In the experiment, the subjects (N=127) were randomly assigned to each treatment condition and each was shown a video scene where they believed a person in a nearby room had been a victim of an attack.
3. While 89% of the subjects eventually made some attempt at help, the speed varied with the experimental treatment.
   (a) The maximum response occurred when the subject was the only bystander; however, when others were present, responsibility to help was not clearly defined and people were hesitant to help.

V. Ethical Issues in Research

A. Participant observation research raises the biggest ethical questions which center upon two issues.
   1. Is an observer required to inform subjects that are being observed? The answer--generally no.
   2. Are subjects entitled to biographical immunity to protect their identity? The answer--yes.

B. The major ethical issue in experiments focuses on the fact that deception is almost always involved which may be stressful and harmful to the research subjects.

C. Survey research raises few ethical issues due to the highly voluntary nature of participation in surveys.

MATCHING

A. Longitudinal design

B. Experiment

C. Dependent variable

D. Induction

E. Replication

F. Deduction

G. Independent variable

H. Correlation

I. Social desirability bias

J. Operational definition

K. Participant observation

L. Hypotheses

M. Guinea-pig effect

N. Survey

O. The field

_____ 1. Two factors tend to occur together.

_____ 2. The cause.

_____ 3. A real life situation.

_____ 4. Expensive and time consuming.

_____ 5. The ethical issue is deception.

_____ 6. Most common sociological research methodology.

_____ 7. People do not act normally when observed.

_____ 8. Ethics of bio-graphical immunity.

_____ 9. From theory to observation.

_____ 10. Misrepresenting the truth.

FILL IN THE BLANK QUESTIONS

1. Science is not divorced from _____ _____ but is an extension of it.

2. Repeating a research project in order to verify the results is called _____.

3. Science has the goals of accurate _____ and _____ of reality.

4. Science is a never ending circle of inquiry in which the investigator moves continually between _____ and _____.

5. In sociological research, causation occurs when the presence of the independent variable increases the _____ of the dependent variable occurring.

6. Survey research is the ideal methodology for providing evidence on _____, _____, and _____.

7. _____, _____, and _____ are the three major elements of participant observation research.

8. The strength of the _____ _____ method is the detail about the context of behavior it is able to gather.

9. Patterns discovered by Kantner and Zelnick documented the extremely _____ and _____ nature of teenage sexuality.

10. The assertion that a man is too much of a man to fulfill his expected role is explained by Liebow's theory of _____.

11. Schwartz and Gottlieb found the most favorable conditions under which a victim may receive help from a stranger is when one is a _____ and _____ bystander.

12. The _____ is a methodology that has the disadvantage of using unrepresentative samples in highly artificial situations.

13. The _____ specifies how variables are to be measured.

14. _____ is the frequency with which an attitude or behavior occurs.

15. Brinkerhoff and White found that as marijuana use increased the students grades _____.

MULTIPLE CHOICE

1. Science differs from other methods of acquiring knowledge in that science:

   a. requires empirical evidence.
   b. is systematic.
   c. is divorced from common sense.
   d. is modern.

2. The first step that should be taken in the research process
    after a topic of interest has emerged:

    a. review the literature.
    b. define the problem more specifically.
    c. choose a research design.
    d. gather data.

3. The variable in a hypothesis that precedes or causes the
    other variable in the hypothesis is called the:

    a. sample variable.
    b. dependent variable.
    c. independent variable.
    d. causal variable.

4. The rules that we use to measure variables:

    a. sampling.
    b. operational definitions.
    c. observations.
    d. induction.

5. This strategy calls for a group of people to be surveyed
    at several points in time:

    a. random sampling.
    b. developing an operational definition.
    c. random design.
    d. longitudinal design.

6. The research strategy which involves asking a large number
    of people the same set of standardized questions is called:

    a. participant observation.
    b. fieldwork.
    c. survey research.
    d. experiment.

7. Social scientists who use the inductive method follow this
    sequence of steps:

    a. data, generalizations, theory.
    b. theory, generalizations, data.
    c. data, theory, generalizations.
    d. generalizations, data, theory.

8. Consider this hypothesis: students who use marijuana will have lower grades. Which is the independent variable?

    a. sex.
    b. year in school.
    c. marijuana use.
    d. grades.

9. Let's suppose that you have been asked to help draw a sample of students with the object being to evaluate a newly pro-posed grading system. Which statement would you want to guide your sample selection?

    a. with a population of 25,000 students, a sample of 25 is okay.
    b. since seniors are more experienced, only include seniors in the sample.
    c. randomly select 500 students from all students registered for the sample.
    d. a random sample of 500 students from among those taking a course in Introductory Sociology will be used.

10. These persons are often used as interviewers, especially when few age-race effects of interviewer are present:

    a. young males.
    b. young, middle-class females.
    c. middle-aged, middle-class white females.
    d. middle-aged, middle-class white males.

11. In the study of marijuana use and grades, closeness to parents was what kind of a variable?

    a. independent.
    b. dependent.
    c. control.
    d. social desirability.

12. Which of the following statements describes a trend?

    a. Divorce is more common than it used to be.
    b. Teenage marriages end in divorce more often than older marriages.
    c. 22 out of 1000 married women divorced last year.
    d. The divorce rate is the number of divorces per 1000 married women.

13. Which is NOT an assumption made by social scientists about causality?

   a. some behavior can just never be understood.
   b. it may be necessary to understand a chain of circum-
      stances to explain behavior.
   c. a probabilistic notion of causality.
   d. a model of multiple causation.

14. This method of obtaining data has serious limitations because a researcher cannot expose subjects to an independ-ent variable that might harm them:

   a. survey.
   b. questionnaire.
   c. controlled experiment.
   d. field studies.

15. In a study of marijuana use and grades, it was decided to categorize the students into subgroups such as sex, year in school, or major. This technique is called:

   a. introducing a causal variable.
   b. introducing a control variable.
   c. cross-tabulation.
   d. developing a cross-sectional design.

16. Participant observation includes three elements. Which is NOT one of these elements?

   a. interviewing.
   b. participating.
   c. observing.
   d. large and representative samples.

17. Suppose that you have been asked to help conduct a study of students' interests and concerns. Data are to be obtained by analyzing the kinds of magazines that are found in the rooms of students. What kind of research strategy would this demonstrate?

   a. controlled experiment.
   b. survey.
   c. participant observation.
   d. artifact study.

18. The two major goals of science are:

    a. description and explanation.
    b. description and prediction.
    c. generalization and description.
    d. control and prediction.

19. The major criticism of the research that looked at the possible side effects of birth control pills or the study of black men who had syphilis:

    a. poor samples.
    b. asking about unimportant issues.
    c. studies were unethical and irresponsible.
    d. studies should have been longitudinal.

20. Excellent device for demonstrating causal relationships:

    a. participant observation.
    b. cross-sectional design.
    c. longitudinal design.
    d. controlled experiment.

21. Researchers who do survery research have to be concerned about their response rates. Which is an acceptable rate usually found in high quality, relatively well-financed survey projects?

    a. 100%.
    b. 80%.
    c. 60%.
    d. 40%.

22. Kantner and Zelnick did important surveys of never-married teenagers in 1971, 1976, and in 1979. These studies documented especially sharp increases in sexual activity for which group?

    a. older, black teenagers.
    b. older, white teenagers.
    c. younger, white teenagers.
    d. younger, black teenagers.

23. The research by Schwartz and Gottlieb is one of the recent studies in the bystander tradition spawned by the Kitty Genovese incident. Subjects in this experiment were most likely to offer aid when:

    a. others were present, and others knew the student was there.
    b. others were present, nobody knew the student was there.
    c. no others were present, others knew the student was there.
    d. no others were present, nobody knew the student was there.

24. Participant observation is a research strategy which grew out of:

    a. Thomas's emphasis on verstehen sociology.
    b. Durkheim's emphasis on discovering social facts.
    c. Comte's emphasis on positivism.
    d. Goffman's studies of backstage performances.

25. Science has been described as a continuously turning wheel. Which is NOT true of this wheel?

    a. never-ending.
    b. no beginning point and no end.
    c. you must start with observation.
    d. investigator moves continuously between observations and theory.

26. One clear advantage of participant observation is:

    a. the researcher can see behavior in context.
    b. it is excellent for analysis of cause-and-effect.
    c. it is limited to small, non-representative samples.
    d. it can be done with large, random samples.

27. The best method for gathering data in a study of consumer preferences needed for a national advertising campaign is:

    a. participant observation.
    b. the controlled experiment.
    c. survey research.
    d. social artifacts.

28. Participant observation is considered appropriate for all BUT one of the following:

    a. studying undesirable behavior.
    b. studying behavior rather than attitudes.
    c. studying individuals rather than social contexts.
    d. studying uncooperative populations.

29. The MOST important rule in survey research is:

    a. to do library research.
    b. to write clear and unambiguous questions.
    c. to draw samples.
    d. to analyze tables.

30. The study reported in the text on the relationship between marijuana use, grades, and time spent with parents found that:

    a. marijuana users get higher grades.
    b. marijuana users get poorer grades.
    c. no relationship exists between marijuana use and grades.
    d. time spent with parents raises marijuana use and thus contributes to higher grades.

ESSAY QUESTIONS

1. Fully discuss the nature of science and compare science to common sense.

2. Explain the ethical issues that arise in social research using the experiment, the survey, and participant observation research.

3. Compare and contrast the longitudinal and cross sectional research designs.

4. Outline the advantages of sample survey research as compared to the controlled experiment and participant observation research.

5. Discuss the relationship between observation and theory.

Chapter 3
Culture

LEARNING OBJECTIVES

1. Discuss the difference between society, culture, material culture, and nonmaterial culture.

2. Define and distinguish between the following terms: values, norms, folkways, mores, laws, sanctions, informal sanctions, and formal sanctions.

3. Define and discuss the difference between subculture, counterculture, elite culture, and popular culture.

4. List those values Americans say are important and note those values sociologists identify as being central and significant to the understanding of American culture.

5. Identify and describe the major American values of the 1980's.

6. Use the concepts of sociobiology and biological determinism to discuss the existence of cultural universals.

7. Discuss how culture is uniquely human.

8. Discuss the role language plays in the development of human culture.

9. Outline the linguistic relativity hypothesis.

10. Explain what is meant by cultural relativity and ethnocentrism.

11. Outline how the environment, technology, isolation, and diffusion influence cultural variability and the rate of cultural change.

12. Note how the dominant cultural theme of Inis Beag can inhibit social change.

CHAPTER OUTLINE

   I. Introduction

       A. Humans have devised different methods for adapting to their environments and solving their basic and unusual problems. With time these methods become patterned, shared, and transmitted across generations as a design for living. The basic patterns of the world show re-markable stability and it is these stable patterns that sociologists identify as <u>culture</u>.
           1. There are two categories of culture: <u>material culture</u> and <u>nonmaterial culture</u>.

       B. Language is the ability to communicate in symbols.
           1. Language is a carrier of culture, it embodies values and meanings.
               (a) A loss of language may mean a loss of culture.
           2. Language also shapes and confines our perceptions.
               (a) The linguistic relativity hypothesis argues that grammar, structure, and categories used in a language affect how one sees reality.
           3. The use of a particular language can serve as a symbol in and of itself.
               (a) Distinct languages can symbolize group or cultural differences.

  II. Carriers of Culture

       A. Shared ideas about desirable goals are called <u>values</u>.
           1. While many values may be universal, ex., stability, security, strong family ties, etc., the guidelines for achieving them varies dramatically from cul-ture to culture.

       B. Cultural guidelines or shared rules of conduct are called <u>norms</u>.
           1. Norms specify the means for achieving socially valued ends.
               (a) <u>Sumner</u> originated the concept of customary and habitual ways of doing things called <u>folkways</u>.
               (b) <u>Mores</u> are norms that have strong feelings of right and wrong associated with them.

(c) <u>Laws</u> are norms that are officially enforced and sanctioned.

C. Social control refers to the forces and processes that encourage conforming to the norms of society.
  1. Conformity is encouraged by <u>sanctions</u>--rewards for conformity and punishments for nonconformity.
     (a) Sanctions may be formal or informal.
     (b) Normative behavior and actual behavior may differ.

D. Variations in lifestyle are typical of modern societies.
  1. Groups sharing the overall culture but maintaining distinctive values, norms, and life-styles are called <u>subcultures</u>.
  2. Groups whose unique values, norms, and lifestyles conflict with the dominant culture are called <u>countercultures</u>.

E. <u>Society</u> refers to the population that shares the same territory and is bound together by economic and political ties.

III. American Culture

A. American values, those things Americans feel are worth pursuing, can be ascertained in two different ways.
  1. Survey research asking Americans what they value the most shows that a good family life, good health, and freedom of choice are very important.
  2. Observation of American behavior shows four major categories of values significant to understanding our culture.
     (a) The importance of work and activity.
     (b) The importance of practicality and efficiency.
     (c) The importance of achievement and success.
     (d) The importance of being moral.
  3. An important changing value that has taken on much prominence in the last decade is self-fulfillment.
     (a) This raises a question of the proper balance between freedom and constraint and between commitment to self and commitment to others.
  4. American society is characterized by great diversity and many subcultures. Highly visible subcultures center upon geographic or regional variations in lifestyles.
     (a) Another set of subcultures exist in high schools. These include: socials/preppies, intellectuals/eggheads/dexters and freaks.
     (b) American countercultures include radicals, hippies, beats, and punkers.

        (1) Countercultural influences challenge the dominant values and often a synthesis can occur as in the dialectic.

    (c) Elite culture refers to art, opera, etc., while popular culture is what people like and what people do.

IV. Determinants of Human Behavior

  A. The common biology of human beings probably explains much of what is common to various cultures. The important question is whether these commonalities are adaptations to similar problems or whether they are encoded in our genetic makeup.

    1. Biological explanations are most likely to be offered for patterns called <u>cultural universals</u>.

      (a) One such universal pattern is dominance.

    2. Most early sociologists favored an evolutionary view of the human species.

      (a) Recent interest has focused upon the role of evolution in human behavior.

        (1) <u>Sociobiology</u> focuses upon the biological and evolutionary bases of social behavior and assumes that some human behavior has evolved as genetic adaptation.

        (2) Culture is thus influenced by biological imperatives just as biology is also influenced by culture.

        (3) Most social scientists remain skeptical about the extent of biological determinism.

      (b) The basic sociological position remains that although some behavior may have a genetic base, most human behavior and most group differences are the result of cultural factors.

  B. Language is the most important biological characteristic of the human species and language is seen as the foundation of culture.

    1. Higher order primates have limited reasoning and symbolic capabilities. They are handicapped by an inability to transmit their learning from generation to generation.

    2. Culture is uniquely human due to our ability to pass on acquired knowledge and habits to our offspring.

      (a) Our superior capacity for language provides a distinct advantage – in short, culture is cumulative only because of language.

      (b) Language frees humans from the slow process of genetic evolution and provides a more rapid and flexible form of adaptation called <u>cultural evolution</u>.

    C. The importance of culture in explaining human behavior is critical.
        1. Biological factors explain what is common to humankind across societies, but culture explains why people and societies differ from one another.
        2. Culture is not instinctive, it is not transmitted genetically, rather it is composed of learned ways of responding to the environment.
        3. Each culture provides its own set of guidelines for solving recurrent human problems. These guidelines vary from culture to culture.
            (a) Thus each cultural trait must be evaluated within the context of its own set of guidelines or culture. This is called <u>cultural relativity</u>.
                (1) <u>Ethnocentrism</u>, or using the values of ones own culture to judge another culture, can pose a barrier to interaction by discrediting or diminishing the value of the way others think and feel.
                (2) Conformity and social control are enhanced within a given society by ethnocentrism.

V. Cultural Variation and Change

    A. Cultural variation and change can in part be explained by reference to such factors as the environment, social isolation, technology, and dominant cultural themes.
        1. The physical and natural environment of an area sets the stage for the cultural adaptations of a society.
            (a) Environmental conditions can include climate, terrain, and natural resources.
        2. Isolation or the absence of contact with other societies tends to perpetuate cultural patterns and slow the rate of change.
            (a) Isolation may be geographical or social in nature.
                (1) The unique culture of the island of Inis Beag arose and is maintained by physical and social isolation.
            (b) Isolation tends to produce ethnocentrism.
        3. Technology, or the technological position of a society, can enhance the degree of cultural variation between societies. It can also have an impact on the rate of social change within a society.
        4. Dominant cultural themes give a distinct character and direction to a culture, thus contributing to greater cultural variation.
            (a) A dominant cultural theme may also function like ethnocentrism to create barriers to interaction.

5. Social change can be accelerated by <u>diffusion</u>, the spread of cultural traits when one culture comes into contact with another.
    (a) The industrial revolution and western practices of colonialism have produced rapid social change through diffusion.

MATCHING

A. Values

B. Subculture

C. Ethnocentrism

D. Culture

E. Isolation

F. Elite Culture

G. Norms

H. Counterculture

I. Evolution

J. Cultural Relativity

K. Language

L. Folkways

M. Society

N. Diffusion

O. Mores

_____ 1. The major carrier of culture.

_____ 2. Units of territorial organization.

_____ 3. Shared rules of conduct.

_____ 4. A trait must be evaluated within the context of its own culture.

_____ 5. The spread of cultural traits.

_____ 6. Shared ideas of desirable goals.

_____ 7. Hippie and beats.

_____ 8. Inis Beag.

_____ 9. The customary, normal, habitual way a group does things.

_____ 10. Art, opera, symphony.

FILL IN THE BLANK QUESTIONS

1. Human behavior and group differences are best understood as products of _____.

2. The _____ _____ _____
   argues that grammar, structure, and categories used in
   language affects ones perception of reality.

3. The traditional form of Catholicism practiced on Inis Beag
   is best described as a _____ _____
   _____ .

4. Rewards for conformity and punishments for deviance are
   called _____ .

5. The resistance to the E. L. A. reflects the notion that
   ones language can serve as a _____ .

6. Norms associated with strong feelings of right and wrong
   are called _____ .

7. Within the United States, a baseball bat would be classified as an item of _____ _____ .

8. Culture is cumulative only because of _____ .

9. Radicals and punkers belong to _____
   while socials/preppies belong to _____ .

10. _____ focuses upon the biological and evo-
    lutionary bases of social behavior.

11. An American reacting negatively to the unique culture of
    Inis Beag could be guilty of being _____ .

12. Recent research indicates that _____ is
    the major American value of the 1980's.

MULTIPLE CHOICE

1. Included as an element of material culture:

   a. tools.
   b. beliefs.
   c. values.
   d. norms.

2. An informal norm that specifies customary normal habitual
   ways of behaving:

   a. more.
   b. law.
   c. folkway.
   d. value.

3. A group of people who share the dominant culture of society
    but who also maintain a distinct set of values, norms, and
    lifestyles:

    a. counterculture.
    b. subculture.
    c. society.
    d. nationality.

4. A capacity NOT shared by humans with other species:

    a. distinguish and sign gestures.
    b. combine gestures into rudimentary sentences.
    c. speak true language.
    d. potential for abstract reasoning.

5. NOT a contributor to cultural variability and change:

    a. technology.
    b. isolation.
    c. environment.
    d. biological inheritance.

6. Which of the following terms is used for shared ideas of
    desirable goals in a culture, such as good health, sta-
    bility and security?

    a. ideologies.
    b. values.
    c. beliefs.
    d. norms.

7. Professor Brown wore blue jeans to a faculty reception.
    Several friends kidded Brown about his dress. Brown had
    violated a:

    a. more.
    b. law.
    c. folkway.
    d. value.

8. John has noticed that his boss smiles and is pleased when
    John gets to work at the office a bit early, or stays a bit
    late. John is being influenced by:

    a. values.
    b. informal sanctions.
    c. formal sanctions.
    d. mores.

9. An example of a counterculture:

    a. religious groups.
    b. occupational groups.
    c. ethnic groups.
    d. punkers, or delinquent gangs.

10. When Americans abroad say that "they really find these
    people strange" they are:

    a. being ethnocentric.
    b. expressing cultural relativism.
    c. identifying with a counterculture.
    d. expressing a wish for more cultural variability.

11. Betty has just taken a position with a different
    corporation. She is quite frustrated because the office
    machines are different, the business forms are unfamiliar,
    and her co-workers use many terms that she hasn't heard
    before. She is reacting to:

    a. a subculture.
    b. diffusion.
    c. a counterculture.
    d. mores.

12. The distinct life-styles and values of high school preppies,
    jocks, intellectuals, and freaks are discussed in your text
    as examples of adolescent:

    a. countercultures.
    b. subcultures.
    c. minority cultures.
    d. deviant subgroups.

13. Values and norms can be evaluated in terms of their gener-
    ality and in terms of immediacy. Which is true:

    a. norms have more immediate but less general influence
        on behavior.
    b. norms have less immediate and less general influence
        on behavior.
    c. values have more immediate and more general influence
        on behavior.
    d. values have less general and less immediate influence
        on behavior.

14. Marxists pay particular attention to this factor when they attempt to explain cultural change and variability:

    a.   technology.
    b.   environment.
    c.   values and norms.
    d.   biological factors.

15. Which theory sees in the presence of countercultures the operation of a dialectic?

    a.   structural functionalism.
    b.   sociobiology.
    c.   symbolic interactionism.
    d.   Marxism.

16. Sociobiology is emerging as an important theoretical perspective in the U.S. At this time most social scientists:

    a.   openly identify with this theory.
    b.   are still wary of this theory.
    c.   have adopted this theory but still reject evolution as an important process.
    d.   are rejecting culture as a source of variation in human behavior.

17. Ethnocentrism means using norms and values of our own culture as standards to judge the practice of others. Which is true about ethnocentrism:

    a.   it is always bad.
    b.   it seldom acts as a barrier to understanding.
    c.   it is not altogether bad.
    d.   it is instinctual.

18. Cultural evolution is based on the assumption that:

    a.   the ability to learn and to pass on knowledge to new generations is the major way people adapt to change.
    b.   social structures evolve and become more complex as a result of adaptation.
    c.   biological evolution is the basis for cultural change.
    d.   cultural change is the result of conflict and revolution.

19. Which of the following is NOT identified as a central value of Americans?

    a. loyalty to the group at all costs.
    b. good health.
    c. freedom of choice.
    d. living up to one's potential.

20. The punk counterculture is particularly attractive to:

    a. middle-class youth.
    b. young women.
    c. young men.
    d. working-class youth.

21. NOT a major factor in the development of sexual repression on Inis Beag:

    a. cultural diffusion.
    b. harsh environment.
    c. limited land supply.
    d. religion that stresses fear of damnation.

22. Rights for non-English speakers are NOT supported by the Courts in this setting:

    a. the workplace.
    b. the voting booth.
    c. the courtroom.
    d. the classroom.

23. The closest primate parallel of human culture observed among macaques was:

    a. aggression toward strangers.
    b. adapting to the sea.
    c. practicing monogamy.
    d. development of a symbolic language.

24. The alternative language in the United States that is causing MOST of the concern over the English Language Amendment to the constitution is:

    a. German.
    b. French.
    c. Spanish.
    d. Black English.

25. Norms have to do with expectations while sanctions are re-
    wards or punishments. Real norms, contrasted with ideal
    ones:

    a.   have expectations but need not have sanctions.
    b.   have sanctions but need not have expectations.
    c.   don't require either expectations or sanctions.
    d.   require both expectations and sanctions.

26. If social change continues at a rapid rate, with inequal-
    ities increasing in our society, we can expect to have:

    a.   fewer subcultures.
    b.   more subcultures.
    c.   more subcultures and countercultures.
    d.   more countercultures.

27. While many Americans continue to be influenced by tradi-
    tional values, research has provided evidence of a new
    value that is prominent now. It is the value that
    stresses:

    a.   hard work and activity.
    b.   self-fulfillment.
    c.   practicality and efficiency.
    d.   achievement and success.

28. Which is NOT a basis for the most prominent subcultures
    in the U.S.?

    a.   intelligence.
    b.   region.
    c.   ethnicity or race.
    d.   class.

29. This factor operates to perpetuate differences in
    societies:

    a.   diffusion.
    b.   geographical isolation.
    c.   adoption of technology.
    d.   rejection of cultural themes for cultural universals.

30. The United States is quite diverse in its ethnic, religious, racial, and economic composition. As a result, members of these different groups:

    a. often are in conflict with the dominant character-
       istics of the larger culture.
    b. tend to be viewed as deviants.
    c. often give the appearance of nonconformity, but are
       really conforming to the norms of different subcultures.
    d. are often alienated from much of American culture.

ESSAY QUESTIONS

1. Identify those values that are central and significant to the understanding of American culture and then discuss the impact of the rapid social change of the last decade upon these values.

2. Discuss the role language plays in the development of human culture.

3. What is ethnocentrism, how does it arise and how might it be seen as both helpful and harmful to a given society?

4. Discuss the role played by the environment, isolation and technology in producing cultural variation.

5. Differentiate between culture, material culture, and non-material culture. Select an item of material culture and note how it is both a result of culture and an influence upon culture.

Chapter 4
Social Structure, Institutions, and Society

LEARNING OBJECTIVES

1. Explain what is meant by the term social process and differentiate between exchange, cooperation, competition, and conflict.

2. What is the norm of reciprocity and how does it influence exchange relationships?

3. Differentiate between social process and social structure.

4. Describe the relationship between social structure, status, and role.

5. Discuss the difference between role strain and role conflict, and note the mechanisms for resolving the difficulties arising from participation in multiple roles.

6. Discuss five different factors influencing how well roles may be carried out.

7. Explain what is meant by the concept of a social institution and describe the five basic institutions.

8. Outline the emergence of separate institutions and discuss the extent to which institutions are independent or interdependent.

9. Compare and contrast the conflict and functional views of the role of social institutions.

10. Explain the differences between the four types of societies.

11. Discuss the impact of forced relocation and the subsequent changes on the social institutions of the Ojibwa of Grassy Narrows.

CHAPTER OUTLINE

I. Social Processes

    A. All interaction can be included in the concept of <u>social processes</u>: the forms of interaction through which people relate to one another. Social processes are concerned with the dynamic aspect of society. Four such processes regularly occur.

        1. <u>Exchange</u> occurs when people voluntarily undertake interaction in the expectation of receiving some reward.

            (a) Exchange is one of the most basic processes of social interaction.

            (b) Exchange relationships are governed by the <u>norm of reciprocity</u>.

                (1) Unequal benefits may result from exchange.

        2. <u>Cooperation</u> occurs when both parties work together for something that none could reach individually.

        3. <u>Competition</u> is a form of interaction that involves a struggle over scarce resources. The struggle is governed by shared rules.

            (a) When shared rules are violated competition may erupt into conflict.

                (1) Competition often results in change.

        4. When individuals or groups in competition attempt to neutralize, injure, or eliminate their rivals, <u>conflict</u> occurs.

            (a) A certain amount of conflict is always present in society.

                (1) Positive and negative consequences may follow.

                (2) Conflict between groups may raise solidarity within the respective groups.

                (3) Conflict within a group is seldom positive.

II. Social Structures

    A. When interaction occurs over and over in a similar way it is referred to as <u>social structure</u> or a network of statuses or positions whose interactions are regulated by social norms.

    B. A <u>role</u> is a set of norms which specify the rights and obligations associated with a status.

        1. <u>Status</u> is a specialized position within a social structure.

      2. A status and its roles do not exist independently of other statuses and roles.

      3. <u>Sanctions</u> are rewards for conformity or penalties for nonconformity.

         (a) Role behavior is reinforced by the use of sanctions.

C. The degree to which roles may be carried out depends upon five factors.

      1. Incompatible demands may occur when multiple roles are performed by the same person.

         (a) <u>Role strain</u> occurs when incompatible demands are built into the same status.

         (b) <u>Role conflict</u> occurs when incompatible demands exist between two or more statuses.

      2. The adequacy with which role expectations are communicated also affects performance.

      3. The adequacy of personal resources, the level of motivation, and the adequacy of environmental resources also influence role performances within social structure.

III. Institutions as Social Structures

A. <u>Institutions</u> are enduring social structures that provide ready-made answers to basic human problems.

      1. The basic institutions are the family, economy, government, education, and religion.

         (a) Historically all institutions were subsumed within the family institution.

            (1) Increasing complexity in society led to the development of more specialized institutions.

            (2) The Mormon Church had to alter many of its practices in order to be integrated into the dominant institutions of American society.

      2. Institutions can lose their regulating vitality when rapid social change occurs.

         (a) The Ojibwa of Grassy Narrows had their institutions destroyed by policies enacted by the Canadian government.

            (1) The result was massive social disorganization as social norms, roles, and values no longer applied to everyday living.

         (b) In many cases the social trauma experienced by individuals can only be cured by altering the institutions of society.

B. The role played by institutions is integrated differently by structural functional and conflict theorists.

      1. Structural functional-theory argues that institutions regulate human behavior and provide the basis for social order through encouraging conformity,

stability, and predictability in social
interaction.
2. Conflict theory acknowledges the regulatory role
played by institutions but interpret this as
reducing innovation and freedom while favoring
one group over another.
(a) Institutions are thus seen as functioning as
mechanisms for disguising inequality.

IV. Types of Societies

A. <u>Society</u> is defined as a territorially organized population bound together by political and economic
dependence.
1. Historically many types of societies have developed
with major changes in their social evolution
coming mainly from changes within the economic
institution.

B. <u>Hunting</u>, <u>fishing</u>, <u>and</u> <u>gathering</u> <u>societies</u> are characterized by subsistence economies where there is no
surplus, technology is limited and small bands are
organized by kinship ties.

C. <u>Horticultural</u> <u>societies</u> occurred with the first breakthrough from subsistence economies – the development
of agriculture.
1. Technology is limited but effective in producing a
surplus which allows for the formation of a class
hierarchy and the emergence of institutions outside
of the family.

D. <u>Agricultural</u> <u>societies</u> emerged as greater surpluses
were produced by expanded technology.
1. Many people were freed from direct agricultural
production producing a greater degree of inequality, a complex class system, permanent urban
settlements, and the further differentiation of
institutions from the family.

E. <u>Industrial</u> <u>societies</u> occurred when surpluses were
greatly increased by mechanical, electrical, and
petroleum energy sources.
1. Urban life displaced rural patterns of living.
2. Surpluses were redistributed and inequality
lessened.
3. Institutions became further differentiated.

MATCHING

A. Role

B. Industrial societies

C. Social structures

D. Role conflict

E. Horticultural societies

F. Structural-functional
    theory

G. Status

H. Agricultural societies

I. Social processes

J. Conflict theory

K. Institutions

L. Role strain

M. Status network

N. Conflict

O. Hunting, fishing, and
    gathering societies

_____ 1. Institutions pro-
           vide the basis
           for social order.

_____ 2. Contradictory ex-
           pectations in two
           or more statuses.

_____ 3. Specialized posi-
           tion within a
           social structure.

_____ 4. Enduring struc-
           tures meeting
           basic human
           needs.

_____ 5. The dynamic as-
           pects of society.

_____ 6. Incompatible
           roles within the
           same status.

_____ 7. Institutionalized
           patterns help
           maintain
           inequality.

_____ 8. Permanent
           settlements.

_____ 9. Neutralize, in-
           jure, or
           eliminate.

_____ 10. Bare subsistence,
            no surplus.

FILL IN THE BLANK QUESTIONS

1. The women of Grassy Narrows were forced to become _____ of goods, rather than _____.

2. When the norms governing interaction are violated, the social process of _____ may turn into _____.

3. The first breakthrough from subsistence economy to economic surplus was the development of _____.

4. The subject matter of sociology is _____ _____ _____.

5. _____ _____ _____ that de-fines our roles relative to others, provide continuity, and are an essential aspect of human society.

6. If you do something for somebody, they are then obligated to return the favor. This is called the _____ _____ _____.

7. When contradictory expectations are built into the same status, _____ _____ can occur.

8. Institutions are enduring social structures that provide ready-made answers to _____ _____ _____.

9. _____ is when people work together to achieve shared goals.

10. The reading of the Mormon Challenge illustrated the example of institutional _____.

11. Often the individual is not the cause of a social problem, instead the cause lies within the _____ _____.

12. An important determinant of institutional development is society's ability to produce an economic _____.

MULTIPLE CHOICE

1. In simple societies, all important needs are met through this institution:

   a. kinship group.
   b. religion.
   c. economy.
   d. education.

2. A network of statuses, or positions, whose interactions are regulated by social norms is called:

   a. norms.
   b. value.
   c. role.
   d. social structure.

3. A specialized position within the social structure is called a:

   a. status network.
   b. social structure
   c. status.
   d. group.

4. An enduring social structure that provides ready-made answers to basic human problems:

   a. role.
   b. value.
   c. institution.
   d. group.

5. The kind of society with the most marked degree of homogeneity:

   a. horticultural.
   b. hunting, fishing, and gathering.
   c. agriculture.
   d. industrial.

6. When an individual faces conflicting role demands from two
    or more different statuses occupied simultaneously, we
    speak of:

    a. role competition.
    b. role stress.
    c. role strain.
    d. role conflict.

7. John is good at math and helps Bill. Bill, who is a good
    typist, knows that he will be expected to help John type a
    term paper. This illustrates:

    a. role strain.
    b. norm of reciprocity.
    c. role conflict.
    d. cooperation.

8. Pete is unhappy at work. His supervisor is inconsistent
    and keeps giving Pete different jobs to do and expects Pete
    to get them all done. Pete is suffering from:

    a. role strain.
    b. value conflict.
    c. role conflict.
    d. role segmentation.

9. The ABC agency is trying to attract customers away from the
    XYZ agency. Which process is at work?

    a. conflict.
    b. cooperation.
    c. exchange
    d. competition.

10. This process can have negative results. But when it is
    present between groups, members within groups may be drawn
    closer together:

    a. exchange.
    b. cooperation.
    c. conflict.
    d. competition.

11. In a positive form these reinforce conforming role behavior. In a negative form they discourage non-conformity. They are:

    a. roles.
    b. values.
    c. sanctions.
    d. norms.

12. Institutions can be thought of as enduring:

    a. cultures.
    b. social structures.
    c. relationships.
    d. norms.

13. As hunting and gathering gives way to agriculture, one can expect:

    a. a decrease in population size.
    b. a decrease in division of labor.
    c. an increase in inequality.
    d. a drastic reduction in the peasant population.

14. Conflict theorists emphasize that institutions have this negative affect:

    a. reduce innovation.
    b. help to pattern conduct.
    c. help people learn what is approved.
    d. produce conformity and stability.

15. It is thought that this institution leads the way in triggering institutional change and complexity.

    a. family.
    b. economy.
    c. religion.
    d. government.

16. Role failure among the Ojibwa was due to:

    a. low motivation.
    b. too few resources.
    c. role conflict.
    d. environmental factors.

17. Both conflict and functional theory have attempted to explain how and why institutions change. What is the contribution of these theories?

    a. conflict theory is most useful.
    b. functional theory is most useful.
    c. the two theories address different questions and each is useful.
    d. neither has proven to be very useful.

18. Which of the two major theoretical perspectives are commonly used to analyze institutions?

    a. conflict theory and structural-functional theory.
    b. symbolic interaction and conflict theory.
    c. structural-functional theory and symbolic interaction.
    d. consensus theory and dramaturgy.

19. The leading cause of deaths in the community of Grassy Narrows was:

    a. alcohol or drug-induced violence.
    b. pneumonia.
    c. industrial accidents.
    d. famine.

20. NOT included as a basic institution:

    a. family.
    b. economy.
    c. government
    d. leisure.

21. The Mormons who migrated to Utah challenged traditional institutions. This economic organization practiced by Mormons challenged America's economic institution:

    a. polygamy.
    b. People's Party.
    c. United Order.
    d. Edmunds Act.

22. The agricultural revolution that led to the development
    of agricultural societies occurred about:

    a. 500 years ago.
    b. 5,000 years ago.
    c. 50,000 years ago.
    d. 100,000 years ago.

23. Which has NOT been a result of the industrial revolution?

    a. more people engaged in industrial production.
    b. increased urbanism.
    c. increased institutional complexity.
    d. substitution of mechanical for animal energy.

24. The MOST important change that resulted in the destruc-
    tion of Ojibwa institutions was in:

    a. 1873 with the signing of indian treaties.
    b. 1925 when the paper mill began operating.
    c. 1963 when they relocated to Grassy Narrows.
    d. 1985 when they lost a legal battle with the
       Canadian government to reclaim land.

25. Ted, who is a manager for a retail business, decides to
    stimulate competition among the sales staff. Which result
    is LEAST likely because of Ted's efforts?

    a. higher sales.
    b. reduced personal stress.
    c. reduced cooperation.
    d. innovation.

26. One of the more recent social structures to be institution-
    alized in Western society:

    a. family.
    b. economy.
    c. religion.
    d. medicine.

27. Competition is thought to be especially problematic in this
    setting:

    a. on the job.
    b. in the classroom.
    c. informal groups such as friendships and marriage.
    d. in athletics.

28. Political leaders sometimes use this social process to get people to draw together and achieve greater solidarity:

    a. exchanges with other countries.
    b. cooperation with other countries.
    c. competition within the country.
    d. conflict with other countries.

29. Each institution can be seen as providing a solution to a universal problem. This institution provides for community coordination and defense:

    a. family.
    b. government.
    c. religion.
    d. education.

30. Your text asks whether institutions are agents of stability or oppression. The answer it gives is that:

    a. they create stability and do not rob us of our freedom.
    b. they rob us of our freedom but do not create stability.
    c. in order to create stability they must reduce our freedom.
    d. stability can exist only when there is freedom from regulation and oppression.

ESSAY QUESTIONS

1. Discuss the historical role played by economic surplus in the change from hunting, fishing, and gathering societies to industrial societies.

2. What is the norm of reciprocity and how does it influence exchange relationships?

3. Define role strain and role conflict and discuss three methods of resolving the difficulties arising from participation in multiple roles.

4. Describe the historical process that accounted for the emergence of the five basic social institutions in modern society.

5. Review the problems at Grassy Narrows and discuss how the situation that resulted could not be blamed upon the individuals involved, and how it was the fault of government policies that resulted in the destruction of traditional Ojibwa institutions.

Chapter 5
Groups, Associations, and Organizations

1. Differentiate between group, aggregate, and category.

2. Explain how size and proximity influence group interaction.

3. Note the characteristics of the following communication patterns: all channel network, circle pattern, and wheel pattern.

4. Discuss how social cohesion and social control function in small groups.

5. Explain the difference between a tame shift, risky shift, and groupthink.

6. Discuss the methods used to break down group cohesion among American POW's in the Korean War.

7. List the characteristics of primary and secondary groups.

8. Differentiate between the following: expressive activities, instrumental activities, social networks, strong ties, and weak ties.

9. Explain what a voluntary association is and what advantages accrue to their members.

10. Discuss the correlates of voluntary association participation.

11. Differentiate between complex organizations and bureaucracy.

12. Spell out the current trends in the growth of bureaucracies and complex organizations.

13. Contrast the classic model of organizations with the garbage can model.

14. Briefly describe each of the drawbacks attributed to bureaucracy.

15. Discuss how complex/bureaucratic organizations differ from the "alternative forms" of organizations.

16. Explain how the Japanese model of organizations combines elements of traditional western bureaucracies and elements stressed/exhibited by Japanese culture.

17. Outline the future of paternalism in Japan.

18. Discuss how network intervention can influence a community.

CHAPTER OUTLINE

I. Groups

   A. When two or more persons interact together within a shared social structure and recognize mutual dependency it is called a group.
      1. Members share a social structure specifying statuses, roles, and norms as well as a feeling of mutual dependency.
         (a) This differentiates groups from categories and aggregates.

   B. Group influence is vital in determining behavior, perception, and values.
      1. This may happen consciously (Asch) or unconsciously.

   C. Interaction in groups is influenced by a host of factors.
      1. As the size of the group increases, the time available for individual participation decreases and the distribution of skills to solve problems increases. Interaction becomes more impersonal, more structured, and less personally satisfying.
      2. Interaction is more likely to occur between group members who are in proximity or physically close to one another. This has been demonstrated by observing housing patterns, small groups, and committees.

3. Interaction of group members can be either facilitated or retarded by patterns of communication.
   Three basic patterns are: the all channel network,
   circle pattern, and wheel pattern.
   (a) Physical location and seating patterns influ-
       ence communication patterns in groups.
4. Social cohesion is defined as the degree of attraction members feel towards a group. The amount of
   interaction and lack of turnover contribute greatly
   to group cohesion.
   (a) American prisoners of war in Korea were unable
       to form cohesive groups due to the way their
       captors manipulated membership and social
       structure.
5. Social control exercised by groups is usually informal and includes sanctions such as ridicule,
   humiliation, contempt, and the threat of exclusion.
   (a) Exclusion is the most effective technique.
6. An outgrowth of group processes is decision making.
   (a) Groups make decisions by achieving consensus.
       The convergence to consensus may take several
       forms.
       (1) The risky shift is convergence upon an ad-
           venturous decision while the tame shift is
           convergence upon a conservative decision.
       (2) Groupthink is an apparent convergence that
           occurs when members stifle critical
           thought. Real opinions are hidden in order
           to be supportive in the decision making
           process.

D. One can belong to a variety of types of groups.
   1. Primary groups (Cooley) are characterized by
      intimate, face-to-face association and cooperation.
      (a) The major function of primary groups is pro-
          viding social integration and emotional support
          for individuals. This form of behavior is
          called expressive activity.
          (1) Primary groups tend to be intimate, face-
              to-face, permanent, small in size,
              informal, and are characterized by loyalty
              and nonrational decision making.
   2. Secondary groups are formal, large, impersonal, and
      are formed to accomplish some specific task, i.e.,
      instrumental activity.
      (a) Secondary groups engage in temporary, formal,
          and anonymous interaction.
   3. Preindustrial society featured primary groups that
      served both expressive and instrumental needs.
      (a) Modern society has shifted a great deal of
          interaction to secondary groups even to the
          extent of using some secondary groups to
          meet expressive needs.

(1) Some see this as a weakening of social control in society.

II. Social Networks

A. A social network is an individual's total set of relationships with others.
   1. Social networks consist of either strong ties or weak ties.
      (a) Strong ties are characterized by intense, intimate sharing and weak ties have low intensity or intimacy.

B. Voluntary associations are nonprofit organizations designed to allow individuals to pursue their shared interests collectively.
   1. Participation in voluntary associations is related to personal satisfaction, self-esteem, political effectiveness, and a sense of community.
   2. Voluntary associations can mediate between primary and secondary groups. Participation meets intimacy needs while providing a greater sense of control over our immediate environment. This is called the mediation hypothesis.
   3. Voluntary association participation can be predicted by urban residence, social class, age, gender, and religion.

C. Social ties also occur within communities where close physical proximity encourages social interaction.
   1. Weak ties with neighbors increases social control and cohesion while decreasing deviance and fear of crime.
   2. Some are advocating network intervention to create social ties in communities.
      (a) This could be done by fostering neighborhood networks, voluntary associations, weak ties, or support groups.

III. Complex Organizations

A. Complex organizations are large formal organizations with complex status networks.
   1. Complex organizations have made massive improvements in the standard of living while contributing to a more impersonal social environment.
   2. Bureaucracy is a special type of complex organization. It is characterized by explicit rules and a hierarchical authority structure, all designed to maximize efficiency.
      (a) Weber developed a framework to analyze bureaucratic structures. It consists of the following characteristics: division of labor and specialization, hierarchy of authority, system

of rules and regulations, impersonality, efficiency, and employment through technical
qualifications.
3. Organizations never reach the ideal type noted by
Weber.
(a) The garbage can model sees real organizations
in a more human light where organizations are
like a garbage can full of alternative goals
and procedures. Most become discarded or lost
while others may be resurrected and acciden-
tally implemented.
(b) The degree of bureaucratization is related to
how predictable or unpredictable organizational
activities are.
4. Organizations may be criticized because they stifle
initiative (ritualism), reduce worker satisfaction
(alienation), or create structured inequality.
5. Complex organizations are growing rapidly throughout the world in business, industry, and
government.
(a) The bureaucratic form is adopted by many groups
because it provides efficiency and legitimacy.

IV. Beyond Bureaucracy

A. Many alternative organizations have arisen in recent
years in an effort to counter the hierarchical authority relations typical of bureaucratic organizations.
1. Collectives emphasize democracy and consensus, min-
imize rules, shun authority, rely on personal and
moral appeals, eliminate advancement and status
distinctions, use nonmaterial rewards, and de-
emphasize specialization and technical expertise.
(a) The demand for consensus and democracy means
some sacrifice in efficiency.

B. A more bureaucratic alternative is the Japanese model
that draws upon western efficiency and Japanese tradi-
tions. This model has four principle components.
1. Permanent employment means a commitment to employ
the worker for life while paternalistically meeting
their economic and noneconomic needs.
2. The bottom up management or ringi system features a
process by which ideas are introduced at the lower
levels of organization and are processed upward
giving greater legitimacy to decision making.
3. There is a strong emphasis on developing strong
group identification and company loyalty through
fostering a great deal of small work group
cohesion.
4. The distinctive nature of the Japanese system is
seen to be breaking down and some see the emergence of typical bureaucratic working conditions
within a few decades.

CHAPTER 5

MATCHING   I

A.   Network intervention

B.   Secondary group

C.   Groupthink

      _____ 1. Mediation
           hypothesis

D.   Expressive

      _____ 2. Consensus centers
           upon a more
           adventurous plan.

E.   Voluntary   association

      _____ 3. A systematic
           attack on group
           cohesion.

F.   Group

      _____ 4. Major sources of
           intimacy.

G.   Brainwashing

      _____ 5. A very human view
           of organizations.

H.   Primary group

      _____ 6. Activities provid-
           ing integration
           and emotional
           support.

I.   Garbage can model

      _____ 7. People temporarily
           clustered
           together.

J.   Weak ties

      _____ 8. Convergence occurs
           when true feelings
           are not shared.

K.   Risky shift

      _____ 9. Temporary, imper-
           sonal, and formal
           interaction.

L.   Bureaucracy

      _____ 10. Activities that
           are task oriented.

M.   Instrumental

N.   Aggregate

O.   Complex organizations

MATCHING II

A. Bureaucratic growth

B. Specialization

C. Control and supervision

                                        _____ 1. Meeting socio-economic needs without bureaucratic regulation.

D. Secondary group

                                        _____ 2. Original model of bureaucracy.

E. Alternative organizations

                                        _____ 3. Division of labor.

F. Voluntary associations

                                        _____ 4. Paternalistic lifetime commitment.

G. Ringi system

                                        _____ 5. Acquaintances.

H. Ritualism

                                        _____ 6. Bottom-up management.

I. Standardize activities

                                        _____ 7. Hierachy of authority.

J. Weber

                                        _____ 8. Multinational conglomerates.

K. Strong ties

                                        _____ 9. Intense, intimate, emotional.

L. Groupthink

                                       _____ 10. Rigid thinking.

M. Japan

N. Make bureaucracy more efficient

O. Weak ties

CHAPTER 5

FILL IN THE BLANK QUESTIONS

1. The breakdown of traditional primary groups has forced us to rely upon _____ _____ even for expressive needs.

2. Much of the alienation that people in modern societies feel can be attributed to _____.

3. As the _____ of a group increases, practical utility may be gained at the expense of individual satisfaction.

4. Within collectives the demand for consensus and full participation means some sacrifice of _____.

5. Through participation in _____ we meet some of our needs for association and intimacy while achieving greater control over our immediate environment.

6. Social cohesion is influenced by the amount of _____ and the absence of _____.

7. Two distinct features of groups are shared _____ _____ and mutual _____.

8. The most effective group control technique is _____.

9. Group memberships are vital in determining our _____, _____, and _____.

10. The major purpose of primary groups is _____ _____.

11. The degree of attraction members feel towards a group is called _____ _____.

12. The most efficient communication pattern is the _____ _____ _____ which allows for maximum participation.

MULTIPLE CHOICE

1. This effect causes group members to perceive a stimuli in a similar way:

   a. size.
   b. convergence.
   c. proximity.
   d. social cohesion.

2. Groups that are characterized by intimate, face-to-face interactions:

    a. primary groups.
    b. secondary groups.
    c. aggregate.
    d. association.

3. This consists of all people to whom we are linked by ties of affection, association, or business:

    a. primary group.
    b. social network.
    c. association.
    d. business.

4. NOT a characteristic of bureaucratic organizations by design:

    a. inefficiency.
    b. numerous divisions.
    c. many roles.
    d. ties of authority and subordination.

5. NOT included as a characteristic of the Japanese model of organizations:

    a. permanent employment.
    b. bottom-up management.
    c. top-down management.
    d. emphasis on small-group responsibility.

6. _____ activities or roles provide integration and emotional support to group members.

    a. instrumental.
    b. cohesive.
    c. expressive.
    d. primary.

7. Dorm residents, Greeks, bald-headed men are examples of:

    a. groups.
    b. categories.
    c. aggregates.
    d. associations.

8. When pressures to agree are strong, people hide their real
    opinions. This is known as:

    a. risky shift.
    b. groupthink.
    c. tame shift.
    d. a bureaucratic design.

9. The closest approximation to an ideal primary group:

    a. work group.
    b. family.
    c. peer group.
    d. adult friendships.

10. John is going to open a new business. He wants to organize
    the work so that each person has specific responsibilities
    and can become an expert in that work. Which characteris-
    tics of bureaucracies should be emphasized?

    a. division of labor and specialization.
    b. hierarchy.
    c. system of rules
    d. impersonality.

11. If social workers wanted to work with people having the
    fewest strong ties, they should most likely concentrate on
    people who:

    a. have less education.
    b. are urban.
    c. are young.
    d. are male.

12. Which of the following is LEAST likely to be a weak tie?

    a. a neighbor.
    b. an in-law.
    c. a husband
    d. a fellow club member.

13. It is thought that voluntary associations mediate (provide
    a bridge) between primary and secondary groups. This is
    called the:

    a. primary group hypothesis.
    b. secondary group hypothesis.
    c. mediation hypothesis.
    d. integration hypothesis.

14. This person is given credit for developing the framework for understanding bureaucracies:

   a.   August Comte.
   b.   Karl Marx.
   c.   Max Weber.
   d.   George Mead.

15. Theory would tell us that collectivist organizations will be LEAST effective if this factor is present:

   a.   high personal involvement.
   b.   consensus.
   c.   ritualism.
   d.   democracy.

16. Theorists have proposed that there may be a shift taking place from a reliance on primary groups to a reliance on secondary groups. From society's point of view, what is the most likely result of this shift?

   a.   social control will most likely increase.
   b.   some persons may crave more emotional support than they will receive.
   c.   people will become less reliant upon secondary groups, too.
   d.   people may turn to secondary groups for both instrumental and expressive needs.

17. Both the number of bureaucracies and their characteristics concern many people. Based on current trends, what is the best hypothesis about bureaucracies?

   a.   both the number and their degree of complexity will increase.
   b.   the number will increase but most will be converted to alternative organizations.
   c.   the number will decrease and so will their degree of bureaucratization.
   d.   the number will decrease but their degree of bureaucratization will increase.

18. Which model of organizations argues that personal whim, accident, or irrationality often determines whether a goal or procedure gets implemented?

   a.   bureaucratic model.
   b.   garbage can model.
   c.   collectivistic model.
   d.   whimsical model.

71

19. The communication pattern with the greatest equality of participation:

    a. circle.
    b. chain.
    c. wheel.
    d. all-channel.

20. Which is true about American prisoners of war during the Korean War?

    a. most defected to communism.
    b. almost none died in captivity.
    c. about 30% were informants.
    d. there were many organized attempts at escape.

21. The MOST important factor affecting a person's number of primary ties is:

    a. sex, with males having more ties.
    b. education level.
    c. residence.
    d. age.

22. This factor is NOT associated with membership or participation in voluntary associations:

    a. region.
    b. social class.
    c. age.
    d. gender.

23. Most persons in the U.S. are employed by:

    a. government.
    b. large, complex organizations.
    c. farmers.
    d. small businesses.

24. Approximately what percent of households move in the United States each year?

    a. 16 percent.
    b. 9 percent.
    c. 32 percent.
    d. 21 percent.

25. These are a major source of solidarity and cohesion, rein-
    forcing our integration in society:

    a. aggregates.
    b. groups.
    c. categories.
    d. bureaucracies.

26. This factor encourages group members to take a "risky shift"
    but not a "tame shift":

    a. size.
    b. proximity.
    c. diffusion of responsibility.
    d. communication patterns.

27. Which was NOT needed in the very effective brainwashing of
    American soldiers during the Korean War?

    a. potential leaders separated from followers.
    b. move prisoners about frequently.
    c. promote self-criticism.
    d. torture.

28. Persons are most likely to participate in deviant acts
    when:

    a. primary groups encourage deviance.
    b. primary groups discourage deviance.
    c. secondary groups encourage deviance.
    d. secondary groups discourage deviance.

29. The primary factor affecting the degree of bureaucratiza-
    tion found in an organization is:

    a. size.
    b. age.
    c. complexity.
    d. degree of uncertainty.

30. As the size of a group increases, group cohesiveness tends
    to:

    a. remain constant.
    b. increase substantially.
    c. increase only slightly.
    d. be reduced.

CHAPTER 5

ESSAY QUESTIONS

1. Discuss the correlates of voluntary association
    participation.

2. Explain how the mediation hypothesis works.

3. How do complex organizations or bureaucracies differ from
    the so called collectives?

4. Discuss how social cohesion and social control function in
    small groups.

5.   Compare and contrast primary groups and secondary groups.

Chapter 6
Socialization

LEARNING OBJECTIVES

1. Define socialization.

2. Know the difference between nature and nurture.

3. Describe the effects of childhood neglect and deprivation.

4. Distinguish between the structural and interaction school of symbolic interaction theory.

5. Define the term self concept, identify the part of the self and describe the operation of the looking glass self.

6. Discuss the relationship between role taking, role playing, significant other, and generalized other.

7. Describe how we develop role identities, a situated identity, and an identity salience hierarchy.

8. Discuss how possessing multiple role identities can create a mutable self.

9. Describe how individuals actively negotiate and create their own identities.

10. Differentiate between the self and a self concept.

11. Note the assumptions underlying behaviorism, its uses in society, and the criticisms leveled against it.

12. Identify the basic assumptions of developmental theories.

13. Discuss how socialization continues through the life course.

14. What is self-esteem and how is it influenced by social interaction?

15. Describe how each of the agents of socialization influences behavior.

CHAPTER OUTLINE

I. Society and the Self

   A. Socialization theory draws upon two major disciplines—psychology and sociology.
     1. Psychologists emphasize the development of <u>personality</u>.
     2. Sociologists are more concerned with <u>socialization</u>.
     3. The self is a complex blending of individual motivations and socially desirable responses.
     4. One must understand both personality and socialization to comprehend the nature of the <u>self concept</u>.
       (a) Both the self and the self concept are characteristic of individuals, yet are products of social interaction.

II. Learning to be human: The beginning steps

   A. The necessity of nurture.
     1. We have a biological endowment referred to as <u>nature</u>.
     2. Love, attention, and interaction or <u>nurture</u> are required for us to survive and to achieve our inherited potential.
     3. Without nurture physical, mental, and social maturation suffer. Key studies by <u>Spitz</u> and <u>Harlow</u> demonstrate these effects.

III. <u>Symbolic interaction</u> is a theoretical framework that emphasizes the subjective meanings of human acts and the processes through which we develop and communicate shared meanings.
   A. The <u>Interaction School</u> holds that people are actively involved in creating and negotiating their own roles and self concepts.

   B. The <u>Structural School</u> focuses upon the self as a product of social roles in which one is constrained and shaped in important ways by society.
     1. A <u>role identity</u> is the concept we have of ourself in a specific role. A self concept is the composite of ones role identities.

        (a) The concept of a <u>situated</u> <u>identity</u> implies that
           we have no unified identity, but instead we
           have multiple role identities that are used in
           specific situations.

        (b) We rank role identities in an <u>identity</u> <u>salience</u>
           <u>hierarchy</u> thus allowing us to choose the most
           preferable role in a given situation.

C.   <u>Zurcher</u> argues a middle ground between the two schools
      and offers the concept of the <u>mutable</u> <u>self</u> where we
      develop a self concept based more upon personality fac-
      tors than upon institutionalized statuses and roles.

    1. The <u>looking</u> <u>glass</u> <u>self</u> is <u>Cooley's</u> term for a self
       concept that is based upon how we think we appear
       to others.

      (a) We actively define our self concept through the
         interpretations of our perceptions of others
         and by selecting from among a range of looking
         glasses.

        (1) These interpretations are real in their
           consequences (<u>W.</u> <u>I.</u> <u>Thomas</u>).

    2. Mead argued that we learn norms and acquire our
       self concept through <u>role</u> <u>taking</u>. This involves
       imagining ourselves in the role of the other in
       order to figure out what criteria others will use
       to judge our behavior.

      (a) This is a lifelong process with role playing
         and role taking being influenced first by the
         <u>significant</u> <u>other</u> and later by the <u>general-</u>
         <u>ized</u> <u>other</u>.

      (b) The individual is an active agent in the con-
         struction of his or her own self concept. The
         self is negotiated through the selective use of
         looking glasses and significant others.

        (1) <u>Self-esteem</u> is the evaluative component of
           the self concept, it is our judgment about
           our relative self worth compared to others.

IV. Other Theories

   A. <u>Behaviorism</u> is a psychological theory that assumes
      individual acts are conditioned by events external to
      the individual.

    1. We learn to repeat behavior that brings pleasure
       (rewards) and avoid behaviors that give us pain
       (punishment).

    2. Behavior modifying techniques have been used exten-
       sively. Short term results appear to be effective,
       but in the long run attitudes and values persist
       with the old behavior often emerging again.

   B. <u>Developmental</u> <u>theory</u> assumes that there are a series of
      stages of cognitive development that correspond to
      physiological maturation.

         1. Cognitive development, pioneered by <u>J. Piaget</u>, assumes that one must master early ways of knowing before one can advance to higher levels of reasoning.

V. Socialization Over the Life Course

    A. Socialization is a lifelong process that begins in childhood and continues as we learn new roles and re-negotiate our self concept throughout our lives.
        1. <u>Primary socialization</u> is personality development and role learning that occurs during early childhood.
        2. Continuing socialization over the life course requires that we engage in the process of <u>anticipatory socialization</u>.
        3. <u>Resocialization</u> occurs when we abandon our self concept and way of life for one that is radically different.
        4. <u>Total institutions</u> are facilities in which all aspects of life are strictly controlled for the purposes of radical resocialization; they include prisons, mental hospitals, and the military.

VI. Agents of Socialization

    A. The family.
        1. The most important agent of socialization is the family, which provides the basic nurturance required for normal human development.
        2. Early learning in the family setting includes the mastery of language, the acquisition of basic skills, and preparation for experiences outside the family.
        3. Personality and self-concept are strongly influenced by childhood experience including the family's race, social class, and religion.

    B. Schools.
        1. Schools function to impart specific skills, necessary abilities, and society's central cultural values.
        2. The school also teaches impersonal rules, regulations, and authority patterns necessary for careers.

    C. Peers.
        1. Extended levels of education coupled with working parents creates a social vacuum which may be filled with peer interaction in which learning is non-deliberate and non-authoritative.
        2. Peers constitute the first agent of socialization the child actively chooses.

      3. Peer interaction facilitates the development and validation of the self-concept while providing an arena for the effective presentation of self.

D. The mass media.
      1. Throughout life the mass media bombards us with messages.
      2. Media information is an important means of supporting and validating what we already know.
      3. Adults actively filter media content through the mechanism of selection perception.
      4. Children spend a great deal of time watching television while still in their formative years.
         (a) The actual effects of television on children are quite controversial and highly debated.
         (b) Much of the debate centers upon the impact of television violence on children.
            (1) Eron found a strong correlation between television viewing and violence in young men who preferred to watch violent programs as children.
            (2) Television violence appears to desensitize the viewer, put violence in a positive light, and present violent role models.

E. Religion plays an important role in every society. In our society different religious values may account for significant variability in socialization experiences.

F. The workplace.
      1. A significant part of our lives is spent at work.
      2. Kohn contends that work influences our self concept and behavior.
         (a) Traits developed on the job are also valued in the home.
      3. Occupation is the dominant status in most people's lives and as such influences their self concept and non-work roles.

G. Others.
      1. Throughout life a large number of other organizations, networks, and associations contribute to adjustment and learning. These may include clubs, organizations we join, or even our neighborhood.

CHAPTER 6

MATCHING I

A. Zurcher

B. Mead

C. Goffman

D. Eron

E. Harlow and Harlow

F. Piaget

G. Cooley

H. Kohn

I. W. I. Thomas

J. Spitz

_____ 1. Total institutions.

_____ 2. Media violence and children.

_____ 3. Looking glass self.

_____ 4. Mutable self.

_____ 5. Deprivation in children.

_____ 6. Situations defined as real are real in their consequences.

_____ 7. Deprivation in monkeys.

_____ 8. Cognitive development.

_____ 9. Role playing and games.

_____ 10. Work and self concept.

MATCHING II

A. Mutable self

B. Negotiated identity

C. Resocialization

D. Total institutions

E. Role taking

F. Developmental theory

G. The "I"

H. Looking glass self

I. Self concept

J. The "Me"

K. Personality

L. Generalized other

M. Self esteem

N. Situated identity

O. Identity salience
    hierarchy

_____ 1. When we abandon
         our self concept
         and way of life for
         something radically
         different.

_____ 2. Putting ourselves
         in the role of
         another.

_____ 3. Our awareness of
         social norms and
         values.

_____ 4. A self concept
         based more on per-
         sonality character-
         istics than on in-
         stitutional sta-
         tuses and roles.

_____ 5. The evaluative part
         of the self
         concept.

_____ 6. The unique abili-
         ties and attributes
         of the individual.

_____ 7. The role identify
         in a specific
         situation.

_____ 8. Spontaneous and
         creative part of
         the self.

_____ 9. A self concept that
         is based on how we
         think we appear to
         others.

_____ 10. Facilities in which
          all aspects of life
          are strictly con-
          trolled for the
          purposes of radical
          resocialization.

CHAPTER 6

FILL IN THE BLANK QUESTIONS

1. _____ _____ _____ is the
    ranking of an individual's various role identities in order
    of importance.

2. The _____ school focuses upon the self as
    a product of institutionalized social roles.

3. Psychologists are primarily concerned with the development
    of _____ while sociologists focus upon

    _____ _____.

4. Parents, siblings, and teachers may be referred to as
    _____ because they are decisive in forming
    the child's self concept.

5. Piaget proposed a _____ theory that
    assumes a series of stages that correspond to physiological
    maturation.

6. Primary socialization refers to _____
    development and _____ learning
    which occur in early childhood.

7. The _____ _____ is the
    composite expectations of all the other role players with
    whom we interact.

8. The _____ school focuses upon the active
    role of the individual in creating the self and the self
    concept.

9. Because each of us has multiple statuses and roles, we have
    multiple _____ _____.

10. _____ _____ is the role
    learning that prepares us for roles that we are likely to
    assume in the future.

11. The self is a complex blending of unique _____
    and _____ _____ responses.

12. _____ is the process of learning roles, sta-
    tuses, and values necessary for the participation in social
    institutions.

MULTIPLE CHOICE

1. The term used to describe a situation in which children are reared in a condition of neglect, isolation, and an absence of mothering:

    a. maternal deprivation.
    b. environmental deprivation.
    c. deprivation dwarfism.
    d. total institution.

2. The emphasis in socialization is on:

    a. development of personality.
    b. participation in informal group activities.
    c. learning roles, statuses, and values.
    d. nurturant activities.

3. The theoretical framework that emphasizes interaction, negotiation, and role taking:

    a. moral development.
    b. developmental theory.
    c. behaviorism.
    d. symbolic interaction.

4. During this socialization, a child develops personality and self-concept, acquires language, and becomes aware of significant others:

    a. primary socialization.
    b. resocialization.
    c. anticipatory socialization.
    d. continuing socialization.

5. The most important socialization agent:

    a. the family.
    b. peers.
    c. schools.
    d. mass media.

6. Self concept is best defined as:

    a. the process of learning the roles, statuses, and values necessary for participation in social institutions.
    b. an individuals internalization of social norms.
    c. the unique abilities and attributes of individuals.
    d. an individual's thoughts and feelings regarding his/her personality and social roles.

7. John had planned his schedule so that Sunday evening would be free for studying, but he decided to go to a movie with several friends when they stopped by and asked that he come with them. John was following his:

    a. me.
    b. looking glass self.
    c. I.
    d. id.

8. Jill is attending her first school dance. She doesn't know the new steps, imagines that her date is disappointed in her, and knows that she is a complete disaster. This is an example of:

    a. the looking glass self.
    b. peer pressure.
    c. impression management.
    d. positive reinforcement.

9. John thinks of himself as a professor at work but a husband and father at home. This concept refers to John's role identity used in a particular situation:

    a. situated identity.
    b. self esteem.
    c. I.
    d. role taking.

10. Prisons and drug treatment centers make deliberate efforts to force people to change their established self concepts and ways of behaving. This process is referred to as:

    a. socialization.
    b. primary socialization.
    c. behaviorism.
    d. resocialization.

11. Self-esteem is our own judgment of our worth. Which is true about self esteem?

    a. we think better of ourselves than others do.
    b. very changeable from situation to situation.
    c. we typically downgrade ourselves.
    d. people with high self-esteem are conservative and resist new ideas.

12. Mead's term for the composite expectations of all the other role players with whom we interact is:

    a. generalized other.
    b. significant other.
    c. role identity.
    d. socialization.

13. In the case studies of socially isolated children, the main independent (causal) variable was:

    a. stimulus deprivation.
    b. uncaring parents.
    c. inadequate self-concept.
    d. poor nutrition.

14. Which is NOT a premise of symbolic interaction theory?

    a. importance of symbolic communication.
    b. self-concept a product of negotiation.
    c. necessity of role playing.
    d. emphasis on reinforcers of behavior.

15. An evaluation of the results obtained through behavior modification indicates that it had the LEAST impact on:

    a. animal behavior.
    b. treatment of the mentally ill.
    c. lasting changes in attitudes and values.
    d. persons in drug and alcohol treatment centers.

16. This school emphasizes the power of roles to influence ones self concept:

    a. interaction.
    b. structural.
    c. behavioral.
    d. developmental.

17. Which is NOT true about anticipatory socialization?

    a. emphasis is on ideal norms, not real norms.
    b. advance preparation for roles we are likely to assume
        in the future.
    c. helps ease role transitions.
    d. usually possible to fully prepare in advance for new
        roles.

18. Persons who have learned the norms and values of their cul-
    ture but choose to "march to the best of a different
    drummer" have developed a self-concept BEST explained by:

    a. structural-functional theory.
    b. the structural school of symbolic interaction theory.
    c. the interaction school of symbolic interaction theory.
    d. exchange theory.

19. According to Provence and Lipton who compared physically
    healthy, institutionalized infants with infants raised at
    home, the institutionalized infants showed definite signs
    of mental retardation:

    a. during the first few weeks of life.
    b. by three months of age.
    c. by twelve months of age.
    d. by 24 months of age.

20. Which of the following is NOT emphasized by symbolic inter-
    action theory?

    a. stages of cognitive development.
    b. interaction.
    c. negotiation.
    d. role taking.

21. Which is NOT a total institution?

    a. monasteries.
    b. factories.
    c. prisons.
    d. mental hospitals.

22. Important sociologist who described the "I" and "me" aspects of self:

    a. Jean Piaget.
    b. B. F. Skinner.
    c. W. I. Thomas.
    d. George Mead.

23. In studies of aggression among persons in the U.S., this factor has been identified as the BEST predictor of how aggressive a male would be by 19 years of age:

    a. violence of television programs he preferred when 8 years of age.
    b. number of siblings.
    c. social class.
    d. race.

24. The average American child spends how many hours a day watching television?

    a. 2 hours.
    b. 3 hours.
    c. 5 hours.
    d. 8 hours.

25. Generalizing from what has been learned about neglected children, the effects of neglect:

    a. have been overestimated.
    b. are severe and never reversible.
    c. are severe but in some cases reversible.
    d. always end in premature death.

26. As children grow older, we can expect them to:

    a. continue to respond to the expectations of significant others.
    b. shift entirely from the expectations of significant others to the generalized other.
    c. respond to the expectations of both significant others and the generalized other.
    d. become autonomous and respond neither to significant others nor to the generalized other.

27. If it is true that a person in modern society is more likely to develop a mutable self, this means that:

    a. institutionalized roles will become less important for an identity.
    b. people will discontinue playing social roles.
    c. self-concept will cease to be important.
    d. people will become less flexible and adaptable.

28. When individuals are described as active in "negotiating" their own identity, this means that:

    a. complete freedom of choice exists in accepting or rejecting judgments of others.
    b. dominant roles become less important.
    c. the influence of parents ceases to exist.
    d. people select dominant roles in which they are likely to succeed and selectively perceive the judgments of others.

29. Which kind of socialization is MOST likely to prepare people for responsibilities they will face as parents, spouses, and workers?

    a. primary socialization.
    b. anticipatory socialization.
    c. resocialization.
    d. socialization in total institutions.

30. The Unification Church (Moonies) uses all of the following recruitment strategies on new members EXCEPT:

    a. explaining the importance of salvation.
    b. isolating new recruits from outsiders.
    c. controlling the interaction of new recruits.
    d. giving new recruits activities to perform such as "street hawking."

ESSAY QUESTIONS

1. How is it that individuals come to accept the norms and values of their culture?

2. Discuss the relationship between nature and nurture.

3. In what ways can we argue that symbolic interaction, behaviorism, and developmental theory have much in common as they explain the socialization process?

4. How can the individual be seen as both a passive and an active agent in the socialization process?

5.   What are the three major kinds of socialization and how
     do they operate over the life course?

Chapter 7
The Sociology of Everyday Life

LEARNING OBJECTIVES

1. Define what is meant by the phrase "the sociology of everyday life" and discuss the basic premise of this approach.

2. Discuss the different directions that the EDL approach takes to everday interaction.

3. Outline the basic assumptions of EDL including the concepts of: dialectic, biography, naturalistic inquiry, thick description, and thin description.

4. How are encounteres problematic and what issues must be resolved to manage a problematic encounter?

5. Differentiate between a frame, keying, and altercasting.

6. Discuss how the theater is an analogy to everyday life.

7. What is ethnomethodology? What is its central concern and what hypotheses and techniques are utilized?

8. What is identity work and what strategies does it entail?

9. Define and differentiate between aligning actions, accounts, excuses, justifications, and disclaimers.

10. What is a spoiled identity and what strategies can be employed in an attempt to protect ones self-esteemP

11. Note the three major decisions one must make upon hearing
     of their impending death.

12. How does the desire for approval govern everyday life?

CHAPTER OUTLINE

 I. The sociology of everyday life, or the EDL perspective,
     focuses on the social processes that structure our experi-
     ence in ordinary face-to-face situations.

     A. Concerns for everyday life focus on two different
         dimensions. One is the patterned regularities that
         govern everyday life and the other is the management
         of the ambiguous or problematic situations.

     B. The routine nature of daily life is often taken for
         granted, yet distinct patterns exist for such phen-
         omena as riding an elevator or simply the personal
         space around us.
         1. Civil inattention can be used in public places
             to discourage intimacy.

     C. Social life depends upon routine and predictable pat-
         terns of behavior (Goffman).
         1. These help us organize and interpret our daily
             lives.
         2. The most important routines are carried out
             through talk.

II. The EDL perspective utilizes four assumptions.

     A. Culture is problematic in that many situations are
         unclear as to which rules apply and when.
         1. This requires a constant stream of choices.

     B. Choice may be seen as a dialectic where a conflict
         exists between individual freedom and social
         constraint.
         1. The outcome of these conflicting choices is never
             certain.

     C. Each individual possesses a unique biography based
         upon his or her own personal history.
         1. No two persons are entirely identical.

     D. Naturalistic inquiry is the attempt to understand the
         subjective social worlds of individual actors in
         specific situations.
         1. Thick description is used in preference to thin
             description.

III. The management of everyday life requires the individual to
      utilize a series of strategies and techniques.

    A. Each encounter requires two basic steps.
       1. Determining what is going on.
          (a) A _frame_ is roughly identical to a definition
             of the situation.
             (1) It is a set of explanations about the
                 nature of the interaction taking place.
             (2) The frame is open to negotiation between
                 actors.
             (3) _Keying_ is the process of revising the frame
                 for an encounter by redefining what is
                 going on. Douglas' work on nudity is a
                 good example.
       2. The second step is to determine what identities
         will be granted.
          (a) The identities are tied to the specific
             situation.
          (b) This is called identity negotiation.
             (1) _Altercasting_ is the process of trying to
                 manipulate others into taking on certain
                 identities. This is a verbal process.

    B. _Dramaturgy_ (Goffman) views social situations as scenes
       manipulated by the actors in order to convey the de-
       sired impression to the audience.
       1. Interaction is seen through the analogy of the
         theater with its stage, sets, props, actors,
         audience, front region, and back region.
       2. In real life ones mode of dress, body language,
         and nonverbal cues are all utilized to manipulate
         the definition of the situation.

IV. _Ethnomethodology_ (Garfinkel) consists of the everyday stra-
      tegies that individuals use to study and organize their
      world.

    A. Interaction begins with a working hypothesis about what
       is going on. We then watch others' reactions.
       1. A central focus of this approach is to discover the
         common understandings individuals use in makiing
         sense of otheir world.
          (a) One such major hypothesis is that people are
             who they appear to be.
          (b) Another hypothesis is that others share our
             symbolic worlds.
             (1) This is a crucial assumption of all
                 interaction.
          (c) Bringing common understandings into the open
             may be done by the use of _break_ _experiments_.
             (1) Interaction is broken down when one delib-
                 erately fails to share symbolic worlds.

V. Identity work consists of managing identities to sustain our self-esteem.

   A. We manage our identities to maximize social approval.

   B. Two techniques of identity work are avoiding blame and gaining credit.
      1. Breaking rules may require that we protect our self-esteem to avoid blame.
         (a) Aligning actions are verbal efforts to restore trust and assure meaningful interaction in the face of some problematic situation.
            (1) Accounts are explanations of unexpected or untoward behavior. Two types are excuses and justifications.
            (2) A disclaimer is a verbal device employed to ward off defeat in advance of doubts and negative reactions that might result from his or her conduct.

   C. Spoiled identities are those identities that are actively rejected by society.
      1. One can manage these identities by three techniques.
         (a) Physically withdrawing from interaction.
         (b) Trying to pass.
         (c) Denying the accuracy of the label.

MATCHING

A. Disclaimers

B. Zurcher

C. Excuses

D. Keying

E. Goffman

F. Justifications

G. Accounts

H. Break experiment

I. Aligning actions

J. Civil inattention

K. Frame

L. Ethnomethodology

M. Garfinkel

N. Identity work

_____ 1. Redefining an encounter.

_____ 2. Verbal efforts to restore trust.

_____ 3. Verbal efforts to ward off defeat.

_____ 4. Everyday strategies individuals use to study and organize their world.

_____ 5. Admitting a bad act that was supposedly unavoidable.

_____ 6. Admitting a bad act and rationalizing it by appeal to another rule.

_____ 7. An answer to the question--what is going on here.

_____ 8. Explanations of unexpected or untoward behavior.

_____ 9. Polite acknowledgement and then social withdrawal.

_____ 10. Managing identities to support and sustain our self-esteem.

CHAPTER 7

FILL IN THE BLANK QUESTIONS

1. Norms about personal space are closely related to _____ _____.

2. Viewing interaction episodes as a _____ leads to the proposition that interaction is never completely programmed.

3. _____ _____ tells us why the actors did what they did and what it meant.

4. When we have to reframe an event, it is called _____.

5. _____ is when you verbally give another indications of their role in this particular scene.

6. Dress and body language are all examples of _____ _____.

7. Ethnomethodologists stress the importance of _____ _____ for smooth interaction.

8. Deliberate attempts to cause trouble to uncover the common sense expectations underlying social behavior are called _____ _____.

9. The two basic types of aligning factors are _____ and _____.

10. One handles a spoiled identity by physically _____, trying to _____ and _____ the label.

MULTIPLE CHOICE

1. Which is likely to violate civil inattention in a public place?

   a. an averted gaze.
   b. silence.
   c. social withdrawal.
   d. striking up a conversation.

2. A methodological technique preferred by those who engage in the study of the sociology of everyday life:

   a. surveys.
   b. thin description.
   c. thick description.
   d. experiment.

3. Roughly identical to a definition of the situation:

   a. a frame.
   b. biography.
   c. keying.
   d. altercasting.

4. A deliberate attempt to challenge common sense expectations that underlie social interaction:

   a. break experiment.
   b. cueing.
   c. framing.
   d. identity negotiation.

5. Managing identities to support and sustain our self-esteem is called:

   a. ethnomethodology.
   b. framing.
   c. naturalistic inquiry.
   d. identity work.

6. Naturalistic inquiry is the:

   a. study of human behavior in terms of the nature/nurture controversy.
   b. attempt to understand the subjective social worlds of individual actors in specific situations.
   c. application of natural selection to the field of sociobiology.
   d. study of all aspects of human nature.

7. John stops briefly to say hello to a worker whom he super-
vises and is surprised to find that the worker wants to tell
him about a personal problem. John excuses himself as
quickly as possible. Which principle is illustrated by
John's behavior?

a. the dialectic.
b. total institution.
c. biography.
d. personal space.

8. A parent asks the eldest child how he/she feels about
accepting more responsibility in a family. This
illustrates:

a. altercasting.
b. dramaturgy.
c. thick description.
d. thin description.

9. Professionals such as medical doctors and lawyers make it a
point to have their offices appear neat and well organized.
They are showing a concern for their:

a. front region.
b. dialectic.
c. back region.
d. biography.

10. A chairperson of one sociology department always arrived at
meetings early so that he could claim the chair at the end
of the table. He was concerned about:

a. body language.
b. cueing status.
c. dress.
d. personal space.

11. An experienced office worker tells a new employee: "Above
all avoid blame when things go wrong, and always take credit
for all work that goes right." This cynic has described:

a. identity work.
b. ethnomethodology.
c. identity negotiation.
d. dramaturgy.

12. Professors who wish to keep their relationships with their students on a business-only basis often refer to their students as Miss Smith or Mr. Washington. This is an application of which social process?

    a. aligning action.
    b. altercasting.
    c. identity work.
    d. keying.

13. The sociology of everyday life is closely identified with this theory?

    a. conflict.
    b. symbolic interaction.
    c. functionalism.
    d. behaviorism.

14. Which is NOT an assumption of the everyday life perspective?

    a. the dialectic.
    b. biography.
    c. cultural universals.
    d. naturalistic inquiry.

15. Which person is regarded as the "chief architect" of dramaturgical theory?

    a. George Mead.
    b. Erving Goffman.
    c. Max Weber.
    d. Karl Marx.

16. Ethnomethodology is closely linked to the work of:

    a. Herbert Spencer.
    b. Erving Goffman.
    c. Harold Garfinkel.
    d. Auguste Comte.

17. NOT an assumption or a corollary of ethnomethodology:

    a. people are who they appear to be.
    b. others will trust our appearances.
    c. others share our symbolic worlds.
    d. belief that appearances can be deceiving.

18. The sociology of everyday life is an approach that examines social structures:

    a. at the macrosociological level.
    b. from the point of view of individual actors.
    c. in terms of the norms and values that guide group behavior.
    d. That are institutionalized in society.

19. Observation suggests that distances of up to _____ are reserved for intimates in this country:

    a. 3 feet.
    b. 6 inches.
    c. 4 feet.
    d. 18 inches.

20. The ultimate back region for most people:

    a. work.
    b. school.
    c. church.
    d. home.

21. NOT included among those with spoiled identities:

    a. mother on welfare.
    b. traitor.
    c. person with AIDS.
    d. severely handicapped person.

22. Douglas concluded that the most basic motivation of nude bathers was:

    a. aggression.
    b. sex.
    c. identity with nature.
    d. social approval.

23. This theory dominated sociology in the 1950s but came under serious question in the 1960s:

    a. ethnomethodology.
    b. dramaturgy.
    c. sociology of everyday life.
    d. structural functionalism.

24. The proportion of states that now allow dying persons to execute a living will is:

    a. 1/10.
    b. 1/4.
    c. 1/3.
    d. 1/2.

25. Based upon what sociologists have learned about personal space, professionals would probably interpret the need to share offices as:

    a. punishing.
    b. rewarding.
    c. inefficient.
    d. very practical.

26. One can expect that people who break the rules will attempt to protect their self-esteem. If they know that they are likely to break a rule in advance, they are likely to:

    a. offer a disclaimer.
    b. give an excuse.
    c. give a justification.
    d. remain silent.

27. Generalizing from what has been learned about spoiled identities, a person arrested for a sex crime is MOST likely to:

    a. confess quickly.
    b. deny that he/she has anything in common with sex offenders.
    c. refuse to be interrogated.
    d. offer a disclaimer.

28. Generalizing from what was learned about children living in cities in the 1900s, which is NOT likely to be an effective motivator of children?

    a. a variety of jobs.
    b. exciting places to spend money.
    c. personal profit from work.
    d. chance to work with parents.

29. Based upon what has been learned about identity negotiation, a humanistic approach toward the terminally ill would:

    a. free them from pain.
    b. encourage suicide.
    c. encourage personal choices.
    d. hide them from knowledge that they are dying.

30. According to your text, the "ex-wife at the funeral":

    a. successfully imposed her definition of the situation on the new wife.
    b. relied on the husband's relatives to frame the definition of the situation.
    c. was forced to key the definition imposed by the new wife.
    d. used nonverbal cues to manage the funeral setting.

ESSAY QUESTIONS

1. Explain how dramatugry, ethnomethodology, and identity work all fit into the EDL perspective.

2. Discuss the four basic assumptions of the EDL perspective.

3. Explain how dramaturgy works in everyday life.

4. Discuss the assumptions underlying ethnomethodology.

5. What is the relationship between identity work and self-esteem?

Chapter 8
Deviance, Crime, and Social Control

LEARNING OBJECTIVES

1. Explain what is meant by social control using the concepts of internalization, informal control, and formal control.

2. Differentiate between nonconformity and deviance and discuss how deviance is relative.

3. Contrast the structural-functional, symbolic interaction, and conflict approaches to the study of deviance.

4. Specify how Merton uses the concepts of anomie and social structure to explain deviance. Note two shortcomings of this approach.

5. Describe Merton's four modes of adaptation to anomie.

6. Identify the key elements of differential association, self-esteem, and control theories.

7. Define each of the following and note the role it plays in labeling theory: primary deviance, secondary deviance, power to label, and moral entrepreneurs.

8. Identify each of the following: crime, deviance, victimless crime, fear of victimization, and street level justice.

9. Critique labeling theory.

10. Discuss how conflict theory explains deviance.

11.   Note two important ways that crime statistics are
       inaccurate.

12.   Identify and outline the current statistical trend for each
       of the following: murder, rape, robbery, assault, property
       crimes, and white collar crime.

13.   Explain the role played by age, gender, race, and class in
       the commission of crimes.

14.   Describe the function of each level of the criminal justice
       system.

15.   Differentiate between retribution, reformation, specific
       deterrence, general deterrence, and prevention.

16.   Discuss the problem of capital punishment.

CHAPTER OUTLINE

  I.   Conformity, Nonconformity, and Deviance

    A.   Social control consists of the forces and processes
         that encourage conformity. Three factors combine to
         create social control.
         1.   Internalization is the process of building conform-
              ity to norms and values from our groups into our
              self concept.
         2.   Informal social control is self-restraint exercised
              because of a fear of what others may think.
         3.   Formal social controls are administrative sanctions
              such as fines and imprisonment.

    B.   Deviance refers to norm violations that exceed the
         tolerance level of the community and result in negative
         sanctions.
         1.   Few acts are intrinsically deviant and most
              deviance depends upon the definition of the
              situation. The definition of what is deviant is
              relative.

    C.   Structural-functional theory sees deviance arising from
         a lack of integration in the structure of society.
         1.   Merton drew upon Durkheim's concept of anomie,
              where the norms of society are no longer clear or
              applicable, to develop the strain theory of
              deviance.
              (a) There is a dislocation between the strongly
                  held social goal of economic success and the
                  means for achieving success that creates a

condition of anomie that encourages individuals
to commit deviant acts.
- (b) Adaptation to anomie may take the form of
  conformity or it may take the deviant forms of
  innovation, ritualism, retreatism, or
  rebellion.
- (c) Deviance is thus seen as arising from the
  social structure and not from individuals.
- (d) Critics argue that Merton sees deviance as an
  unnatural state arising from extraordinary circumstances when in fact deviance is a natural
  state of human affairs.
    - (1) Conflict theorists argue that deviance
      comes only from competition over scarce
      resources.
    - (2) Others see Merton's use of social class as
      an explanation for some deviance as
      inaccurate.

D. Symbolic interaction sees deviance as being learned
   through interaction and involving the development of a
   deviant self concept.
1. Differential association theory assumes that
   deviance is learned through the same mechanisms as
   conformity, i.e., through interaction with
   intimates (Sutherland).
   - (a) Deviance is thus learned in ones neighborhood,
     on the job, or among friends and will occur
     when individuals find that they are rewarded
     more for criminality than for conformity.
2. Self-esteem theory argues that people choose conformity or deviance depending upon which will
   enhance their self-esteem the most.
   - (a) Most individual's self-esteem is enhanced by
     conformity but some find little reward in
     conformity and enhance their self-esteem by
     deviant acts.
3. Social control theory assumes that deviance is a
   natural condition which may be controlled by strong
   bonds that tie an individual to society.
4. Labeling theory is concerned with the processes by
   which the label deviant is attached to specific
   behaviors of individuals.
   - (a) Becker contends that deviant behavior is
     behavior that people so label. Thus the label
     that people attach to an act is more important
     than the act itself.
     - (1) The labels are attached by control agents
       upon the deviant.
   - (b) Primary deviance is an individual's first
     impulsive act of nonconformity. When a person
     accepts a deviant self concept and elects to
     play that role, secondary deviance occurs.

(1) Powerful groups in competition may label others as deviant to protect itself. Those with the power to create and enforce new definitions of deviance are called moral entrepreneurs.
(c) Three major criticisms are commonly mentioned regarding labeling theory.
(1) The relativistic approach to deviance limits its use to minor or victimless crimes.
(2) Labeling also overlooks the causes of primary deviance.
(3) It cannot explain repeated deviance by the yet unlabeled.
5. Conflict theory argues that economic pressures lead to crime and that class interests determine who is labeled as criminal.
(a) The law rationalizes and supports the status quo by failing to punish any but the poor law breaker.
(1) Lower class crime is thus a response to deprivation and exploitation.

II. Crime as Deviance

A. Crimes are deviant acts that are subject to criminal or civil penalties. In violating criminal or civil codes, crimes can be classified as violating significant norms and thus constitutes deviant behavior.
1. Crime rates are measured by two basic means.
(a) The Uniform Crime Report summarizes crimes known to the police in seven major categories.
(1) Critics cite the lack of uniform reporting standards and practices as a distorting influence. Other categories of crime appear to be greatly underreported again distorting the findings.
(b) The National Crime Survey is a victimization survey used to supplement the police reports.

B. Crimes involving the use of force or threat of force are called crimes of violence.
1. Murder is the most violent and rarest of major violent crime.
(a) Homicide rates have been relatively stable for nearly a decade with minorities and the poor in society being the typical perpetrator and/or victim.
(1) Over half of all murder victims are acquainted with their murderer.
2. Forcible rape accounts for only 7% of violent crime.
(a) Victims are likely to be acquainted with the assailant.

       (b) Reported rapes are increasing due to changes in reporting patterns and revised legal procedures.

    3. Robbery involves personal confrontation and the threat or use of force.

       (a) Robbery rates are increasing, especially those involving weapons.

    4. Assault or an attack for the purposes of inflicting severe bodily injury constitute nearly half of all violent crime.

       (a) Violent assault has increased rapidly in the last decade.

C. Property crimes are by far the most frequently reported crimes.

D. Crime rates this decade are higher than the previous decade.

E. There are four major correlates of crime: age, sex, race, and class.

    1. Males, consistent with their sex roles, are greatly overrepresented in crime, especially violent crime.

       (a) Women tend to be more involved in minor crimes and their rates in these areas have increased faster than those of men. Still, women are not typically involved in violent crimes.

    2. Social class, as such, is not seen as a direct cause of crime itself. It appears that class is directly related to the type of crime committed.

       (a) Lower class crime is typically of a direct and interpersonal nature while middle or upper class crime tends to center upon the misuse of power.

          (1) Enforcement and incarceration are typically reserved for the lower class criminal.

    3. Blacks and hispanics are greatly overrepresented in crime statistics.

       (a) Most of the explanations for minority crime lie in the living conditions of disorganized neighborhoods and deprivation experienced by minority group members.

          (1) Minorities appear to be more likely to commit some crimes and are far more likely to be singled out for attention by the criminal justice system.

    4. The highest crime rates are for the population 15 to 24 years of age with black males between the ages of 18 to 20 being the most likely to commit crimes.

       (a) Younger people may experience lower self-esteem, a greater gap between aspirations and opportunity and lack effective ties to conventional society.

F. Victimless crimes are illegal acts of exchange for
which there is no complaintant. Crimes typically
included here are prostitution, gambling, homosexuality, etc.
1. Efforts against victimless crimes are costly and
time consuming activities that direct resources
from violent crime.
(a) Enforcement continues due to strong public
pressure on the criminal justice system.

G. White collar crime is crime committed by people of
respectability and high social status in the course
of their profession.
1. White collar crime is far more costly than common
crime.
2. White collar crime is obviously class related and
for the most part these crimes go undetected and
unreported.

H. About one-fifth of all U.S. households are victims of
crime each year.
1. The relatively common experience plus media sensa-
tionalism can cause widespread fear.
2. National surveys show fear of victimization is far
greater than the statistical probability of being
victimized. Some see this as eroding the quality
of life especially for vulnerable categories such
as the elderly.

III. Formal Social Controls

A. The role of the police is to investigate and arrest
persons suspected of committing crimes.
1. The police are in a unique and powerful position
due to their ability to make arrests under conditions of low visibility and great discretion.
(a) The discretionary powers are best reflected in
street-level justice or the decisions made by
police in the initial stages of an
investigation.
(1) This form of justice is relatively
invisible and hard to evaluate.
(2) There is much concern that these practices
reflect prejudice and bias.

B. The court system involves the prosecution of people who
have been arrested as suspects in the commission of a
crime.
1. Decision stages in the court system are critical in
that negotiation and plea bargaining account for 90
percent of all convictions. They occur before a
trial can be held.
2. Negotiation and plea bargaining are often involved
in setting the sentence for the guilty.

3. Sentencing varies greatly from jurisdiction to jurisdiction with prejudice and class bias playing a strong role.

C. The prison system is assigned the task of administering punishment to those convicted of crimes. Five rationalizations for punishment are retribution, reformation, deterrence, general deterrence, and prevention.
  1. Prisons today are greatly overcrowded and function to perpetuate criminal careers while subjecting many to cruel and inhumane conditions.
    (a) Only one quarter of convicted offenders go to prison. The others are put into a community-based corrections program that includes probation and parole.
  2. Capital punishment is a highly controversial topic and is enjoying strong support despite overwhelming evidence that it has absolutely no effect on the crime rate.
    (a) Some evidence suggests that capital punishment may increase the amount of violence in society. This is called the brutalization effect.
    (b) The only rationale for capital punishment is the social desire for vengance or retribution.
    (c) In practice, capital punishment appears to reflect a strong degree of racial prejudice.

MATCHING   I

A.   Police

B.   Murder

C.   Women

D.   Robbery

E.   Rape

F.   Assault

G.   Property crimes

H.   Lower class

I.   Mafia

J.   Middle class

K.   Lower-class minorities

L.   Victimless crimes

M.   White collar crime

N.   Street-level justice

O.   Fear of victimization

_____   1. Most frequently committed crime.

_____   2. Prostitution, gambling, pornography.

_____   3. A relatively rare form of crime, 2% of U.C.R. crimes.

_____   4. More frustrated, angry, and despairing.

_____   5. This crime has shown an increased tendency towards violence in the last decade.

_____   6. Commit more interpersonal crime.

_____   7. In 50% of the cases victims and perpetrators were acquaintances.

_____   8. No increase in their participation in violent crime.

_____   9. Particularly has a negative effect on women, nonwhites, and elderly.

_____ 10. Commit crimes involving power.

MATCHING   II

A.   Courts

B.   Social control theory

C.   Specific deterrence

D.   Primary deviance

E.   Moral entrepreneurs

F.   Police

G.   Retribution

H.   F.B.I.

I.   Secondary deviance

J.   General deterrence

K.   Blacks and Hispanics

L.   Victimless crime

M.   Prevention

N.   White collar crime

O.   Reformation

_____ 1. Revenge the victim.

_____ 2. Most of this type of crime goes un-reported and undetected.

_____ 3. Negotiated plea bargaining.

_____ 4. Uniform Crime Report.

_____ 5. Designed to scare society.

_____ 6. Street-level justice.

_____ 7. Incapacitating offenders.

_____ 8. Police must find both the crime and the criminal.

_____ 9. Those who create and enforce new definitions of deviance.

_____ 10. Designed to scare the offender.

FILL IN THE BLANK QUESTIONS

1. Being expelled from class for cheating exemplifies
_____ _____ social control while
fearing humiliation in front of your classmates demonstrates
_____ social control.

2. Self-control occurs because individuals _____
the norms and values of their groups.

3. Minor rule violation connstitutes _____ and
significant norm violation is called _____.

4. In Merton's scheme, slavishly going through the motions pre-
scribed by society is called _____.

5. Sutherland's theory of _____ _____ assumes
that _____ is learned when ones associates favor
_____ more than they do _____.

6. The perspective called _____ _____
assumes that deviance is normal.

7. Becker contends that deviant behavior is any behavior people
_____ _____.

8. The first impulsive act of deviance is called _____
_____.

9. According to labeling theory, it is society's differential
treatment that produces _____ _____.

10. People who are arrested for criminal acts are overwhelmingly
and disproportionately _____,
_____, and _____ _____
_____.

11. _____-class individuals predominately commit
interpersonal crimes while _____-class
individuals commit crimes using power.

12. The structural-functional approach to deviance sees deviance
as being _____ to society.

13. America's emphasis on achievement and success leads to
_____ according to Merton.

14. Labeling theory tends to ignore the causes of _____
_____ in favor of a focus on the reactions to
deviance.

15. According to conflict theory, crime is actually _____
prevalent among the poor.

MULTIPLE CHOICE

1. Social control, the forces that bring about conformity, rests largely on:

   a. self control and informal social controls.
   b. self control and formal social controls.
   c. formal social controls.
   d. self control.

2. Social scientists speak of deviance when:

   a. any norm is violated.
   b. when one feels guilty about a norm violation.
   c. when people violate society's significant norms.
   d. when persons in a group violate norms together.

3. Which is NOT true about behavior that is defined as deviance?

   a. many acts are intrinsically seen as deviant in all cultures.
   b. often depends on the circumstances.
   c. often depends on the individual's characteristics.
   d. often depends on the group whose norms and values are chosen as standards.

4. Continued and deliberate deviance that results from labeling:

   a. primary deviance.
   b. innovation.
   c. secondary deviance.
   d. white collar crime.

5. Becker's concept "moral entrepreneur" refers to:

   a. persons who are labeled.
   b. those who successfully impose labels on others.
   c. social scientists who look for causes of deviance.
   d. persons who commit victimless crimes.

6. Self-esteem theory suggests:

   a. deviance is more likely among persons with low self-esteem.
   b. self-esteem is a protection against deviance.
   c. people choose deviance or conformity depending on which will do the most to enhance their self-esteem.
   d. self-esteem affects primary deviance but is unrelated to secondary deviance.

7. Some parents may work very hard at getting their children to internalize the norms and values of their group. This means that they want their children to conform because of:

   a. informal social controls.
   b. self control.
   c. formal social controls.
   d. fear of the authorities.

8. Citizens sometimes complain that employees in government agencies are more concerned about following the rules, even when this doesn't make sense, than they are about helping citizens. Robert Merton would refer to these employees as:

   a. ritualists.
   b. conformists.
   c. innovators.
   d. retreatists.

9. Successful campaigning by the Federal Bureau of Narcotics caused this behavior to be labeled as deviant and illegal:

   a. drinking alcohol.
   b. use of prescription drugs.
   c. driving while intoxicated.
   d. smoking marijuana.

10. Data for the Uniform Crime Reports are obtained from:

   a. crimes known to police.
   b. random sample of householders who report any crimes that they have experienced.
   c. confidential reports by police informants.
   d. self report techniques.

11. An example of white collar crime:

    a. prostitution.
    b. homosexuality.
    c. false advertising.
    d. murder.

12. The decisions the police make in the initial stages of an investigation are referred to as:

    a. harrassment.
    b. distributive justice.
    c. street-level justice.
    d. discretionary justice.

13. This theory of deviance was initially formulated by Durkheim:

    a. anomie.
    b. cultural transmission theory.
    c. social control theory.
    d. sociobiology.

14. According to Robert Merton's strain theory, innovation as deviance occurs when:

    a. persons accept both society's goals and means.
    b. persons accept society's goals but not the means.
    c. persons reject both society's goals and means.
    d. persons accept society's means but not the goals.

15. These theorists see deviance as an inevitable product of competition in society:

    a. anomie.
    b. conflict.
    c. cultural transmission.
    d. labeling.

16. This theory assumes that deviance is learned:

    a. anomie.
    b. differential association.
    c. labeling.
    d. social conflict.

17.   This theory of deviance assumees that strain is universal:

      a.   anomie.
      b.   differential association.
      c.   control theory.
      d.   labeling.

18.   Labeling theory assumes all of the following EXCEPT:

      a.   deviance is relative.
      b.   the label people attach to an act is less important
           than the act itself.
      c.   those who do the labeling are usually more powerful
           than those who are labeled.
      d.   persons who accept deviant labels are likely to make
           the transition to secondary deviance.

19.   Which is true about the murder rate in the U.S.?

      a.   a relatively rare form of crime.
      b.   rate has changed dramatically in recent years.
      c.   chance of being a victim greatest for white males.
      d.   most victims are middle class.

20.   Nearly half of all violent crimes are:

      a.   murder.
      b.   rape.
      c.   robbery.
      d.   aggravated assault.

21.   The state that regards the possession of marijuana as a
      felony but permits gambling and prostitution:

      a.   California.
      b.   Texas.
      c.   Nevada.
      d.   New Jersey.

22.   About what percent of criminal convictions are actually
      processed through public trials?

      a.   10 percent.
      b.   30 percent.
      c.   50 percent.
      d.   75 percent.

23. Some persons in the U.S. fear being a victim of a crime more so than do others. Which of these is LEAST likely to fear being a victim?

   a. male.
   b. black.
   c. over age 65.
   d. city size more than 1,000,000.

24. Property crimes occur _____ times more often than crimes of violence:

   a. twenty.
   b. five.
   c. two.
   d. nine.

25. Researchers have found that this theory helps to explain how the reactions of powerful others to deviant acts is related to future deviance:

   a. labeling.
   b. anomie.
   c. differential association.
   d. control theory.

26. Only about 3% of the population reports being a crime victim each year, but if one is a victim he/she is MOST likely to be a victim of a:

   a. robbery.
   b. rape.
   c. aggravated assault.
   d. property crime.

27. If this theory is correct, we would expect crime among the lower class to rise during economic recessions when it becomes difficult to meet basic needs:

   a. anomie.
   b. differential association.
   c. self-esteem.
   d. conflict.

28. Murder is among the most violent of criminal acts. Victims are most likely to be:

    a. unknown to their attackers.
    b. rural residents.
    c. black.
    d. female.

29. Some persons are much more likely to be arrested for criminal acts. A characteristic of persons MOST likely to be arrested is:

    a. old.
    b. male.
    c. female.
    d. white.

30. The self-report measures of deviance among Seattle 17-year-olds found that, compared to lower-class youth, middle-class youth were:

    a. more deviant.
    b. slightly less deviant.
    c. considerably less deviant.
    d. very similar in the amount of self-reported deviance.

ESSAY QUESTIONS

1. Discuss how deviance is relative.

2. Outline and critique labeling theory using specific
    examples.

3. Discuss the problem of capital punishment.

4. Use three examples to explain how Merton uses the concepts
    of anomie and social structure to account for deviance.

5. Contrast the structural-functional and conflict approaches
    to the relationship between crime and social class.

Chapter 9
Stratification

LEARNING OBJECTIVES

1. Explain the relationship between inequality and
    stratification.

2. Define what is meant by ascribed status and achieved
    status, and discuss the role played by each in caste
    and class systems.

3. Identify each of the following terms and note how it
    is used by Marx in his explanation of social classes:
    bourgeoisie, proletariat, class consciousness, and false
    consciousness.

4. Explain what Weber means by reference to the concepts of
    class, status, and power.

5. Outline the structural-functional theory of social stra-
    tification and the Marxian or conflict view of stratifi-
    cation. Don't forget to note the major shortcomings
    of each approach.

6. Discuss how inequality evolves according to Lenski and
    point out how this approach draws upon both structural-
    functional and conflict theory.

7. Define SES and explain how sociologists use occupation
    and self-identification to measure social class.

8. Point out inequities in the distribution of wealth and
    income in the U.S. and describe how social class makes
    a different in the lives of individuals.

9. Differentiate between the following terms: social mobility, intergenerational mobility, and intragenerational mobility.

10. Outline how the indirect inheritance model functions, noting the factors that influence mobility.

11. Specify both the macro and micro factors in social mobility.

12. Outline the dominant characteristics of the upper class, the working class, and the poor.

13. Explain the following terms: absolute poverty, relative poverty, culture of poverty, and underclass.

14. Point out how poverty may be seen as functional.

15. Discuss the role played by ideology in justifying inequality in the U.S.

16. How do intelligence and achievement motivation operate to overcome barriers to social mobility?

CHAPTER OUTLINE

I. Structures of Inequality

A. Sociologists study that form of inequality called stratification in which social categories within society are ranked according to the amount of scarce resources they receive. Inequality becomes stratification under the following conditions.
1. The inequality is institutionalized.
2. The inequality is based upon membership in a category rather than on personal attributes.

B. Two basic forms of stratification structures are caste and class systems.
1. Caste structures exist where scarce resources are distributed on ascribed statuses.
(a) Caste systems are best suited to stable, pre-industrial societies.
2. Class systems are more flexible and exist where scarce resources are distributed primarily on the basis of achieved statuses.
3. A class system is an ordered set of categories, the actual number of which depends upon one's theoretical approach.

(a) <u>Marx</u> identified only two main classes. They are <u>bourgeoisie</u>, or those who own the means of production, and the <u>proletariat</u>, who own nothing and must compete among themselves to sell their labor to the bourgeoisie.
   (1) Class is thus determined by ones relationship to the means of production.
   (2) Marx believed that a revolutionary movement to eliminate class differences would be likely to occur when <u>false conscious-ness</u> was replaced by <u>class consciousness</u>.
(b) <u>Weber</u> proposed three independent dimensions upon which to rank individuals. Like Marx, he chose <u>class</u> but he added status and party as two additional dimensions.
   (1) <u>Status</u> is social honor expressed in ones lifestyle which is not to be confused with an economic ability to purchase goods and services.
   (2) People from the same class are united in a unique lifestyle.
   (3) <u>Power</u> is the ability to get others to act against their own wishes.
   (4) Modern sociologists draw heavily upon Weber in constructing a composite measure of <u>social class</u> where a category of people share roughly the same class, status, and power.
   (5) Social class thus includes an emphasis on class, status, power, and an element of self-awareness.

II. Explanations of Inequality

   A. Structural-functional theory was applied to social stratification by <u>Davis</u> and <u>Moore</u> who concluded that stratification is necessary and justifiable because it contributes to the maintenance of society.
      1. Society has important roles to fill and inequality functions to fill these roles, thus contributing to the maintenance of society.
         (a) Society must encourage those with talent to undergo extensive training to fill these roles.
         (b) Inequality in the form of significant financial rewards serves to motivate the talented to undergo training and to fill key roles.
         (c) Rewards are influenced by the unpleasantness and importance of the task as well as the talent required.
      2. Criticisms against functional interpretations of stratification systems focus upon three major parts.
         (a) It can be used as an ideology that justifies inequality.

(b) The theory does not consider how society is structured against many who are poor and are talented.

(c) Income levels do not really reflect the functional importance of a position.

B. Marxian <u>conflict</u> <u>theory</u> explains inequality in terms of exploitation.

1. The bourgeoisie seeks to maximize profit by minimizing the amount of wages paid to the proletariat.

(a) Inequality is thus a product of the division of labor and the ownership and control of private property.

(1) Individuals who control the work of others also have power to pursue their self-interest.

2. Criticisms against Marxist theory center upon the fact that people are unequal to begin with and that inequality is a major motivation for human labor.

C. Lenski draws upon both functional and conflict theory in proposing an evolutionary theory.

1. The level of inequality in society is directly related to the level of production.

(a) Inequality is necessary at lower levels of productivity and unnecessary at higher levels of productivity.

(1) Inequality persists in situations of high productivity as individuals seek to maximize their rewards at the expense of others.

(2) Recent times marks the first instance of decreasing inequality with the expansion of the middle class.

III. Inequality in the United States

A. The picture of inequality obtained depends upon how inequality is measured.

1. <u>Warner's</u> classic study used several dimensions of lifestyle to pinpoint six class levels.

(a) Subsequent analysis shows his work relied upon one indicator, occupation.

2. Self-identification simply asks people to identify what class they belong to.

(a) Answers vary considerably based upon the form of the question asked.

3. Occupational prestige scales yield reliable and consistent results that order occupations in a prestige ranking.

(a) <u>Socioeconomic</u> <u>Status</u> <u>(SES)</u> ranks individuals on combinations of variables, chief among which is occupation.

B. Economic inequality is present at high levels in all
    contemporary societies.
    1. Inequality in household income has changed little
        in the last 35 years.
    2. <u>Wealth</u> is highly concentrated and has been in
        America since at least the beginning of the 19th
        century.
        (a) The top 1% in income owned 21% of all assets
            in 1972.
        (b) The top 20% of households held 76% of all
            wealth in 1962.

C. The consequences of social class are quite apparent in
    that class influences almost every behavior and
    attitude one has.
    1. While wealth and income inequality patterns are
        quite stable, some patterns have changed.
        (a) Middletown studies show that class differ-
            ences are declining.
        (b) Two factors are noted: an increase in real
            income and a greater increase in public
            services.

IV. Social Mobility in the United States

A. <u>Social mobility</u> is a change in occupation or social
    class position. It may be measured as <u>intergenera-</u>
    <u>tional</u> or <u>intragenerational</u> mobility.
    1. Mobility may be upward or downward.
    2. Macro factors in mobility are changes in society
        that produce mobility.
        (a) Principle among these is a change in occupa-
            tional structure.
    3. Micro factors deal principally with individual
        characteristics.

B. The <u>indirect inheritance model</u> focuses upon micro level
    factors, especially the role of the family.
    (a) Education is a key to mobility and ones social
        class standing.
        (1) The best predictor of education is ones
            parents' education.
    (b) Parental education and social class directly influ-
        ence the educational aspirations of a child.
        (1) Aspirations are bolstered by home attitudes,
            help, and family resources.
    (c) Two factors not directly influenced by the family
        that influence mobility are <u>achievement motivation</u>
        and intelligence.

C. An <u>ideology</u> is a set of norms and values that ration-
    alize the existing social structure. Ideologies are
    built into the dominant culture of society.
    1. The major ideology justifying inequality in this

country is the <u>American Dream</u> which states that success comes entirely from one's own efforts and that failure can only be blamed upon the individual.

III. The Rich, the Working Class, and the Poor

    A. The upper class is best characterized by inherited wealth.
        1. The wealth is cumulative and is managed to produce even more wealth.

    B. The working class falls below the middle class and above the lower class.
        1. Most members of the working class have finished high school and are employed in poorly paid jobs requiring little skill.
        2. Many working class families have been victims of unemployment, automation, and plant closings.
        3. <u>Rubin</u> summarizes the working class lifestyle as follows:
            (a) Children grow up in run-down, crowded homes with tired parents.
            (b) They leave home, enter marriage at an early age, end up in dead-end jobs, and become pregnant.
            (c) Economic problems make happy marriages quite difficult.
                (1) Males often turn to domestic tyranny or alcohol out of frustration.
                (2) Economic uncertainty dominates the life of the working class.

    C. The poor or those living in poverty lack the amount of money or resources to meet the minimum requirements of a decent standard of living.
        1. In 1986 the figure for poverty stood at 32.4 million people.
        2. Poverty cuts across many dimensions of age, sex, and race.
            (a) In 1986 53% of the poor were elderly, children, and the disabled.
                (1) The persistently poor are typically those living in a household headed by a black woman or the elderly.
        3. Poverty can be seen as either <u>absolute</u> <u>poverty</u> of <u>relative</u> <u>poverty</u>.
            (a) Few people in America are absolutely poor.
        4. The affluent, citing the American Dream, blame the poor for their own condition. They are seen as lazy, inept, immoral, or disabled.
            (a) White poor often accept this ideology while black poor are more likely to see structural factors lying at the root of poverty.

    (b) <u>Lewis</u> uses the concept of a <u>culture</u> <u>of</u> <u>poverty</u> to explain the persistence of the poor.
- (1) The poor develop values that are functional to their current living conditions because middle class values do not work for most of the poor.
- (2) These alternative values enable the poor to survive but they do not lead to mobility.

    (c) <u>Myrdal</u> used the term <u>underclass</u> to refer to these unemployed and unemployable who have been left behind as the economic structure of America changes.

5. <u>Gans</u> sees the existence of the poor as being functional.
- (a) Being poor ensures that someone will be available for low status jobs.
- (b) The existence of poverty can serve to warn us if we fail to adhere to the official ideology of the American Dream.

6. Most sociologists conclude that structural problems in the American economy create a mismatch between jobs and the people available to fill them.
- (a) Policies toward the problem of inequality follow three routes: taxing inheritances, outlawing discrimination, and creating special education programs.

CHAPTER 9

MATCHING

A. Class structure

B. Status

C. Conflict theory   _____ 1. Status is fixed at birth.

D. Ideology   _____ 2. A society based upon achieved status.

E. Relative poverty   _____ 3. Those who own tools and materials.

F. Bourgeoisie   _____ 4. Social honor.

                                       _____ 5. A composite measure of income, education, and occupation.
G. Absolute poverty

H. Caste structure   _____ 6. Davis and Moore.

I. Under class   _____ 7. American Dream.

                                       _____ 8. American norms and values.
J. Structural-functional theory

                                       _____ 9. Inability to provide the requirements for life.
K. Estate taxes

L. Proletariat   _____ 10. Those who sell their labor.

M. Middle class   _____ 11. Culture of poverty.

N. Ascribed status   _____ 12. Origins of inequality in the division of labor.

O. SES

P. Lenski's evolutionary theory

FILL IN THE BLANK QUESTIONS

1. The two basic forms of stratification structures are
    _____ and _____.

2. In periods of rapid social change a _____
    system provides more flexibility.

3. _____ _____ is a lack of aware-
    ness of one's real position in the class structure and
    _____ _____ is an awareness
    of one's true class identity.

4. The three dimensions upon which to rank people, proposed
    by Weber, are _____, _____,
    and _____.

5. The structural-functional theory argues that _____
    are the means used by society to ensure people fill essen-
    tial roles.

6. _____ theory has been criticized as an
    ideology that justifies inequality.

7. _____ theory explains inequality as
    exploitation.

8. Conflict theory overlooks the fact that many people are
    motivated by _____.

9. Lenski's evolutionary theory argues that the level of
    _____ is directly related to the level of
    _____.

10. Social class differences are less than they were 50 years
    ago because of an increase in _____
    _____ and the extension of _____
    _____.

11. A macro approach to social mobility would focus upon changes
    in the _____ structure while a micro approach would
    focus upon _____ factors.

12. The role played by the family in influencing mobility is
    stressed in the _____ _____
    _____.

13. Two factors influencing mobility that are not directly re-
    lated to ones social class background are _____
    _____ and _____.

14. _____ is a set of values and
    norms that rationalize the existing social structure.

15. For children reared in _____ families, the fantasies and dreams of marriage typically remain unrealized.

MULTIPLE CHOICE

1. Inequality becomes stratification when all of the following conditions exist EXCEPT:

   a. the norms of resource distribution support inequality.
   b. inequality is institutionalized.
   c. individual characteristics are important for stratification.
   d. inequality is based on membership in a category.

2. The express purpose of the sumptuary laws declared by Elizabeth I of England was to:

   a. prevent disorder and confusion about class membership.
   b. raise funds to build a navy.
   c. emphasize the importance of religion in life.
   d. give women the right to vote.

3. This term means that a person may have a higher or lower occupation or social class than the parents did:

   a. career mobility.
   b. intergenerational mobility.
   c. intragenerational mobility.
   d. social mobility.

4. Family status and income provide children with surroundings and goals that ensure that they end up at the same place as parents. This is referred to as:

   a. caste system effects.
   b. achievement motivation effects.
   c. intergenerational mobility.
   d. indirect inheritance model.

5. Oscar Lewis coined the term "culture of poverty" to explain why some people stay poor. Which value is emphasized in the culture of poverty?

    a. live for the moment.
    b. thrift.
    c. investment in the future.
    d. hard work.

6. Relative poverty refers to the inability to:

    a. support oneself in the style to which one has become accustomed.
    b. meet the requirements of life.
    c. meet society's conception of a decent standard of living.
    d. provide food and shelter.

7. The number of social classes in the U.S. according to W. Lloyd Warner is:

    a. two.
    b. three.
    c. none.
    d. six.

8. Which is NOT a consequence of social class in the U.S.:

    a. middle-class women are more likely to be overweight.
    b. babies born in poor neighborhoods are more likely to die before their first birthday.
    c. people who fail to graduate from high school are more likely to get a divorce.
    d. people with poor education score lower on measures of mental health.

9. The major ideology that justifies inequality in the U.S. is:

    a. liberalism.
    b. the American Dream.
    c. conservatism.
    d. imperialism.

10. Although some changes have occurred, which of the following is still true for the working-class families studied by Rubin in 1974:

    a. most still do not graduate from high school.
    b. those who graduate from high school do not go on to college.
    c. most continue to get married at 17 or 18.
    d. they continue to face economic insecurity.

11. Why are some people poor? Is it their own fault? The black poor are MORE likely than the white poor to believe that being poor is caused by:

    a. lack of thrift.
    b. loose morals.
    c. lack of effort.
    d. structural factors.

12. The Earl of Swithin has so little money that he works as a clerk in a law office. He may be said to be:

    a. high on status and low on class.
    b. high on status and high on class.
    c. high on class and low on status.
    d. high on party and low on status.

13. In Marx's framework those who own the tools and materials necessary for their work are the:

    a. bourgeoisie.
    b. middle class.
    c. proletariat.
    d. government leaders.

14. Which of the following is NOT an assumption of the Davis and Moore functional theory of stratification:

    a. some roles in society are more important.
    b. inequality in rewards is the means society uses to ensure that people play important roles.
    c. inequality is seen as exploitation.
    d. inequality is seen as a rational response to a social problem.

15. A major criticism of the conflict perspective on stratification is that it:

    a. is an ideology that justifies inequality.
    b. makes the assumption that unequal financial rewards are needed to motivate people.
    c. ignores the fact that people are unequal.
    d. places too much emphasis on the importance of inequality as a major motivator of human labor.

16. According to Lenski's evolutionary theory, what is the relationship between the level of inequality in a society and the level of productivity?

    a. the higher the productivity, the lower the inequality.
    b. the higher the productivity, the higher the inequality.
    c. inequality is necessary at both low and high levels of productivity.
    d. there is no relationship between inequality and productivity.

17. Alternative theories exist to explain why we have inequality and poverty. Governments, sometimes guided by social science theory and research, have developed policies with regard to the elimination of inequality. Which has NOT been a direct approach of social policy in the U.S.?

    a. taxing inheritance.
    b. outlawing discrimination.
    c. seeing the family as the root of both advantage and disadvantage.
    d. creating special education programs.

18. A major criticism of conflict theory is that it overlooks:

    a. the role of inequality as a motivation for work.
    b. the importance of technology in the economy.
    c. the extent of self seeking by the powerful.
    d. the forces of social change.

19. The occupation with the highest prestige in the U.S. is:

    a. physician.
    b. college professor.
    c. accountant.
    d. police officer.

20. If Americans are asked whether they belong to the upper, middle, lower, or working class, nearly half of the middle class and some of the lower class will say that they are:

    a. upper class.
    b. middle class.
    c. lower class.
    d. working class.

21. Which is true about inequality in the distribution of household income in the U.S.?

    a. it has declined dramatically in recent years.
    b. it has increased dramatically in recent years.
    c. it has changed little in the last 35 years.
    d. it is present now but was not present in the early years of our history.

22. In 1972 a team of investigators did a restudy of Middletown (Muncie, Indiana) and reported a marked CONVERGENCE on all measures except one - namely:

    a. percent unemployed.
    b. infant mortality.
    c. mental health.
    d. obesity.

23. Most millionaires in the U.S. pursued careers in:

    a. sports.
    b. business.
    c. professions.
    d. education.

24. What percent of the U.S population was classified as poor in 1986?

    a. 3 percent.
    b. 52 percent.
    c. 14 percent.
    d. 20 percent.

25. The single BEST predictor of eventual class in the U.S.:

    a. race.
    b. parents' education.
    c. education.
    d. intelligence.

26. Marx and Weber each included this dimension in their analysis of stratification:

    a. class.
    b. status.
    c. party.
    d. family.

27. The BEST single predictor of eventual social class is education and the best single predictor of one's education is:

    a. parents' education.
    b. parents' occupation.
    c. ambition.
    d. intelligence.

28. The wealth of those with small estates is MORE likely to be invested in:

    a. stocks and bonds.
    b. their homes.
    c. businesses.
    d. other investments.

29. Which is NOT a characteristic of working-class families?

    a. steady work but at jobs that require low skill.
    b. graduation from high school and some college is common.
    c. unemployment is high.
    d. many working-class jobs are threatened by automation.

30. American beliefs about stratification can be summed up by saying that Americans believe:

    a. in equal shares rather than fair shares.
    b. in fair shares rather than equal shares.
    c. that equal shares are fair shares.
    d. that fairness is a dirty word.

CHAPTER 9

ESSAY QUESTIONS

1. Discuss the relationship between the bourgeoisie, the
   proletariat, class consciousness, and false class consciousness in Marxian conflict theory.

2. Define SES and explain how sociologists use occupations and
   self-identification to measure social class.

3. Describe how the indirect inheritance model of mobility
   functions, note each of the specific factors.

4. Explain how poverty can persist in American society.

5. Discuss the role played by ideology in justifying inequality.

Chapter 10
Racial and Ethnic Inequalities

LEARNING OBJECTIVES

1. Compare and contrast the concepts of race and ethnicity.

2. Recount the history of racism and note how race relations constitute a semicaste system.

3. Define the following: majority group, minority group, conflict, accommodation, acculturation, and assimilation.

4. Discuss how prejudice is facilitated by personal and institutional factors.

5. Describe how the self-fulfilling prophecy works.

6. Define discrimination, note its different forms, and outline the relationship between prejudice and discrimination.

7. Fully identify each of the following: social distance, segregation, and extraordinary solutions.

8. Outline the historical development of the melting pot and anglo conformity in America.

9. Note the distinctive historical, social, and economic characteristics of black Americans.

10. Discuss the political, educational, and economic changes experienced by black Americans in the last two generations.

11. Highlight the distinctive historical, social, and economic characteristics of Hispanics, Native Americans, Jews, Japanese, and other Asians.

12. Briefly outline the use of extraordinary solutions to the problems of American racial and ethnic minorities.

13. Identify America's newest immigrants and give a prognosis for their eventual acceptance.

14. Discuss how American minority groups engage in intergroup conflict.

15. Explain the relationship between prejudice and residential segregation.

16. Note changes in prejudice and discrimination in America during the last two decades.

CHAPTER OUTLINE

   I.   Race, Racism, and Ethnicity

        A. Race refers to a category of people who are treated as distinct because of physical characteristics to which we have assigned social importance.
            1. Physical characteristics are no longer considered scientifically valid and our current racial categories are socially defined.

        B. Ethnicity refers to a category of people who are distinct because of their inherited cultural characteristics and thus become ethnic groups also.

        C. Racism is the belief that inherited physical characteristics provide a legitimate basis for inequal treatment.
            1. Racism arose after the enlightenment and due to the inequality experienced may be considered a special instance of stratification.
            2. The stratification characteristics of a semicaste system apply to minority group, majority group relationships where the majority group maintains a strong advantage in the distribution of scarce resources.
                (a) Both race and class are critical factors in the maintenance of the semicaste system.
            3. Within minority groups the patterns of stratification are apparent in that income and wealth are unequally distributed.

II.   Patterns of Intergroup Conflict

    A.   Intergroup conflict and continued interaction often be-
come an exercise in dominance and power.
        1.   A <u>majority</u> <u>group</u> is culturally, economically, and
politically dominant and a <u>minority</u> <u>group</u> is culturally, economically, and politically subordinate.
        2.   Relations between minority and majority groups may
follow several patterns including <u>conflict</u>, <u>accom-
modation</u>, <u>acculturation</u>, or <u>assimilation</u>.

III. Maintaining Group Boundaries

    A.   Interaction with minority group members can be con-
trolled with regard to the intimacy and proximity
involved.
        1.   <u>Social</u> <u>distance</u> is the degree of intimacy in re-
lationships between two groups and is reflected
in ones social desirability ranking.
        2.   <u>Prejudice</u> is irrationality based negative atti-
tudes towards categories of people.
            (a) Prejudice relies heavily upon stereotypes and
operates through the mechanism of the <u>self-
fulfilling</u> <u>prophecy</u>. If we stereotype a category of people, treat them according to the
stereotype, then they will probably become much
like the stereotype.
            (b) Prejudice is learned along with other norms,
values, and beliefs.
            (c) Personal factors accounting for why some indi-
viduals are prejudiced are <u>authoritarianism</u>
and <u>scapegoating</u>.
            (d) Prejudice can become institutionalized into
the structure of society where the attitudes
permeate the major institutions and social
class structure.

    B.   Prejudice is an attitude and discrimination is behavior
in which individuals are treated unequally on the basis
of their membership in categories.

    C.   Group differences are easier to maintain if social dis-
tance is enhanced by <u>segregation</u> or the practice of
physically separating minority and majority group
members.
        1.   Segregation may unfairly structure interaction be-
tween the majority and minority groups but it may
promote strong ingroup solidarity for the respec-
tive groups.

    D.   Discrimination need not be explicit or blatant; it
occurs with the normal operation of ostensibly neutral
processes and systematically produces unequal results
for majority and minority groups.

E. Additional solutions exist in the form of rigid separa-
tion, concentration camps, expulsion or extermination.
These are referred to as <u>extraordinary solutions</u>.

IV. Racial and Ethnic Relations in the United States

A. White immigration began in the 16th century with the
English emerging as the majority group, a position not
relinquished to this day.
1. Those arriving after English domination engaged in
acculturation and assimilation. Despite this fact,
a myth arose in which it was believed that a physical and cultural blending of groups called a <u>melt-
ing pot</u> would occur.
2. What in fact occurred is a process of acculturation
called <u>Anglo-conformity</u> in which new immigrant
groups came to adopt English language and customs.
(a) Today, fewer Americans identify with an ethnic
group.

B. Blacks constitute 12% of the population and are the
largest racial minority.
1. Black migration was involuntary and blacks are
among the earliest of American immigrants.
(a) Slavery located most blacks in the south.
Migration to northern industrial centers began
in World War One and accelerated greatly after
World War Two.
(1) The last forty years have seen major gains
for the black minority with outlawed segregation in the armed forces, desegregation
of schools, passage of the Civil Rights
Act, and the passage of affirmative action
legislation.
2. Political gains commenced with the passage of the
Fourteenth Amendment, but they only became reality
with the massive civil rights movements occurring
in the 1960's and 1970's.
(a) Black voter registration skyrocketed and black
mayors have been elected in a number of major
cities.
3. Educational gains have centered upon the near equal
high school graduation rates between whites and
blacks. Major differences still exist throughout
undergraduate and graduate level degree programs.
4. Economic gains for blacks remain a major problem.
Greater opportunities have existed for working and
middle class blacks while lower class blacks have
found greater poverty and now constitute a distinct
underclass.
(a) While major improvements have been made by
blacks, they are still significantly disadvantaged in higher education and income
categories.

       (b) Black family income is below white levels. Factors include the high proportion of black families headed by females. Low remarriage rates further compound the problem.

       (c) Familial structure and lack of opportunity create a vicious circle entrapping a significant segment of the black population in permanent poverty.

C.   Hispanics include Cubans, Puerto Ricans, and Chicanos.

    1.   Cubans first arrived in large numbers in 1960 with the displacement of the Cuban middle class by the Cuban revolution. Subsequent immigration has been from among the more disadvantaged.

    2.   Puerto Ricans live primarily within the greater New York City area and have a high incidence of female-headed households and have one of the lowest family incomes of any racial or ethnic group.

       (a) Many Puerto Ricans suffer the triple disadvantage of being Hispanic, black, and poor.

    3.   Chicanos for the most part were not immigrants. Many are third generation Americans who became citizens with the annexation of the southwestern states.

    4.   Major problems confronting Hispanics center upon their segregated urban native language which hinder acculturation and assimilation. Prejudice and discrimination heighten and maintain their minority status.

D.   Jews have experienced thousands of years of prejudice and discrimination, thus helping to maintain a highly segregated and distinct culture.

    1.   Jews through work and education enjoy mobility rates twice that of any other minority.

    2.   Discrimination and prejudice against Jews and separatism by Jews are all declining, thus leading some to suggest that Jews may no longer be considered as minorities.

E.   Asian Americans constitute 1.5% of our population and are one of the most economically active minority groups.

    1.   Older Asian immigrants enjoy the highest average income of any racial or ethnic minority.

       (a) Post World War II immigrants follow the patterns of their predecessors.

          (1) Current Asian refugees are quickly establishing self-sufficiency.

    2.   One of the most virulent outbreaks of discrimination against Japanese Americans was their internment in World War II.

    F.   Native Americans still remain predominately unaccul-
turated and unassimilated.
1. Prejudice and discrimination against Native Americans took the exclusive form of extraordinary
solutions.
2. This treatment, combined with the reservation system, has created a shattered culture with individuals who cannot find a home in modern society
or in their past culture.

    G.   The newest immigrants are the Haitians, Laotians, and
Vietnamese.

    H.   Intergroup conflict or conflict between the different
minority groups occurs over scarce resources.
1. This process is accelerated by the developing
ethnic pride and awareness.

V. Continuity and Change

    A.   With greater steps securing minority rights in the past
two decades, prejudice has declined with the decline in
discrimination.
1. Prejudice has softened and has become more condi-
tional, nonetheless whites are still uncomfortable
with blacks and vice versa.

MATCHING   I

A.   Discrimination

B.   Scapegoat

C.   Segregation
                                       _____   1. Extraordinary
                                                     solutions.

D.   Amalgamation
                                       _____   2. Inherited physical
                                                     characteristics.

E.   Racism
                                       _____   3. Banks, landlords,
                                                     etc., discriminate.

F.   Race
                                       _____   4. Blocked goal
                                                     attainment.

G.   Racial steering
                                       _____   5. End of identity as
                                                     a distinct group.

H.   Prejudice
                                       _____   6. Common cultural
                                                     characteristics

I.   Accommodation
                                       _____   7. Physical and cul-
                                                     tural blending.

J.   Melting pot
                                       _____   8. Permit intimate
                                                     social interaction.

K.   Ethnicity
                                       _____   9. Negative and
                                                     irrational.

L.   Assimilation
                                   _____ 10. Behavior, not an
                                                     attitude.

M.   Expulsion or extermination

N.   De facto segregation

O.   Social distance

MATCHING   II

A.   Cubans

B.   Asian Americans

C.   Mulatos

D.   Native Americans

E.   Chicanos

F.   White ethnics

G.   Anglo conformity

H.   Puerto Ricans

I.   Defensive pluralism

J.   Vietnamese

K.   Blacks

L.   Haitians

M.   Japanese

N.   Canadians

O.   Jews

_____ 1. Declining ethnic
          identity.

_____ 2. A specific form of
          U.S. acculturation.

_____ 3. Most are not immi-
          grants, 50% are 3rd
          generation
          residents.

_____ 4. American concentra-
          tion camps.

_____ 5. Largest racial
          minority.

_____ 6. Most disadvantaged
          minority.

_____ 7. Highest average in-
          comes of any major
          minority group.

_____ 8. First wave came in
          1960.

_____ 9. Rate of upward
          mobility twice that
          of other
          immigrants.

_____ 10. Seventy-three per-
          cent live in New
          York City.

FILL IN THE BLANK QUESTIONS

1. Although there are physical differences between the races, the differences that count are those with _____ importance.

2. A _____ group is culturally, economically, and politically dominant while a _____ group is culturally, economically, and politically subordinate.

3. The process of _____ includes learning the language, history, and manners of the dominant group.

4. Despite frequent association or physical closeness, _____ _____ can be maintained by prejudice and discrimination.

5. _____ refers to attitudes, _____ refers to behavior.

6. Both _____ and _____ are personal factors contributing to prejudice.

7. In a society were discrimination is illegal and overt racism unacceptable, _____ _____ may still keep the minority groups subordinated.

8. Two key characteristics of black Americans are that their immigration was _____ and blacks were among the _____ of all immigrants.

9. The sizable group of blacks at the bottom of the class hierarchy who have not benefited from overall black improvement is called the black _____.

10. Decreased discrimination and high rates of intermarriage suggests that _____ may no longer be considered a minority.

11. Native Americans have, for the most part, remained the _____ and _____.

12. Data show that _____ are the most highly segregated minority group living in urban centers.

MULTIPLE CHOICE

1. A category of people who are socially defined as distinct
    because of inherited physical characteristics:

    a. ethnic group.
    b. race.
    c. majority.
    d. minority.

2. The degree of intimacy in the relationship between two
    groups is called:

    a. social distance.
    b. prejudice.
    c. discrimination.
    d. racism.

3. With this form of intergroup relations the minority group
    adopts elements of the culture of the majority group:

    a. conflict.
    b. accommodation.
    c. assimilation.
    d. acculturation.

4. A situation in which, by acting on the belief that some-
    thing exists, it becomes real:

    a. institutionalized racism.
    b. self-fulfilling prophecy.
    c. discrimination.
    d. scapegoating.

5. An extraordinary solution:

    a. prejudice.
    b. discrimination.
    c. segregation.
    d. rigid segregation.

6. An indirect form of discrimination, one in which ostensibly neutral processes exclude a disproportionate number of minority group members is:

   a. segregation.
   b. institutionalized racism.
   c. bias.
   d. aparthied.

7. Which is NOT true about prejudice?

   a. always negative.
   b. irrational.
   c. a barrier to interaction.
   d. easily gives way to facts.

8. Which of the following was used to justify racism during the age of the enlightenment (19th century)?

   a. religion.
   b. emerging political philosophy.
   c. popular ideas about social Darwinism.
   d. scientific evidence.

9. Which would NOT be considered a minority group?

   a. whites in South Africa.
   b. women in the U.S.
   c. students.
   d. blacks in the U.S.

10. The kind of intergroup relations practices in Canada with its parallel cultures, each with its own institutions is:

    a. conflict.
    b. acculturation.
    c. accommodation.
    d. assimilation.

11. Setting unjustifiable prerequisites that exclude a dispro- portionate number of minority group members and unneces- sary educational requirements for jobs are examples of:

    a. prejudice.
    b. institutionalized racism.
    c. social distance.
    d. racial steering.

12.   Individuals who are authoritarian tend to be:

    a.   submissive to everybody they come in contact with.
    b.   bullying and aggressive toward everybody they come
         in contact with.
    c.   submissive to those with higher status, but bullying
         toward those with less status.
    d.   polite and kind to those with less status, but
         aggressive toward those they think have more status
         than they do.

13.   Which is NOT true of prejudice?

    a.   its foundation is stereotyping.
    b.   it may be positive or negative.
    c.   it exists in spite of the facts.
    d.   personal and institutional factors cause prejudice.

14.   It has been proposed that personal factors can cause
      prejudice. One personal factor discussed in the text is:

    a.   age.
    b.   sex.
    c.   authoritarianism.
    d.   political preference.

15.   How are prejudice and discrimination thought to relate to
      social distance?

    a.   they create social distance.
    b.   social distance creates them.
    c.   they are independent of each other.
    d.   in former years they created social distance, but laws
         prevent this now.

16.   Prejudice is thought to ensure that when people from differ-
      ent groups interact with each other, they see not each other
      but only their conception of what the other is like. If
      this is true, by 1700 unless you were a member of this group
      you were a minority in the American colonies:

    a.   French.
    b.   English.
    c.   Spanish.
    d.   Dutch.

17. Which of the following is NOT a factor that causes prejudice?

    a. cultural norms.
    b. biological differences.
    c. institutional patterns.
    d. personal factors.

18. According to your text, the model which BEST describes the relationship between social class and race in the United States is:

    a. an embedded caste structure.
    b. a semicaste structure.
    c. a semiclass structure.
    d. a segregated class structure.

19. This represented a startling example of prejudice by Americans during World War II:

    a. the internment of West Coast Japanese Americans.
    b. the refusal to allow blacks in the military.
    c. the denial of voting rights for Americans with German ancestry.
    d. the refusal of Japanese Americans to serve in the military.

20. Four combinations of prejudice and discrimination are possible. "Timid bigots" are:

    a. prejudiced and discriminate.
    b. prejudiced but do not discriminate.
    c. not prejudiced but do discriminate.
    d. not prejudiced and do not discriminate.

21. Public policy in the U.S. directed at racism is aimed almost entirely at reducing:

    a. prejudice.
    b. discrimination.
    c. social distance.
    d. stereotyping.

22. The most highly segregated group in U.S cities:

    a. Asians.
    b. Hispanics.
    c. Jews.
    d. Blacks.

23. The largest racial minority in the U.S.:

    a. Hispanics.
    b. Japanese.
    c. Blacks.
    d. Native Americans.

24. Overall, black family income in the United States is about
    _____ percent of white family income:

    a. 35%.
    b. 57%.
    c. 76%.
    d. 87%.

25. Scholars of race relations and stratification in the U.S.
    use this term to describe the system in operation today:

    a. classes.
    b. castes.
    c. institutionalized racism.
    d. semicaste.

26. Instead of a blending of all cultures in the U.S. what has
    happened is a special form of acculturation called:

    a. the melting pot.
    b. Anglo-conformity.
    c. the American dream.
    d. a "peculiar institution".

27. Although the 40 years following World War II have seen rigid
    social change, this goal has NOT been accomplished by black
    Americans:

    a. economic parity with whites.
    b. segregation banned in the military.
    c. school segregation is outlawed.
    d. affirmative-action laws passed.

28. The largest group of Hispanics in the U.S. are:

    a. Cubans.
    b. Puerto Ricans.
    c. Chicanos.
    d. persons from Central America.

29. The second wave of Jewish immigrants to the U.S. came from:

    a. Germany.
    b. Eastern Europe.
    c. Near East.
    d. Far East.

30. The ordinary solutions that societies use to maintain boundaries between majority and minority groups include all of the following EXCEPT:

    a. segregation.
    b. discrimination.
    c. prejudice.
    d. expulsion.

ESSAY QUESTIONS

1. Compare and contrast the concepts of race and ethnicity. In what ways may they be different and in what ways may they overlap?

2. Define and note the relationship between the concepts of prejudice and discrimination.

3. Explain the relationship between prejudice, social distance, and residential segregation.

4. Discuss the relationship between Anglo conformity and rising ethnic awareness.

5. Explain how race relations in America constitute a semi-caste system.

Chapter 11
Sex
and
Gender

LEARNING OBJECTIVES

1. Differentiate between sex and gender.

2. What are gender roles and what are the determinants of a woman's status?

3. Discuss how American gender norms are sex typed for child care, labor force participation, housework, personality, and interaction.

4. Review the differences in life chances and note how women are disadvantaged in education, earnings, occupations, careers, and political power.

5. Outline the disadvantages for males in a male dominated society.

6. Discuss in detail how the socialization process is a major factor in perpetuating patterns of sex stratification.

7. Discuss how expectation states theory operates to the disadvantage of women.

8. Differentiate between sexism and sexual harassment.

9. Note the key differences between liberal, socialist, and radical feminist thought.

10. What is the relationship between viewing violent pornographic materials and men's attitude toward women?

CHAPTER 11

11. Discuss what is meant by the term androgyny.

CHAPTER OUTLINE

I. Sexual Differentiation

   A. In all societies biological sex is the basis for
      differentiation.
      1. Gender refers to the expected dispositions and
         behaviors that cultures assign to each sex.
      2. Androgyny refers to the more or less equal posses-
         sion of masculine and feminine traits.

   B. While the biological sexes are only two, the rights,
      duties, and obligations assigned to men and women, or
      gender roles, differ greatly from culture to culture.
      1. The exact balance between cultural and biological
         determinants of contemporary gender roles is yet
         to be determined.

   C. The behaviors Americans associate with being male and
      female are not universal.
      1. Margaret Mead discovered a great variety of sex
         roles in New Guinea among the Araresh, Mundugumors,
         and Tchambuli tribes.
      2. Universally, women have lower status, less power,
         and less value than men.
         (a) Three factors determine the status of women;
             they are:
             (1) The degree to which bearing, nursing, and
                 rearing children ties her to the house.
             (2) The degree to which economic and child
                 rearing duties overlap in or near the
                 home.
             (3) The degree of physical strength necessary
                 for subsistence activities.

II. American Gender Norms

   A. Many characteristics are sex typed or considered more
      appropriate for one sex than another.

   B. All societies view child care as a female
      responsibility.
      1. This is the major reason women are unequal with
         men.
      2. Most American women have (on the average) less than
         two children. This has created major role changes.
         (a) Alternative roles in the economy and community
             are now possible.

            (1) Nearly one in four women born after 1955 in
                the U.S. will choose to go childless.

C. Every decade since 1900 has seen an increase in the
labor force participation of women.
   1. Women work for a higher standard of living, for a
      career, and for socially valued roles.
      (a) Work is more of an option than an obligation
          for women, with norms specifying that their
          family must come first.

D. Norms specify that household tasks are women's
responsibility.
   1. Traditional gender roles follow the inside/outside
      division of labor.
   2. Women have increased their outside participation
      while men seldom increase their inside labors.

E. Different cognitive skills and personality characteristics are attributed to men and women.
   1. Differences in math and science scores are not
      innate and probably reflect differences in
      socialization.
   2. Personality differences are highly complex and
      subtle.

F. The lower status of women influences their patterns of
interaction.
   1. Women smile more and interrupt less than males do
      in conversation.

III. Differences in Life Chances by Sex

A. Women are equal to men in graduation rates for both
high school and college diplomas.
   1. Women get few Ph.D.'s, especially in law or
      medicine.
      (a) Socialization pressures direct women into
          teaching, nursing, and the humanities while
          men are directed into the sciences.

B. Full time women employees earned 59 cents for every
dollar earned by a man.
   1. Women earn less because they hold low paying jobs
      with few benefits or promotional opportunities.
   2. Internalization of gender appropriate norms dis-
      courage many men and women from seeking jobs
      normally reserved for the opposite sex.
   3. Women are clearly discriminated against by
      employers in hiring, salaries, and promotions.
   4. Despite a few gains, labor force participation
      is still highly sex segregated.
   5. Men also earn more in the same job than do women.

           (a) Family duties curtail career advancements with women having to subordinate their work to their familys' and husbands' needs.
6. Significant prejudices exist against many women in politics.

C. Male power and status are enormous advantages.
1. Conversely, men live shorter, more dangerous lives, have more heart disease, alcoholism, and commit more suicides than women.
2. Masculinity means men form fewer close relationships with children, kin, and friends.

IV. Perspectives on Sex Stratification

A. Socialization practices perpetuate different gender roles.
1. By 24-30 months children can differentiate by sex.
    (a) Because this is learned behavior, future generations can learn more flexible sex roles.
2. Management of multiple roles (wife, mother, career, etc.) causes many women to lower their expectations and subordinate themselves to their home role aspirations.
    (a) Socialization practices also serve to undermine girls' sense of self-esteem and self-worth.
3. Socialization to housework is sharply sex typed and follows the inside/outside division of labor.

B. Expectation states theory argues that status characteristics create expectations in others. By acting upon these expectations, the expectations are confirmed.
1. Males and females expect each other to act accordingly and act in ways to bring this about, thus confirming gender inequalities.

C. The belief that men and women have biologically different capacities and that these form a legitimate basis for the subordination of women is called sexism.
1. Sexism can be seen as part of a general strategy of stratification thru restricting access to scarce resources.

D. Sexual harassment constitutes unwelcome sexual advances, requests for sexual favors, or other verbal or physical conduct of a sexual nature.
1. Sexual harassment is illegal as a condition of employment, a basis for employment decisions, or if it interferes with an individual's work.

E. Both sexism and sexual harassment constitute discriminatory behavior and are an integral part of societal sex stratification.

F. A special case of sex stratification occurs with the combination of pornography and violence against women.
    1. Those exposed to pornography become more callous toward women, sympathize less with rape victims, and believe the rape myth.
    2. The more violent the pornography, the more marked the effect.
    3. While no direct scientific evidence links these attitudes to actual violence against women, scientists, feminists, and many women believe the connection exists.
        (a) This raises important questions for the formation of public policy.

V. Feminist Theories

    A. All feminists view gender inequality as socially constructed and feel that it should be eliminated.
        1. Liberal feminism applies standard moral and political values equally to men and women.
        2. Socialist feminism uses a Marxist critique to argue that the elimination of all private property including the private ownership of children is necessary to create equality for women.
        3. Radical feminism sees men, not social institutions, as the problem.
            (a) This view advocates the severing of all heterosexual relationships and the creation of a separate women's culture.
        4. Socialist and radical theory are a distinct minority.

VI. Prospects for Change

    A. Traditional gender roles are thoroughly institutionalized, yet the last fifteen years have seen important changes.
        1. These changes have increased alternatives for women, eroded some male power, and made men and women compete more between each other.
        2. Changes have increased role strain in that both men and women must add new roles.

    B. Despite some stress and change, traditional gender roles still dominate in the home.

    C. Women's low fertility and high education will help to erode traditional gender roles.
        1. As gender roles become less differentiated, more equality will emerge between men and women.

MATCHING

A.   Housework

B.   Sexual harassment

C.   Sexism

D.   Socialist feminism

E.   Radical feminism

F.   Male gender role

G.   Expectation states theory

H.   Sex typing

I.   Gender roles

J.   Liberal feminism

K.   Gender

L.   Sex

_____ 1. Creating a separate women's culture.

_____ 2. Rights, duties, and obligations assigned by sex.

_____ 3. Biological characteristic, male or female.

_____ 4. Certain behaviors suitable only for men or women.

_____ 5. Unwelcome sexual advances.

_____ 6. Expected dispositions assigned by culture to each sex.

_____ 7. Biological differences are a legitimate basis for subordination.

_____ 8. Inside/outside division of labor.

_____ 9. Hypertension, suicide, and alcoholism.

_____ 10. Equality for women through abolishing private property.

FILL IN THE BLANK QUESTIONS

1. American women can now expect to live _____ years
    after the last child leaves home.

2. It is estimated that twenty percent to twenty-five percent
    of the women born after 1955 will remain _____.

3. The average wife with a full time job puts in an additional
    _____ hours a week of housework compared to _____
    hours for her husband.

4. In conversation, _____ interrupt _____
    more often.

5. In life expectancy, _____ outlive _____
    by an average of seven years.

6. For every dollar a man earns, a woman typically earns
    _____ cents.

7. Socialization for the domestic division of labor is still
    sharply _____ _____.

8. Taking out the garbage is largely a _____
    province.

9. The major studies on violent pornography _____
    but do not _____ a link between pornography
    and some aspects of violence toward women.

10. _____ is the more or less equal possession
    of masculine and feminine traits.

11. _____ is the public policy issue with
    the largest gender gap.

12. Radical feminists want to sever all heterosexual relation-
    ships and create a women's culture based upon _____,
    _____, and _____.

MULTIPLE CHOICE

1. This terms refers to rights, duties, and obligations
    assigned to people in every society:

    a. sex.
    b. gender roles.
    c. life choices.
    d. conventional achievements.

2. Which is NOT a characteristic of gender norms?

    a. noncompliance to gender norms leads to sanctions.
    b. gender norms are internalized.
    c. gender norms can lead to guilt when people fail to comply.
    d. gender norms easily are changed by fact and rational thought.

3. Differences in rewards, rights, opportunities, status, and income are aspects of this system:

    a. sex roles.
    b. sexual stratification.
    c. gender.
    d. life chances.

4. A special form of discrimination that is especially problematic for female workers and students is:

    a. sexual harassment.
    b. denial of access to professional jobs.
    c. the educational gap.
    d. higher levels of unemployment.

5. This perspective holds that status characteristics create expectations in others about males and females:

    a. socialization.
    b. expectation states theory.
    c. prejudice.
    d. feminism.

6. Sexism refers to:

    a. unwelcome sexual advances, requests for sexual favors, or other verbal or physical conduct of a sexual nature.
    b. being prejudiced toward the opposite sex.
    c. the study of the biological differences between male and female.
    d. the belief that men and women have biologically different capacities and that these form a legitimate basis for unequal treatment.

7. If you score high on both masculine and feminine dimensions, you will be categorized as:

    a. androgynous.
    b. undifferentiated.
    c. traditional.
    d. uncertain.

8. John disagrees with his parents who always ask him to mow the yard and wash the car and his sister to help prepare dinner and take care of their younger brother. Sometimes John would like to switch responsibilities with his sister. John is critical of:

    a. gender norms.
    b. his gender.
    c. his sister's poor work.
    d. his parents.

9. People (men and women) who reject traditional sex roles for modern sex roles can be expected to experience:

    a. more flexibility but less role strain.
    b. more flexibility and more role strain.
    c. less flexibility and less role strain.
    d. less flexibility but more role strain.

10. The typical male in this class compared with the typical female can expect to:

    a. earn less money.
    b. have greater difficulty gaining access to a profession.
    c. have less political power.
    d. live fewer years.

11. These people wish to apply standard moral and political values to gender inequality:

    a. liberal feminists.
    b. socialist feminists.
    c. radical feminists.
    d. all feminists.

12. Women tend to have the highest status in:

    a. early industrial societies.
    b. advanced industrial societies.
    c. agricultural societies.
    d. simple horticultural societies.

13. This belief encourages people to think that men and women have biologically different capacities and that these form a legitimate basis for the subordination of women:

    a. Marxism.
    b. sexism.
    c. functionalism.
    d. feminism.

14. This socialization practice functions to channel girls' aspirations differently than boys:

    a. achievement socialization.
    b. learning gender identities.
    c. domestic socialization.
    d. learned expectations.

15. Based upon Bem's theory, androgynous people can be expected to:

    a. be inflexible but high performers.
    b. be flexible but poor performers.
    c. be inflexible and poor performers.
    d. be flexible and high performers.

16. Evidence of the impact of differential socialization is provided by:

    a. unequal salaries for males and females.
    b. the greater strength of boys.
    c. different aspiration levels of girls.
    d. discrimination by employers.

17. Radical feminism is MOST likely to explain differences between the status of men and women on the basis of:

    a. standard moral and political values.
    b. blaming men, not institutions.
    c. biological determinism.
    d. Marxist ideology.

18. Which feminist theory is based on the Marxist perspective that men are the bourgeois and women the proletarians?

    a. liberal feminism.
    b. socialist feminism.
    c. reactionary feminism.
    d. radical feminism.

19. Women's status in societies that have industrialized:

    a. is lower than in any other type of society.
    b. is higher than in any other type of society.
    c. has declined since the beginning of industrialization.
    d. was initially low but shows signs of rising.

20. Which is true today about labor force participation for those aged 25-54?

    a. most men and women work.
    b. equal percentages of men and women work.
    c. less than half of women work.
    d. only about half of men and women work.

21. In terms of life chances, which is NOT true for females in the U.S. today?

    a. have fewer children.
    b. longer life expectancy than males.
    c. educational achievement increased faster than for males.
    d. elimination of the salary gap between males and females.

22. A comparison of SAT scores show that:

    a. boys and girls have equal scores.
    b. girls have better math skills.
    c. boys have better verbal skills.
    d. boys outnumber girls 13 to 1 among those scoring 700 or more on the quantitative test.

23. Which is a cultural universal in terms of roles assigned men and women?

    a. men raise crops and tend livestock.
    b. men are aggressive.
    c. men have more power than women.
    d. women wear make-up and spend hours preening.

24. Approximately what proportion of all women employees are clerical workers?

    a. one out of ten.
    b. one out of three.
    c. one out of two.
    d. three out of four.

25.   A major cost paid by males because of traditional sex roles
       is:

       a.   higher levels of mental illness.
       b.   greater incidence of poverty.
       c.   less political power.
       d.   less intimacy and affiliation with children.

26.   Generalizing from the research on sex role identification by
       Bem, we would expect these people to have high role perform-
       ance in both instrumental and expressive tasks:

       a.   masculine.
       b.   androgynous.
       c.   feminine.
       d.   undifferentiated.

27.   A cross-cultural review of genders and sex roles indicate
       that:

       a.   sex is distinct, but gender roles may vary.
       b.   both gender and sex roles are distinct.
       c.   neither gender nor sex roles are distinct.
       d.   neither gender nor sex roles vary.

28.   Which is NOT a key factor in determining women's status in a
       society?

       a.   the degree they are tied to the home by children.
       b.   intelligence and motivation.
       c.   the degree to which economic activities are compatible
             with staying at home and caring for children.
       d.   the physical strength needed to carry on subsistence
             activities.

29.   Looking to the 1990s and the next century, which is the BEST
       prediction about labor force participation?

       a.   most males and most females will work.
       b.   most males and about one-fourth of females will work.
       c.   participation rates will fall for males and females.
       d.   relatively fewer males will work.

30. Studies show that, when wives in the U.S. work outside the home, the husband's participation in housework:

    a. increases substantially.
    b. increases only slightly.
    c. remains unchanged.
    d. decreases slightly.

ESSAY QUESTIONS

1. Note how sex roles are becoming more androgynous.

2. Discuss how sexual stratification works in our society.

3. Discuss how expectation states theory constitutes a self-fulfilling prophecy for both men and women.

4. Critique each of the feminist theories.

5. Why do women work?

Chapter 12
Age Differentiation and Inequalities

LEARNING OBJECTIVES

1. Briefly outline what aspects of aging interest sociologists.

2. Define the concept of life course and discuss how age-related transitions are a product of social structure.

3. Outline the age norms for the following categories: children, adolescents, young adults, middle age, and those over 65.

4. Discuss how the young are legally and economically disadvantaged.

5. What are the characteristics of a youth subculture and in what historical periods have they existed?

6. Carefully outline the advantages and disadvantages for those 65 and over.

7. To what extent are the young and old tied to their kin?

8. Describe the changing age distribution of the U.S. and note the impact upon public policy for today and for the future.

9. Use the structural-functional and conflict perspectives to explain age stratification.

10. Use modernization theory to account for the impact of the industrial revolution on the power of the elderly in society.

11. Describe how age, sex, and race can contribute to double or triple jeopardy.

12. What is ageism and how does it function in society both legally and illegally?

13. Briefly outline a life course and follow a cohort through time noting key transitions and appropriate rites of passage.

CHAPTER OUTLINE

I. Age Differentiation

    A. All societies assign different roles according to age.
        1. Sociologists are primarily interested in the norms and roles that structure different age categories.
            (a) Concern is also focused upon socially structured inequities.

    B. Aging and age expectations are an important part of social structure.
        1. Critical ages in the U.S. are 6, 16, 18 or 21 and 65. These are products of culture, not biology.
            (a) Bureaucracies reinforce these age norms by requiring schooling and retirement.
        2. Age-related transitions that are socially created, socially recognized, and shared are referred to as the life course.
            (a) A cohort is a category of individuals who share a particular experience at the same point in time.
                (1) Each age category or cohort will experience aging differently because of their unique experiences over the life course.

II. Age Norms

    A. Age norms refer to the attitudes and behavior expected when one "acts their age".
        1. Age norms are general and have few sanctions associated with them.

    B. Norms of childhood establish a rather clear set of rights and responsibilities.
        1. Legal rights guarantee health, education, and protection.
        2. Obligations include playing and accomplishing developmental tasks.
            (a) Children can be objects of abuse.

3. Increasingly more children are being raised in single parent households.

C. Adolescence is a period of irresponsibility.
    1. Four basic obligations are to:
        (a) become independent of their parents.
        (b) test and experiment with new roles.
        (c) acquire adult skills.
        (d) have fun.

D. The role of adult carries more burdens and more benefits.
    1. A <u>rite of passage</u> is a formal ritual marking the end of one status and the beginning of another.
        (a) There is no clear demarcation of the adult role.
            (1) Normally finishing school, becoming employed, married, and a parent suffice.
            (2) The order and timing of these transitions have varied considerably in recent decades.
    2. Middle age (45 to 65) is usually a quieter and more prosperous period than the first 25 years of adult life.
        (a) Fewer role strains and conflicts occur.
        (b) It is a period of consolidation and assessment.
            (1) Some experience a <u>mid-life crisis</u> and reorganize their priorities.
    3. Adults over 65 should be independent, yet nonproductive, nonaggressive, and noncompetitive.
        (a) Retirement is usually a positive stage in the life course despite negative stereotypes of older adults.
            (1) Life satisfaction is correlated with good health, adequate income, and a good family life.

III. Life Chances and Inequalities

A. Adults between 30 and 65 control society thus creating inequities for young and old alike.

B. Young people are not considered responsible and have few legal rights.
    1. Societal beliefs hold that age is a measure of competency and lacking age, the young may be legally discriminated against.
        (a) The lower status of youth is institutionalized into the culture.
    2. Most American youth earn the minimum wage or are unemployed.
        (a) Youthful minorities and young families are most often the victims of these economic practices.

(b) The young are not fully integrated into society and are overrepresented in crime and accident statistics.

3. A youth subculture exists that emphasizes passive escape and style.
   (a) Style is based upon image, demeanor, and argot.
       (1) Mastery of style enhances ones self-esteem.
   (b) The youth subculture is basically a leisure time activity.

C. Those over 65 are not particularly disadvantaged if they are healthy.

1. The average life expectancy at 65 is sixteen additional years.
   (a) The "old old" have lost physical stamina and cannot effectively care for their homes or themselves.

2. Social Security, private pensions, and government programs have drastically increased the income of the elderly in the last three decades.
   (a) Older people have fewer expenses and most now survive adequately with the reduced income of retirement.
       (1) Single women and minorities are the most disadvantaged.

3. Few older people are forced into retirement, and most look happily forward to retiring.
   (a) Age discrimination in the form of ageism works to the disadvantage of middle aged persons seeking employment.
       (1) Ageism is reinforced by the negative stereotypes of older persons.

4. The Elderly vote, more so than any other age group.
   (a) Consensus is not reached due to the cleavages created by race, class, and gender.
       (1) Older people tend to feel politically powerless.

5. Despite the advantages of age and retirement, most older persons are accorded reduced levels of honor and esteem.
   (a) Reductions in vigor, attractiveness, and productivity mean less prestige.
       (1) Historically the elderly have suffered the same indignities.

6. Social integration into society declines with the age related loss of roles.
   (a) Ties with friends and relatives are still critically important although some family roles may force the older person to be dependent upon their children.

(1) Longevity has led to the creation of a "generation squeeze", a condition in which many middle aged adults have responsibilities to both their adult children and their aging parents.

IV. The Changing Balance of Youth and Age

A. America is rapidly becoming a society of older adults.
   1. The proportion of the elderly is increasing as the proportion of the young declines.
      (a) Lower fertility and increased longevity account for the changes in age distribution.

B. Younger people are effectively disenfranchised and adults control the contest for scarce public resources.
   1. Recent federal budget cutbacks have seriously disadvantaged youth while the elderly remain unscathed.
      (a) Poverty has increased among children and decreased among the elderly.
         (1) This reflects the belief that children are the responsibility of their families while the elderly are the responsibility of the government.
         (2) Illegitimacy and divorce compound this problem.

V. Explanations for Age Stratification

A. The young and the old lack status because they are less competent and less productive.

B. Structural-Functional theory sees age stratification as functional.
   1. The young are afforded time to learn and the old are allowed to disengage.
   2. Disengagement theory is a functional theory that argues that the elderly voluntarily disengage themselves from active social participation.
      (a) Disengagement allows for the orderly transition from one generation to the next while reducing the stigma of declining productivity attributed to older workers.
         (1) It is argued that a consensus exists that disengagement is a benefit to all.
   3. Conflict theory sees age stratification as arising from competition over scarce resources, namely jobs.
      (a) Excluding youth and highly paid older workers benefits workers between 20 and 65 as well as their employers.
      (b) Mandatory retirement achieves this end.

4. Current values argue that retirement suits both the aging worker and the economic system.
   (a) Conflict may emerge again as fewer young people exist to support an increasing population of the elderly.
5. <u>Modernization theory</u> (<u>Cowgill</u>) argues that industrialization reduces the power of the elderly by reducing the value of their traditional resources: land, labor, and experience.
   (a) As occupations displace land as the basis for income and prestige, the elderly lose control of the power associated with inherited land.
   (b) Modern productivity robs the elderly and children of a valuable economic role.
   (c) Rapid change makes the experience of older adults outmoded.
6. Disengagement theory and modernization theory are more applicable to explaining the status of the elderly while conflict theory and modernization theory account better for the low status of youth.

VI. Cross-Cutting Statuses: Age, Sex, and Race

A. A person low on two or more of these dimensions of stratification is said to be in <u>double</u> <u>or</u> <u>triple</u> <u>jeopardy</u>.
   1. Aging and gender are especially problematic for women.
      (a) Women outlive men and will spend their last years alone and uncared for.
         (1) Husbands typically die first at home in the care of their wives.
      (b) Men who widow remarry more easily while most older women are seldom able to find a new spouse.
      (c) Increasingly, older populations are becoming feminized.

B. Minorities may be comparatively better off in retirement due to less of a drop in income and the <u>mortality crossover</u>.
   1. Government programs, higher esteem in ethnic communities, and closer family ties may aid the older minority individual.
   2. Minorities still experience major economic dislocations with age and are less likely than anglos to reach retirement.

MATCHING

A. Cohort

B. Middle Age

C. Modernization theory

D. Generation gap

E. Conflict theory

F. Ageism

G. Role theory

H. Disengagement theory

I. Youth subculture

J. Life course

K. Empty nest

L. Rites of passage

M. Adolescence

N. Honeymoon

O. Double or triple jeopardy

_____ 1. Age legitimizes unequal treatment.

_____ 2. Age-related transitions that are socially created, recognized, etc.

_____ 3. A period of great role stress.

_____ 4. Industrialization reduces the value of land, labor, and experience.

_____ 5. A period of assessment.

_____ 6. All those born in 1965.

_____ 7. Formal rituals marking transitions.

_____ 8. Functionalist theory of aging.

_____ 9. An emphasis on passive escape.

_____ 10. Low status on 2 or more dimensions of stratification.

FILL IN THE BLANK QUESTIONS

1. Aging and age expectations are in large part products of
    _____ _____.

2. A _____ is a category of individuals who
    share a particular experience at the same point in time.

3. Current estimates indicate that one out of _____ girls
    will experience sexual abuse by their parents.

4. The most common transition sequence into adult status is to
    finish school, get a _____, then a
    _____ and _____.

5. Some claim that retirement is a _____ role
    due to the _____ of rights and duties.

6. As long as the elderly retain their _____, they
    generally report higher levels of life satisfaction.

7. Discrimination against _____ may be legally
    approved inequality.

8. Style in the youth subculture consists of _____,
    _____, and _____.

9. The average person reaching 65 can expect to live an addi-
    tional _____ years.

10. The mandatory retirement of police officers at age 50 is an
    example of a ___ ___ ___ ___.

11. The "old old" are disproportionately _____ and
    _____.

12. Data have shown that poverty has increased among _____
    and decreased among the _____.

13. On the average women outlive men by _____ years.

14. When surviving minorities reach retirement age, they may
    experience lower mortality rates, this is called the
    _____.

15. The practice of "_____ _____"
    and the availability of the local _____ helped
    to create a youth subculture in 17th century New England.

MULTIPLE CHOICE

1. A category of people who share a particular experience at the same point in time:

    a. family.
    b. cohort.
    c. group.
    d. society.

2. These serve as the "road map" that structures us on the life course:

    a. age norms.
    b. biological characteristics.
    c. chronological ages.
    d. gender norms.

3. Which of the following carries with it more rights and responsibilities than any other age role:

    a. childhood.
    b. adolescence.
    c. old age.
    d. adulthood.

4. Persons who are thought to have a "roleless role" are:

    a. over 65.
    b. adolescents.
    c. children.
    d. middle-aged.

5. Which of the following terms refers to a set of patterned responses to some problems that are unique to a particular group in society:

    a. age expectations.
    b. life chances.
    c. rites of passage.
    d. subculture.

6. When a person has a low status on three different dimensions of stratification we speak of:

   a. triple jeopardy.
   b. status integration.
   c. underachievement.
   d. status disengagement.

7. Age differentiation differs from other bases of differentiation in that:

   a. it is less severe.
   b. it is more severe.
   c. it is independent of prejudice.
   d. other bases of differentiation tend to be mutually exclusive.

8. Which of the following is NOT of primary interest to sociologists who study age:

   a. systematic physical and psychological changes.
   b. social norms.
   c. roles that structure behavior.
   d. the relationship between privileges and inequality.

9. A sociologist completes a study of people of a given age who have had unique experiences. This is a study of the:

   a. life course perspective.
   b. age structure.
   c. age norms.
   d. cohort perspective.

10. The description of a situation in which the middle generation experiences demands from their children and parents is called:

    a. lack of integration.
    b. roleless role.
    c. generation gap.
    d. generation squeeze.

11. Which group of people is NOT caught in a situation of double jeopardy?

    a. white adolescents.
    b. black adolescents.
    c. aged women.
    d. black women.

12. Which of the following would be a rite of passage?

    a. going to the senior prom.
    b. having a baby shower.
    c. going through high school graduation.
    d. getting your first car.

13. Ageism is thought to be correlated with:

    a. job discrimination.
    b. forced retirement.
    c. loss of physical strength.
    d. long life.

14. Generalizing from the results of the last century, a society could anticipate an increased proportion of older people if:

    a. fertility falls.
    b. fertility rises.
    c. mortality falls.
    d. mortality rises.

15. Which theory is supported by the existence of mandatory retirement rules:

    a. physiological theory.
    b. disengagement theory.
    c. conflict theory.
    d. modernization theory.

16. Which conclusion is associated with modernization theory's explanation of age stratification?

    a. youths are excluded so others will benefit.
    b. reduced social participation of the aged is good for the aged and society.
    c. the elderly are excluded so others will benefit.
    d. a decreased status for the elderly because of erosion of their power bases.

17. In everyday usage, most people rely upon this theory of age stratification:

    a. conflict theory.
    b. physiological theory.
    c. disengagement theory.
    d. modernization theory.

18. The modernization theory of aging argues that the elderly have:

    a. low status in modern societies because the value of their traditional resources has eroded.
    b. low status in modern societies because they are no longer productive.
    c. relatively high status in modern societies because of of their past contributions to development and modernization.
    d. a right to share in the wealth produced by modernization.

19. Which age is NOT a critical point in the age distribution for Americans:

    a. 6.
    b. 18 or 21.
    c. 65.
    d. 2.

20. About what percent of children born in the 1980s will live in a single-parent household at some time before they are 18?

    a.   5 percent.
    b. 20 percent.
    c. 90 percent.
    d. 60 percent.

21. Young and older persons share this stereotype of older persons:

    a. friendly and warm.
    b. wise.
    c. bright and alert.
    d. open-minded.

22. In law, people under 18 are called:

    a. children.
    b. infants.
    c. adolescents.
    d. young adults.

23. These people are MOST likely to suffer unemployment:

    a. black youth.
    b. white youth.
    c. white adults.
    d. black adults.

24. Between 1820 and 1985, the proportion of the American popu-
    lation over 65 has gone from:

    a. 2% to 12%.
    b. 10% to 15%.
    c. 10% to 22%.
    d. 16% to 8%.

25. In contrast to sex norms, age norms:

    a. are less specific.
    b. generate more sanctions.
    c. guide the behavior of few people.
    d. affect only a few people.

26. The normative transition sequence in the U.S. is:

    a. finish school, job, children, spouse.
    b. job, finish school, children, spouse.
    c. finish school, job, spouse, children.
    d. spouse, job, finish school, children.

27. If one's parents are typical they LEAST expect an
    adolescent to:

    a. become independent.
    b. be responsible.
    c. experiment with new roles.
    d. have fun.

28. This variable is NOT correlated with life satisfaction
    among those over age 65:

    a. meaningful work.
    b. good health.
    c. adequate money.
    d. satisfying family life.

29. Which of the following is the MOST structurally disadvantaged in American society?

    a. children and adolescents.
    b. children and middle-aged.
    c. adolescents and those over 65.
    d. children and those over 65.

30. Which of the following is the MOST accurate statement about poverty and the elderly?

    a. being old causes many people to be poor for the first time.
    b. social security and medicaid lift some people out of poverty for the first time in their lives.
    c. the proportion of elderly that is poor far exceeds the percent of the total population that is poor.
    d. being old and poor is often the result of being young (or middle-aged) and poor.

ESSAY QUESTIONS

1. How adequately do structural-functional and conflict theories account for the position of today's elderly.

2. Discuss how children are more disadvantaged than the elderly by age stratification.

3. Discuss how the role of the retired can be seen as a role-less role.

4. Explain how those between 30 and 65 control society.

5. Explore the implications of the phenomenon of the feminization of the elderly.

Chapter 13
The
Family

LEARNING OBJECTIVES

1. Outline the six universal functions/responsibilities of the family noted by Murdock.

2. Differentiate between the following concepts: family, kin group, and marriage.

3. Define each of the following terms and note those that are typical of modern society: nuclear family, extended family, neolocal, matrilocal, patrilocal, monogamy, polygyny, poly-andry, patriarchal, matriarchal, and egalitarianism.

4. Outline a profile of the American family.

5. Explain how the divorce rate is calculated and indicate the current trends in divorce.

6. Define romantic love and note the social and historical conditions under which it is most likely to occur.

7. Discuss the origin and characteristics of the "sexual revolution."

8. Describe how the dating game operates and specify the role played by propinquity, homogamy, physical attractiveness, and the love filters.

9. Differentiate between male and female roles in marriage; what has changed and what has remained the same over the last fifty years.

10. Identify the different gender roles for males and females and indicate the different sexual scripts available to women today.

11. Compare and contrast the rewards and liabilities of having and raising children for both mothers and fathers.

12. Outline the correlates of marital satisfaction and stability.

13. Use the conflict, structural-functional, and symbolic interaction approaches to highlight current problems in the family.

14. Explain how stepparenting causes stress in a marriage.

15. Note the structural changes in the American family and indicate the consequences of these changes.

16. Discuss the manifest and latent functions of divorce.

CHAPTER OUTLINE

I. Marriage, Family, and Kinship: Basic Institutions of Society

    A. Murdock contends that the major responsibilities of families are: replacement through reproduction, regulation of sexual behavior, economic responsibility for dependents, socialization of the young, ascription of status, and the provision of intimacy.
        1. Every society provides some institutional structure to meet these responsibilities called the family.
            (a) The family is a relatively permanent group of persons linked together in social roles by ties of blood, marriage, or adoption who live together and cooperate economically and in the rearing of children.
            (b) The family is usually embedded in a larger set of relatives - the kin group.
            (c) Marriage is an institutionalized social structure providing an enduring framework for the regulation of sexual behavior and for childbearing.

(1) While some family ties are biological,
marriage is a key concept in understanding
the family as a social group whereby
society controls the formation of new
family units, kinship relationships, and
inheritance. This ensures continuity in
the existing patterns of stratification,
etc.

2. Families universally regulate sexual behavior, provide care for dependents, and offer emotional and
financial security. In doing so, many cultural
variations occur.

(a) Family patterns include the <u>nuclear</u> <u>family</u>
where the married pair establish an independ-
ent household and the <u>extended</u> <u>family</u> where
they live with other kin.

(b) Residence patterns also vary with the nuclear
family living by itself in the <u>neolocal</u>
pattern. Other patterns include the <u>matrilocal</u>
and <u>patrilocal</u> forms.

(c) Courtship patterns are a reflection of social
values and economic interests.

(1) Arranged marriages are typical where prestige and property are involved with the
parents playing a major role in selecting
mates.

(2) When the economic interests of the parents
are not directly involved and the young
have freedom, there is a decrease in
familial involvement and control.

(3) Parents still exert strong indirect control
through their selection of neighborhood and
schools.

(d) Marriage patterns vary from <u>monogamy</u> to <u>poly-</u>
<u>gamy</u> and even <u>polygyny</u>.

(1) Viewed cross-culturally polygyny has been
the most popular marriage form while the
vast majority of the world's population
practices monogamy.

(e) Authority patterns in western society are norm-
atively <u>egalitarian</u> where the spouses share
equally in decision making, control of family
resources, and childrearing. Alternative forms
include <u>patriarchal</u> and <u>matriarchal</u> patterns.

II. A Profile of the U.S. Family

A. Norms about growing up specify that children should
grow up in intact families.

1. Divorce and illegitimacy allow for only 3/4 of
children to live in intact families.

(a) Children of so called broken homes may be more
prone to divorce and illegitimacy themselves.

B. Americans are the "marryingest" of the industrial nations.
1. Current trends show a strong tendency to delay marriage. This increase in singleness poses serious questions. Are people forsaking marriage or only postponing it?

C. The majority of married couples expect to have children with the number of children desired falling rapidly in the last generation, slightly less than two.
1. Decreases in childbearing have been accompanied by increases in female participation in the labor force.
2. The average woman does not yet place career ahead of family but she does desire more personal freedom and economic security which are adversely affected by the time spent in childrearing.
    (a) Illegitimacy has increased dramatically with nearly one half of all illegitimate births happening to teenage mothers.
    (b) Most mothers of illegitimate children eventually marry.

D. Divorce has become a commonplace phenomena. It is measured by either the <u>divorce rate</u> or the <u>lifetime divorce probability</u>.
1. Both statistics show increases in the past decades, but have apparently stabilized.
2. Divorce rates remain high due, in large part, to more social approval.

E. Most people who get divorced also remarry - often very quickly.
1. Age creates major remarriage problems for women but not for men.

III. Courtship in the United States

A. No other society has believed that love in marriage is as important as in contemporary America.
1. <u>Romantic love</u> is a combination of such physical symptoms as breathlessness and a pounding heart with a sexual yearning for the other and a disregard for practical and economic consequences.
    (a) Romantic love first was recognized in the 12th and 13th Centuries; despite this, it can only flourish when marriage is an arrangement between individuals rather than families.
        (1) This is more typical in systems featuring reduced kinship roles and the nuclear family.

B. Many social structures encourage the development of
love. Generally in our society all young people are
expected to date; it is an obligatory form of social
behavior.
   1. Important norms concerning dating center upon the
      appropriate degree of sexual contact. Norms range
      from abstinence to total permissiveness.
      (a) Within the U.S. two major sexual revolutions
          have occurred; one in the 1920's that saw a
          sharp increase in premarital sexual intercourse
          and a second in the late 1960's which featured
          an increase in permissiveness and the decline
          of the double standard.
          (1) A <u>double standard</u> exists when premarital or
              extramarital sexual activity is acceptable
              for men but not for women.

C. The choice of a marriage partner is influenced by
several factors.
   1. Original attraction will be strongly influenced by
      the spatial nearness of potential partners
      (<u>propinquity</u>), social similarity (<u>homogamy</u>), and
      physical attractiveness.
   2. Dating may progress toward a more serious consider-
      ation of marriage as the respective partners pass
      a series of barriers or filters.
      (a) The filters include propinquity, social back-
          ground, attractiveness, compatibility, and a
          final assessment called a market evaluation
          filter.
   3. The dating game can be viewed as a shopping trip
      where one is evaluating the goods and searching for
      the best bargain.

D. <u>Cohabitation</u> occurs when couples live together without
legal marriage.
   1. Cohabitation rates have increased dramatically in
      the past two decades. Increasingly, cohabitation
      is viewed as a prelude to marriage.
   2. Sociologists view cohabitation as an additional
      stage in the courtship process rather than an
      alternative to marriage.

E. Highly educated women over age 30 are significantly
disadvantaged in the marriage market.
   1. Most compatible men are either married or looking
      for younger women.
      (a) A large number of women in this category do not
          have marriage as a priority.

IV. Roles and Relationships in Marriage

A. Both home and work roles for men and women are changing
in fundamental ways.

       1.   The majority of married women work and it is vital to maintaining their family's standard of living.

       2.   The majority of mothers work even if their children are preschoolers.

          (a) Career involvement and attitude toward work are the best predictors of a working mother.

       3.   Norms still dictate that husbands ought to work and the wives should do the housework.

          (a) The actual division of labor remains unchanged when a wife works.

             (1) Many women experience severe role overload.

B.   Sexual roles have undergone a great deal of change recently.

       1.   Studies show that there is a greater acceptance of oral sex, particularly by women, and women have reached parity with men in their probability of having an affair.

          (a) Another finding indicates that the importance of sex in marriage declines significantly after the first year.

       2.   The sexual script for women has changed dramatically.

          (a) In the 19th Century sex was a male right and a female duty.

          (b) In the post war period of 1950-1970 sex was positive for both men and women but men were seen as enjoying sex without love where women could not.

             (1) The double standard was operative during this period.

          (c) Beginning in the 1970's men and women were seen as having similar approaches to sex.

             (1) Feminist arguments often exhorted women to take charge of their own sexual experience.

          (d) _Rubin's_ study of working class families showed few such changes. Many working class women responded to their husbands' sexual demands out of a sense of duty or powerlessness. Some used sex as a bargaining tool in the marriage.

C.   Parenthood is the biggest gamble most married people will ever make.

       1.   Children are financially and emotionally costly and require a tremendous commitment of time, energy, and money.

       2.   Childrearing duties follow the traditional divisions of labor with the female being chiefly responsible.

          (a) The consequences of this division of labor occur later in life where widowed men receive less support and help from their children than do women.

3. Stepparenting is becoming more frequent with increases in divorce and remarriage in our society. Unfortunately stepparenting is an especially stressful experience for the children and the stepparent involved.
   (a) Encouraging teenagers to leave the home reduces this stress as does the ultimate act--another divorce.
      (1) The divorce rate for families with stepchildren is twice the rate for families without them.
4. The empty nest is that period in the marriage when all the children have left home. With fewer children and increasing longevity, the empty nest typically can last up to 30 years.
   (a) Most parents adjust nicely to the empty nest with reported marital satisfaction increasing especially for women who feel a sense of release and renewal.

D. Increasing longevity and delays in marriage often sandwich the middle aged couple between the demands for help from their parents and their adult children.

V. Determinants of Marital Satisfaction and Marital Stability

A. The strongest predictor of divorce is age at marriage.
   1. Marriages before age 20 are particularly vulnerable to divorce.
      (a) Those married before they are 20 are often poor, lacking in maturity and social skills, and have experienced short engagements.
         (1) These factors combine to make these marriages very stressful.

B. Integration into relationships outside the nuclear family helps to deter divorce by providing additional social support and providing help if needed.
   1. Divorce would sever these relationships and this also deters divorce.

C. Income is positively associated with marital satisfaction and a lower probability of divorce.

D. Children have little impact upon divorce after the first year or two when they are born.
   1. A newborn deters divorce.

E. The increase in the probability of divorce during this century reflects important structural changes in society.

      1. With a shift from agriculture and industrializa-
tion to a service economy, economic assets like
education and experience are not tied to the
family.
      (a) Opportunities in the economy are readily avail-
able outside of marriage - especially for
women.
      (1) Marriages thus have less institutional
support than before.

VI   Theoretical Approaches to the Problems of the Family

   A. Perceptions of family problems and solutions are
directly influenced by a given theoretical framework.
      1. Structural-Functionalists see the emphasis on self,
happiness, and growth as eroding the commitment
to marriage.
      (a) As fathers and mothers voluntarily leave
families, the major task of childrearing is
being undermined. This is seen as being
dysfunctional.
      (1) The increasing number of women and children
in poverty reflects this problem.
      2. Conflict theorists still see the family as oppres-
sive for both women and children who are exploited
and often abused.
      (a) Equal opportunity for women and state enforced
support for children would ease the problems.
      3. Symbolic interactionists see family instability as
having a potentially harmful effect upon ones personal identity.

   B. The family continues to perform vital functions for
society and the individual alike.
      1. Positive signs are the enduring mother/child bond,
high remarriage rates, intergenerational help patterns, and the continuation of stepparenting.

MATCHING

A. Nuclear family

B. Polygyny

C. Sandwich generation

D. Homogamy

E. 19th Century

F. Neolocal

G. 1970's - 1980's

H. Propinquity

I. Dating

J. Egalitarianism

K. 1960's - 1970's

L. Polygamy

M. Extended family

N. United States

O. Monogamy

_____ 1. An obligatory
           form of social
           behavior.

_____ 2. The nuclear family
           lives by itself.

_____ 3. Men and women
           approach sex
           similarly.

_____ 4. Marriage to more
           than one spouse
           at a time.

_____ 5. Sex is a male
           right and a
           female duty.

_____ 6. Married pair
           forms an independ-
           ent household.

_____ 7. Romantic love
           is of prime
           importance.

_____ 8. The double
           standard was
           operative.

_____ 9. Spatial
           nearness.

_____ 10. Caring for your
           parents and
           your children.

CHAPTER 13

FILL IN THE BLANK QUESTIONS

1. The _____ is usually embedded in a larger set of relatives called the _____.

2. _____ is an institutionalized social structure that provides an enduring framework for regulating sexual behavior and childbearing.

3. Encouraging teenagers to leave home helps to reduce the stress of _____.

4. The average woman desires more _____ _____ and _____ _____, both of which are adversely affected by taking time out for childbearing.

5. Nearly one out of five births were to an _____ mother.

6. Integration into the community helps to deter _____.

7. Eighty percent of _____ and seventy percent of _____ remarry after divorce.

8. Increasingly _____ is viewed as an additional stage in the courtship process rather than as an alternative to marriage.

9. With the increase in working mothers, household tasks such as cleaning and cooking are done by _____.

10. After the first year of marriage, _____ is of decreasing importance to most people.

11. Rubin's study of working-class families showed that women viewed their sexual behavior in terms of _____, _____ and as a _____ _____.

12. _____ is really the biggest gamble most married people will ever make.

13. _____ _____ individuals report happier marriages and fewer divorces.

14. Reported marital satisfaction increases as children _____ _____ when women especially report feelings of _____ and _____.

15. The strongest predictor of divorce is _____.

16. Most mothers of illegitimate children will _____ marry.

MULTIPLE CHOICE

1. A key concept in understanding the family as a social rather than a biological unit is:

    a. marriage.
    b. birth of children.
    c. economic activities carried out in families.
    d. the care of children.

2. All cultures discourage:

    a. homosexuality.
    b. extramarital relationships.
    c. premarital relationships.
    d. childbearing outside of marriage.

3. A married pair and their children that have formed an independent household living apart from other kin is called:

    a. extended family.
    b. nuclear family.
    c. kin structure.
    d. kinship.

4. The kind of residence where the nuclear family lives by itself is called:

    a. matrilocal.
    b. patrilocal.
    c. neolocal.
    d. complex residence pattern.

5. The kind of family form practiced by the Mormons in the 19th century was:

    a. monogamy.
    b. polyandry.
    c. polygamy.
    d. polygyny.

6. When premarital or extramarital sexual activity is acceptable for men but not for women, we refer to:

    a. a double standard.
    b. structured social inequality.
    c. sex role inequality.
    d. gender differentiation.

7. Which of the following does NOT qualify as a family?

    a. mother living alone with her child.
    b. a couple with no children.
    c. a man living with several wives.
    d. a person living alone.

8. Juan is a student from another country. There, he lives with his parents, and sometimes aunts and uncles live with them, too. This is an example of:

    a. a nuclear family.
    b. an extended family.
    c. kin structure.
    d. group marriage.

9. John believes that it is alright for him to play around but he expects his wife to be a virgin at marriage. This means that John believes in:

    a. the double standard.
    b. polyandry.
    c. the neolocal family.
    d. romantic love.

10. Susan was attracted to Tim because they had so much in common in the way of religion, social class, age, and interests. What factor was in operation with Susan and Tim?

    a. propinquity.
    b. homogamy.
    c. opposites attract.
    d. physical attractiveness.

11. Harold looks forward to marriage and having children. If Harold is typical, what do results from recent surveys of parents tell us about the responsibilities that Harold and his spouse will hold with regard to children?

    a. he will have more responsibility for economic support.
    b. she will have more responsibility for teaching norms and values.
    c. she will have more responsibility for developing the child's cognitive abilities.
    d. they will have equal responsibility for teaching skills.

12. John and Mary both work at Sears as sales clerks in the same department. Because of their jobs they spend quite a bit of time together and eventually they start dating. Which of the following factors best describes the basis of their original attraction to one another:

    a. physical attractiveness.
    b. homogamy.
    c. propinquity.
    d. value consensus.

13. Control of marriage is exerted through social norms. Which of the following norms is LEAST associated with controlling marriage in the U.S. today?

    a. who should marry.
    b. when one should begin having sexual relationships.
    c. when one should marry.
    d. limiting the range of potential partners.

14. According to your text, the reason most people in the U.S. get married is:

    a. for economic gains.
    b. for romantic love.
    c. to escape from parents.
    d. to escape from loneliness.

15. Theory suggests that as more and more women work for income outside of the home, relationships between husbands and wives will change, too. In which of the following ways has the sexual script in marriage changed in recent years in the U.S.?

    a. the frequency of sexual activity has increased during the past 30 years.
    b. women have reached parity with men in their probability of having an affair.
    c. the double standard persists.
    d. about 50% of all husbands but only about 10% of all wives have had an affair.

16. A great deal of theory and considerable research has focused upon marital satisfaction. Which of these factors has been found to increase the marital satisfaction of couples?

    a. the empty nest.
    b. marrying young, before age 20.
    c. couples with low incomes.
    d. a wife's employment.

17. Theory suggests that mate selection is processual, with people moving through filters. Which of the following sequences is generally followed?

    a. attractiveness, propinquity, compatibility.
    b. attractiveness, compatibility, propinquity.
    c. propinquity, attractiveness, compatibility.
    d. compatibility, propinquity, attractiveness.

18. The Oneida community, founded by John Humphrey Noyes in 1847, was based on:

    a. the principles of religious theocracy.
    b. the principles of Christian communism.
    c. dedication to quality silverware.
    d. unification through democracy.

19. In colonial America, the family's primary responsibility was for:

    a. replacement through reproduction and care of dependent children.
    b. regulation of sexual behavior.
    c. socialization of the young.
    d. ascription of status.

20. This function has taken on increased importance as a dimension of marital relationships in recent decades:

    a. socialization of the young.
    b. provision of intimacy.
    c. economic responsibilities for dependents.
    d. replacement through reproduction.

21. For couples marrying in 1970 or later, the lifetime probability of a divorce is:

    a. 75 percent.
    b. 50 percent.
    c. 25 percent.
    d. 100 percent.

22. About what percent of children in the U.S. live with both parents?

    a. 1%.
    b. 10%.
    c. 50%.
    d. 75%.

23. The "marryingest" country among all industrialized countries
    is:

    a. Canada.
    b. United States.
    c. Japan.
    d. West Germany.

24. The percent of Americans who reach middle age without
    marrying is:

    a.   5 percent.
    b. 10 percent.
    c. 16 percent.
    d. slightly over 22 percent.

25. Parents and kin are likely to control the activities leading
    up to marriage when:

    a. dowries or bride prices are exchanged.
    b. the new spouse will not move in with the family.
    c. prestige is not related to family ties.
    d. the kin group's economic interests are not affected by
        the young people's choices.

26. Viewed cross-culturally, the most popular marriage pattern
    has been:

    a. monogamy.
    b. polygamy.
    c. polygyny.
    d. polyandry.

27. There are no societies in which the cultural norms specify:

    a. patriarchal authority.
    b. egalitarianism.
    c. matriarchal authority.
    d. equality of authority.

28. Which is true about the divorce rate in the U.S.?

    a. the divorce rate has risen steadily in the post-World
        War II period.
    b. the divorce rate is about 10.0 at present.
    c. of persons married in 1890, the proportion ending their
        marriage in divorce was about 40%.
    d. for couples marrying in 1970, the proportion expected to
        be divorced in their lifetime is about 80%.

29. Cohabitation in the U.S.:

a. is increasingly viewed as an additional stage in courtship.
b. occurs with the same frequency in urban and suburban areas.
c. is limited to those with low incomes and educations.
d. is practiced mainly by who have been married before.

30. Of the following, which age at first marriage category is MOST likely to experience greater marital conflict and divorce? Persons who:

a. marry during their teenage years.
b. marry in their early twenties.
c. marry in their late twenties.
d. wait until after the age of 30 to marry.

ESSAY QUESTIONS

1. Briefly outline the six universal functions/responsibilities of the family noted by Murdock.

2. Discuss the difference between family, marriage, and kinship.

3. Define romantic love and note the historical and social conditions under which it is most likely to occur.

4. Outline the correlates of marital satisfaction and stability.

5. Discuss the most critical impact of current patterns of divorce.

Chapter 14
Education

LEARNING OBJECTIVES

1. Briefly recount the history of American education starting from the colonial period and continuing to the current time.

2. Describe the trend toward the increasing bureaucratization of education and note the signs that signal this trend.

3. Contrast the views on local control of education with the view supporting greater standardization.

4. Outline the functional model of education noting the manifest functions, latent functions, and the dysfunctions of our educational system.

5. Use the conflict approach to explain the relationship between social class and credentialism in American education.

6. Discuss, using a systems model, how the diversity of students that enter the school system are influenced by life in school and note the outcome of that process.

7. Indicate, for the individual, the consequences of completing a college education. Include the impact on income, occupation, and values.

8. Describe the current crisis in American education.

9. Differentiate between the concepts of mass education and elite education.

10. Critique the use of I.Q. tests in education.

11. Summarize the current trends in educational attainment for whites, minorities, and women.

CHAPTER OUTLINE

I. Development of Mass Education

   A. Prior to the 19th Century education was reserved for the elite with education for the masses beginning at the elementary school level in the 19th Century. Secondary schools emerged at the start of the 20th Century and college education blossomed after World War II.
      1. In colonial America early schools were church sponsored. Formal schooling in the early colonies was for moral and religious reasons.
         (a) Education for occupations took place in apprenticeships or at ones parents' directions.
      2. The major changes in the 19th century were to standardize education through state control and to increase the time spent in formal education.
         (a) Major pressure for education came from rural areas where education taught good values and work habits as well as preparation for good citizenship.
         (b) The rural model featured an emphasis on dom- inant cultural values through local control.
            (1) Education was to prepare citizens more so than workers.
      3. Mass elementary school education was in place by 1900 with an emphasis on high school emerging in the 1930's and a virtual explosion of colleges in the post World War II era.
         (a) Several wars, the "G.I. Bill", and fear of being drafted increased the demand for college education.

   B. Education has expanded enormously with one consequence being an increase in bureaucratic practices.
      1. The characteristics of this bureaucratization are standardization, hierarchies of authority and the specialization and professionalization of personnel.
      2. The rural model featuring local control over edu- cation has led to vast inequities in the quantity and quality of services provided.

(a) Increasingly, the federal government has intervened in order to create greater standardization among public schools.

II. Education in the United States: Three Models

A.   A structural-functional model of education stresses
the consequences of educational institutions for the
maintenance of society.
1. The manifest functions of education have been
designed to meet multiple needs.
(a) Cultural reproduction occurs when schools
transmit society's culture from one generation to the next.
(b) Social control occurs with the socializing
of the young into patterns of conformity.
(c) Assimilation is achieved by exposing students
from diverse backgrounds to a common curriculum which helps to create and maintain a
common cultural base.
(d) Training and development entails teaching
specific, socially valued skills.
(e) Selection and allocation occurs as schools
sift, cull, and sort students into those
that will be allowed to go on and those which
will not.
(f) Promotion of change is accomplished by aiming
new knowledge and technology at children and by
encouraging critical skills, analytic skills,
and skepticism.
2. Latent functions and dysfunctions refer to consequences which are either unintended or actually
negative.   Some of these are:
(a) A generation gap occurs when the knowledge im-
parted by schools drives a wedge between generations by contradicting values held by
parents.
(b) Custodial care is an important consequence of
compulsory education that enables elders to
command higher wages in the market place and
allows parents to forego their responsibility
of supervising children.
(c) A youth culture is created by isolating young
people from the larger society and confining
them to the company of others their own age.
(d) Schools perpetuate inequality by distributing
educational resources inequitably, especially
for minorities and disadvantaged students.
Education therefore has the consequences of
maintaining and reinforcing the existing social
class hierarchy.

B. Conflict theory offers a critical perspective on the relationship between education and the social class system arguing that modern education serves the interests of the elite.
    1. Capitalism needs a steady supply of skilled, productive workers who are obedient, punctual, and loyal and who accept the ideology that inequalities result from merit and achievement rather than coercion.
        (a) A _hidden_ _curriculum_ socializes young people into obedience and conformity.
        (b) Most scholars are skeptical regarding the claims made by conflict theory arguing that education represents core values, not those imposed by an elite.
    2. The elites further maintain their advantages by fostering the educational practice of _credentialism_ or the use of educational degrees as job requirements to ward off any encroachment of the lower classes upon upper class jobs.
        (a) Credentialism is a way of manipulating the system for the benefit of the well-off.
        (b) Credential inflation favors the elite who can easily afford more education.

C. The _systems_ _model_ _of_ _education_ focuses on the process by which inputs are transformed into outputs.
    1. Two important input factors in the systems model are social class background and early socialization.
        (a) Social class is an important variable in that children raised in middle class homes arrive in school with values better suited to success than do children from the lower socioeconomic classes.
            (1) Parents' social class also influences the neighborhoods in which the children grow up in as well as the quality of the school attended.
        (b) Early socialization experiences also disproportionately help the middle class child. Middle class parents provide help, support, and resources for the most part unattainable by the lower classes.
        (c) Children of affluent families also acquire _cultural_ _capital_ through preschool home experiences.
            (1) This capital enhances ones self-concept.
    2. Two important processes in schooling have a critical effect upon the quality of the output. They are cognitive development and tracking.
        (a) Children undergo a process where their mental skills grow and expand called _cognitive_ _development_.

      (1) Cognitive development is enhanced by com-
          plex and demanding work without close
          supervision and by high teacher
          expectations.

      (2) Lower class and minority classrooms often
          are highly authoritarian and structured
          thus impeding development.

      (3) Development processes in schooling are
          seldom reinforced in the lower class and
          minority home.

(b) _Tracking_ occurs when evaluations relatively
    early in a child's career determine the edu-
    cational programs the child will be encouraged
    to follow. By having classes geared to their
    level, bright and slow learners should benefit
    from increased teacher attention.

      (1) Research shows tracking becomes a self-
          fulfilling prophecy where bright students
          profit much more than slow ones.

      (2) One aspect of tracking is the use of so
          called standardized tests that claim to
          measure mental ability. They have strong
          cultural biases including reasoning, know-
          ledge, competitiveness, familiarity with
          testing, and achievement aspiration, all
          of which depend upon prior experiences.

      (3) Given their inherent biases they might be
          better suited as measures of cultural
          deprivation rather than as measures of
          natural ability.

      (4) Cultural stereotypes held by teachers also
          reinforce the negative aspects of tracking.

3. _Goffman_ contends that schools are "loosely coupled"
   organizations in that what actually occurs has
   little to do with the official rules.

   (a) Students must negotiate roles in this setting.

   (b) This leeway allows for the formation of student
      subcultures.

      (1) The friendship/clique structure provides
          additional meaning to the schooling
          process.

   (c) Symbolic interaction stresses how the indi-
      vidual is an active agent in this process.

4. The output of our educational system has increased
   steadily each year with more people completing high
   school and college than before.

   (a) Two problems are of current concern. They are
      a less than acceptable graduation rate and fear
      over the quality of education as measured by
      standard achievement tests.

III. College Education

    A. Eighty percent of high school graduates do not attend college.
        1. Parents' S.E.S. is the best indicator of college attendance.
           (a) These families value education and can afford it.
        2. The most important personal characteristic is high school academic preparation.

    B. College graduates earn considerably more than high school graduates.
        1. Female college graduates still earn less than high school male graduates.
        2. Black college male graduates reap the largest relative gains.

    C. While some community college students graduate from four year colleges, those starting and completing their education at four year colleges earn considerably more.
        1. A shortage of cultural capital, credentialism, and social class background handicap the typical community college student.

    D. Overeducation occurs when the level of education attained exceeds what is necessary for an occupation. While overeducated individuals seem somewhat dissatisfied with their jobs, they are not hostile or depressed.
        1. Most claim to be happier than if they were not to have gotten their education.

    E. The bottom line for a college graduate is that a college degree is a rewarding and valuable experience.
        1. College graduates are more knowledgeable, more tolerant, less prejudiced, more active socially and politically, and they are more open to ideas.
           (a) College transmits knowledge and values. Graduates are likely to experience the following: a decline in conventional religious preference, an increase in partying, and an increase in political liberalism.

IV. Balancing Equity and Excellence

    A. A national commission on education declared that we were a "Nation at Risk" due to our poor educational system.
        1. In order to achieve excellence more demand on basic studies were urged as were higher standards and a longer school year.
           (a) Most students benefiting from these changes would be the better students.

      (b) A latent dysfunction of an emphasis on excellence is an increased dropout rate.
2. Combating dropouts requires:
      (a) Teachers raising expectations.
      (b) Reducing the size of schools.
      (c) Making a flexible education to include youth who work, bear children, and marry.

CHAPTER 14

MATCHING

A. Educational process

B. Rural school districts

C. Middle class families

D. Selection and allocation

E. Hierarchies of authority

F. Educational credentials

G. Lower socioeconomic classes

H. 1960's

I. Parents' SES

J. Coleman report

K. Dropouts

L. Hidden curriculum

M. Specialization and profes-
    sionalization of personnel

N. Overeducation

O. Perpetuation of inequality

_____ 1. A major dysfunc-
         tion of education.

_____ 2. Schools should en-
         sure the best use
         of the best minds.

_____ 3. Values of indepen-
         dence, self-
         direction, initia-
         tive, etc.

_____ 4. Primary focus of
         the systems model.

_____ 5. Attend college to
         avoid the draft.

_____ 6. Single best pre-
         dictor of attend-
         ing college.

_____ 7. American model
         of education.

_____ 8. Bureaucratization
         in education.

_____ 9. A surrogate for
         social-class
         background.

_____ 10. Socialize the
          young into
          obedience and
          conformity.

FILL IN THE BLANK QUESTIONS

1. Two major long term trends in American education are a shift from _____ to _____ education and increasing _____.

2. Formal schooling in the early colonies was instituted for _____ and _____ reasons.

3. The long term trend of federal intervention in education has meant a reduction in _____ and increasing _____.

4. Conflict theory offers a critical perspective by arguing that education serves to reproduce _____.

5. The _____ _____ prepares young people for life in the industrial working class.

6. Research on tracking shows that _____ students benefit substantially more than _____ students.

7. It is recommended that I.Q. tests be used not as a measure of _____ _____ but as a measure of _____ _____.

8. Middle class children have more _____ _____ for their education.

9. The average _____ college graduate who works full time earns less than a _____ high school graduate.

10. The best personal indicator of success in college is ones _____ _____ academic preparation.

11. College graduates are generally more _____ and less _____ and _____ active in public and community affairs.

12. Three major changes that occur as a result of college education are a decline in _____, an increase in _____ and political _____.

13. An increased emphasis on academic _____ could increase the _____ rate.

14. Raising _____ _____ raises attendance, and the performance levels of both good and poor students.

15. The U.S. Educational system was not designed to produce _____, but to produce _____.

CHAPTER 14

MULTIPLE CHOICE

1. "The Old Deluder Act" passed in 1647 in the Massachusetts Bay Colony was intended to:

   a. increase taxes on tea.
   b. make education compulsory.
   c. require church attendance.
   d. prohibit new political parties.

2. A characteristic of schools that reflects the necessity of formal credentials:

   a. specialization and professionalization.
   b. standardization.
   c. hierarchies.
   d. local control.

3. Harry Smith believes that the public schools should do more to promote discipline and obedience. Which function does he want emphasized?

   a. cultural reproduction.
   b. social control.
   c. assimilation.
   d. training and development.

4. This term is used to describe how schools evaluate, sort, and select students on the basis of achievement and competition:

   a. testing.
   b. counseling.
   c. teaching.
   d. tracking.

5. I.Q. tests are supposed to measure:

   a. what has been learned.
   b. interests held.
   c. innate capacity to learn.
   d. motivation level.
   d. cognitive development.

6. Cultural capital refers to:

   a. inherited social status.
   b. familiarity with elite culture.
   c. economic advantages such as encyclopedias.
   d. cognitive development.

7. Formal schooling in the <u>early</u> colonies:

   a. stressed preparation for work.
   b. was available for both rich and poor.
   c. was instituted for moral and religious reasons.
   d. was considered a necessity.

8. This has been called a surrogate for social-class background:

   a. family name.
   b. tuition grants.
   c. credentialism.
   d. I.Q.

9. The input for schools stressed by the systems model theorists refers to:

   a. people who graduate.
   b. children.
   c. teachers.
   d. federal guidelines.

10. Which of the following is NOT emphasized by the "hidden curriculum":

   a. casual life-style.
   b. rules.
   c. regulations.
   d. routine.

11. Those persons LEAST likely to begin their careers in entry-level positions for which they are overqualified:

   a. blacks.
   b. lower-class.
   c. under 35 years of age.
   d. whites.

12. Jose', a recent college graduate majoring in history, has ended up taking a job as a taxi cab driver in Los Angeles. This illustrates:

    a. tracking.
    b. the employment factor.
    c. poor college advising.
    d. overeducation.

13. A function of education that has been criticized most by conflict sociologists is that education:

    a. makes people literate.
    b. promotes inequality.
    c. teaches values.
    d. teaches specialized skills.

14. Which of the following criticisms of the American educational system has little support:

    a. credentialism is a surrogate for social class.
    b. schools reproduce inequality.
    c. schools are bureaucratic.
    d. schools are a capitalistic tool.

15. An unintended (latent) function of public education is:

    a. social control.
    b. training.
    c. youth culture.
    d. selection and allocation.

16. Conflict theorists argue that modern education primarily serves the interest of:

    a. teachers.
    b. the elite.
    c. students.
    d. coaches and fans.

17. The ability of parents to pass on their social-class attainments depends primarily upon their ability to provide their children with:

    a. appropriate educational credentials.
    b. role models.
    c. curricula.
    d. family names.

18. Which theoretical perspective of education views community colleges as merely another means to track students?

   a. conflict model.
   b. systems model.
   c. status attainment model.
   d. structural-functional model.

19. During the development of the Common Schools (1812-1900), rural parents sent their children to a school to gain:

   a. a liberal arts education.
   b. good values and work habits.
   c. sex education.
   d. good jobs in the cities.

20. Which of the following educational gaps has increased the MOST since 1940 in the U.S.?

   a. white females compared to white males who have graduated from college.
   b. white females compared to white males who have graduated from high school.
   c. black females compared to black males who have graduated from college.
   d. black females compared to black males who have graduated from high school.

21. Public education in the U.S. is still largely financed through:

   a. state taxes.
   b. local taxes.
   c. federal taxes.
   d. grants from industry.

22. On any given school day approximately what percent of children between the ages of 7 and 13 are enrolled in school in the U.S.?

   a. 10%.
   b. 25%.
   c. 50%.
   d. 99%.

23. The correct sequence from low to high dropout rates is:

    a. blacks, whites, Hispanics.
    b. Hispanics, whites, blacks.
    c. whites, blacks, Hispanics.
    d. whites, Hispanics, blacks.

24. Recent estimates indicate that the proportion of the work force in the United States that is overeducated is:

    a. one out of 20.
    b. one out of 10.
    c. one out of 5.
    d. one out of three.

25. Which of the following was NOT a social condition that contributed to the development of mass education at the college level after 1940:

    a. G.I. Bill.
    b. desire to avoid being drafted in the 1960's.
    c. Civil Rights movement and expanding roles for women.
    d. compulsory attendance laws.

26. Evidence indicates that tracking benefits which students the MOST:

    a. bright students.
    b. slow learners.
    c. average students.
    d. bright students and slow learners.

27. Increasingly, the federal government has intervened in public education, especially to:

    a. attack segregation and discrimination.
    b. get schools to use common textbooks.
    c. raise teacher salaries.
    d. influence courses offered.

28. This parental characteristic determines the neighborhoods in which children are raised and the types of schools in which they enroll:

    a. social class.
    b. race.
    c. home environment.
    d. family composition.

29. Which of the following was NOT mentioned by your text as a strategy to increase excellence in schools?

    a. raise teacher expectations.
    b. spend more heavily for education.
    c. reduce the size of schools.
    d. build flexibility into the systems.

30. Scholars from the interaction school of symbolic interactionism remind us that:

    a. our role in school shapes our personality.
    b. we are only young once.
    c. each of us is an active agent negotiating our own school experience.
    d. the school is a rigid bureaucracy that stifles the negotiation of identity.

ESSAY QUESTIONS

1. Explain the conflict between the proponents of standardized education and those favoring local control.

2. Describe the current crisis in American education.

3. Critique the use of "I.Q." tests.

4. What is cultural capital, who has it, and how does it pay off?

5. Discuss how the process of education touches each student in a unique way.

Chapter 15
Political Institutions

LEARNING OBJECTIVES

1. Differentiate between power, authority, coercion, and influence.

2. Describe each of Weber's authority types and the circumstances under which each is most likely to be found.

3. Define democracy and specify the conditions that exist in order for democracy to flourish.

4. Indicate the differences between authoritarianism, totalitarianism, and institutionalized pluralism.

5. Differentiate between political institutions and the state and note how states attempt to institutionalize their authority.

6. Describe the conditions that undermine the voting solidarity of the working classes.

7. Discuss the conditions that are conducive to the maintenance of a two party system.

8. Outline the characteristics of the pluralist, elite, and conflict/dialectic models of American government.

9. What is single issue voting and why is it on the increase?

10. Describe the patterns of political affiliation in the U.S.

11. Discuss the correlates of political participation.

12. Despite the apparent intensity of the issue, why is the abortion issue not very important to most voters?

CHAPTER OUTLINE

I. Power

    A. <u>Power</u> is the ability to direct others' behavior even against their wishes.
        1. <u>Coercion</u> is the exercise of power through force or the threat of force.
        2. <u>Authority</u> is power supported by norms and values that legitimates its use.
            (a) Authority based upon the sanctity of time-honored routines or a reverence for the past is called <u>traditional</u> <u>authority</u>.
            (b) Authority derived from the perceived extra-ordinary personal characteristics of the individual is <u>charismatic</u> <u>authority</u>.
                (1) Charisma may be powerful but it is also inherently unstable because it resides in the individual and is thus mortal. Charismatic authority may evolve into traditional authority.
            (c) Unequal authority based upon rationally established rules constitutes <u>rational-legal</u> <u>authority</u>.
                (1) Rational-legal authority has gradually supplanted traditional authority and is seen as being more flexible and changeable.
            (d) In practice, authority is usually a combination of two or more types.
                (1) In that authority rests upon norms and values, it can usually be exercised without conflict. It ultimately rests upon the legitimation of coercion.
        3. <u>Influence</u> occurs when a person must rely on persuasion and individual personal appeals based upon personal or ideological grounds and not upon social structure. Influence and power often exist side by side.

II. The State

    A. Power does not exist randomly; it is socially structured.
       <u>Political</u> <u>institutions</u> are concerned with the social structure of power.

B. The <u>state</u> is a social structure that successfully claims a monopoly on the legitimate use of coercion and physical force within a territory.
   1. States are responsible for setting collective goals, gathering resources, arbitrating relationships, and maintaining ties with other societies.
   2. The state has jurisdiction for legitimate decision making for society as a whole and maintains control through three types of coercion: police power, taxation, and the maintenance of armed forces.

C. <u>Democracy</u> is a political system that provides regular, constitutional opportunities for a change in leadership according to the will of the majority.
   1. Three general conditions must be met before democracy can flourish. There must be competing interest groups, an absence of fundamental cleavages, and a high level of economic development.

D. <u>Authoritarianism</u> is a political system in which the leadership is not selected by the people and legally cannot be changed by them.
   1. Many different forms and degrees of authoritarian governments exist.

E. A political structure has been institutionalized when the distribution of power is affirmed by norms and values attached to a network of statuses.
   1. If consensus exists the state has authority, without it the state must use coercion and a preponderance of its resources in overcoming resistance and securing obedience.

III. American Political Parties

A. The two party system is focused upon an extra legal practice of the <u>political party</u> or an association specifically organized to win elections and secure access to the power of the state.
   1. Parties use nonviolent means and are both gracious winners and losers.
      (a) They are voluntary associations with open recruitment.
   2. A unique aspect of American parties is the winner take all rule that requires a party to win fifty percent or more of the votes to hold office.
      (a) In a heterogeneous society, majority backing requires a program that combines and balances the interests of many smaller groups.
      (b) Stability in American parties is based upon an appeal to diverse groups and the lack of well defined class boundaries or ideology.

        (c) Working class solidarity is undercut by the heterogeneity of its composition, abundance in the economy, and the American dream.

B. Philosophical differences between the two American parties lead to different patterns of affiliation.
   1. The Democratic party is seen as being more socially responsible and attracts those with higher education and liberal values. Minority voters and nonwhites also vote Democratic.
   2. Republicans are seen as more fiscally responsible and tougher on defense and attract the more conservative voter with a higher income.
   3. In recent years there has been a switch to issue voting and voters who call themselves independent.

C. The pluralist model of power sees a continual process of coalition and competition among many organized groups, none of which is consistently a winner.
   1. PAC's exist to funnel money to interest groups.
     (a) They appear to be effective.

D. The power elite model (Mills, 1956) contends that there is a higher level of decision making where an elite makes all the major decisions in its own interest.
   1. The power elite consists of the people who occupy the top positions in three key bureaucracies: the military, industry, and the executive branch of government.
     (a) Additional factors solidifying the power of the elite lies in their similarity and interchangeability.
       (1) The upper class is highly overrepresented in the power elite.

E. Conflict/dialectic model is based upon Marxian conflict theory in which there is an elite consisting of those who control production. It stands in opposition to a subordinate class easily awakened by the rise of class consciousness and class action.
   1. The dialectic stresses the conflict that arises over changing economic and political conditions.
     (a) Both sides struggle for their vested interests.
       (1) Conflict may also occur between elites.
   2. The conflict model differs from the power elite model in that a much smaller elite dominates and that elite can experience internal tension and aggressive competition.
     (a) Conflict can also exist between the elite and the nonelite.

IV. The Soviet Union

    A. Typically the Soviet system has been defined as <u>totalitarian</u> which is a new kind of authoritarianism, one in which the state tries to pulverize all existing associations in society in order to remake that society and subsequently even man himself according to certain ideal conceptions.

        1. The characteristics of totalitarianism are the existence of an official ideology that covers all aspects of existence, a single political party led by a single individual, a system of police terror to supervise the party and party control over all aspects of daily life through the dominance of all major institutions.

    B. Contemporary thinking sees decision-making as following a model of <u>institutionalized pluralism</u> where bureaucratic heads compete with each other for a share of the budget.

        1. Much of the most intense conflict takes place within policy areas rather than between them.

        2. According to the viewpoint of institutionalized pluralism, the elite acts as a broker mediating the demands of conflicting groups.

V. Individual Participation in American Government

    A. The average citizen is not politically oriented or active, thus some groups have more influence than others. Voters differ from nonvoters on social class, race, and age.

        1. Political participation of any sort is strongly related to social class, people with more education, more income, and more prestigious jobs are more likely to be politically active.

        2. The differences between black and white political participation are due almost entirely to social class differences. In fact, controlling for social class reveals that blacks have increased voter participation.

            (a) Low participation of minorities and the working class can in part be attributed to the absence of a political party that directly represents their interest.

        3. There is a steady increase in political interest, knowledge, opinion, and participation with age.

        4. Overall, elected officials tend to be white men from the professional classes.

    B. Social choice theory argues that individual decisions (like voting) are based on cost/benefit calculations.

        1. Increasingly people find the costs of voting outweigh the benefits.

        (a) Parties with centrist platforms that are often
            quite similar inhibit effective choice and
            ultimately voting.
        (1) Voters often identify self-interest with
            political party.

C. The politically alienated are those who cynically
believe that voting is a useless exercise that has no
influence on decision-making. They are not politically
active.
   1. Alienation among voters has increased substantially
      since the 1960's.

MATCHING

A. Social choice theory

B. American dream

C. Charismatic authority

D. Totalitarianism

E. Power elite

F. Authority

G. Coercion

H. State

I. Political parties

J. Abortion

K. Traditional authority

L. Alienation

M. Pluralism

N. Institutionalized pluralism

O. Influence

_____ 1. A positional theory of power.

_____ 2. Legitimate power.

_____ 3. Voluntary associations with open recruitment.

_____ 4. Perceived extraordinary personal characteristics.

_____ 5. Processes of coalition and competition.

_____ 6. Sanctity of time honored routines.

_____ 7. Cost benefit calculation.

_____ 8. A reliance upon persuasion and personal appeals.

_____ 9. Undercuts working class solidarity.

_____ 10. Where the elite mediates the demands of conflicting groups.

FILL IN THE BLANK QUESTIONS

1. _____ is the ability to get others to do something against their wishes and _____ entails the threat or use of force.

2. Unequal authority based on rationally established rules is _____.

3. Ultimately _____ rests upon a legitimation of coercion.

4. The state is the unit that has the _____ for legitimate decision-making and it controls the use of _____ in society.

5. The state exercises three primary types of coercion through the use of _____, _____ and the maintenance of an _____.

6. All _____ share constitutional procedures for changing leaders and these changes reflect the will of the majority.

7. Under _____, leadership is not selected by the people and legally cannot be changed by them.

8. An important characteristic virtually unique to American democracy is the _____.

9. The _____ model is based upon the key factors: control of vast bureaucracies, similar interests, and background.

10. The _____ model sees underlying tensions between the elite and the nonelite.

11. Today, the differences between black and white political participation are due almost entirely to _____ differences.

12. There is a steady increase in political interest, knowledge, opinion, and participation with _____.

13. In practice, elected officials tend to be _____ men from the _____ classes.

14. One sign of the switch to issue voting is the sharp increase in the proportion of _____ voters.

15. _____ _____ theory argues that decisions are based on cost/benefit calculations.

MULTIPLE CHOICE

1. Which institution is MOST concerned with the social struc-
    ture of power?

    a. family.
    b. religion.
    c. state.
    d. education.

2. The exercise of power through force or the threat of force
    is called:

    a. influence.
    b. will.
    c. coercion.
    d. authority.

3. Decision-making power that is based on the sanctity of time-
    honored routines is called:

    a. coercion.
    b. traditional authority.
    c. charismatic authority.
    d. rational-legal authority.

4. A characteristic virtually unique to the American brand of
    democracy is:

    a. the existence of political parties.
    b. the winner-take-all rule.
    c. a constitution.
    d. the presence of coalitions.

5. C. Wright Mills coined this term for the people who occupy
    the top positions in three bureaucracies:

    a. leaders.
    b. power elite.
    c. generals.
    d. administrators.

6. The pluralist model of American government focuses on:

    a. class-based power differentials.
    b. the legitimation of coercion.
    c. the structure of political parties.
    d. coalitions in state and federal government.

7. Universities and other organizations sometimes recruit
    retired generals or other famous people to help with their
    fund raising. When they do this they are attempting to
    benefit from:

    a. traditional authority.
    b. charismatic authority.
    c. rational-legal authority.
    d. coercion.

8. When researchers study local communities in order to find
    out who has informal power they are focusing upon people
    with:

    a. influence.
    b. rational-legal authority.
    c. coercive power.
    d. traditional authority.

9. Which of the following status relationships is NOT an
    example of a socially structured power relationship?

    a. student/teacher.
    b. parent/child.
    c. officer/soldier.
    d. friend/friends.

10. When people respond favorably to political leaders because
    of their personal characteristics, they are responding to:

    a. charismatic authority.
    b. traditional authority.
    c. legal authority.
    d. influence.

11. This term was specifically developed to describe Nazi
    Germany and Stalin's Russia:

    a. dictatorship.
    b. authoritarian.
    c. communistic.
    d. totalitarian.

12. A monarchy such as that of Queen Elizabeth I or Louis
    XIV of France is best characterized as:

    a. authoritarian.
    b. democratic.
    c. totalitarian.
    d. institutionalizes pluralism.

13. Theory suggests that three conditions must be present before stable democratic governments can exist. The conditions are:

    a. competing interest groups, absence of fundamental cleavages, and economic development.
    b. mass media, public education, and competing interest groups.
    c. competing interest groups, economic development, and mass media.
    d. competing interest groups, strong military, and public education.

14. A vital part of the pluralist model of power is:

    a. the importance of the dialectic.
    b. class consciousness.
    c. shifting coalitions.
    d. a power elite.

15. Those who identify with a conflict/dialectic model of power think that subordinates can gain power by emphasizing this resource:

    a. economic wealth.
    b. alliances with corporate leaders.
    c. class consciousness.
    d. the revolving door principle.

16. In the context of the strip-mine example in the text, the conflict/dialectic model would assume that:

    a. the elite is divided.
    b. there is competition among various interest groups.
    c. each affected group would seek allies among peripherally affected groups.
    d. there is a cohesive group of business and other leaders.

17. The characteristics of a totalitarian society do NOT include:

    a. an official ideology.
    b. a constitution.
    c. a single political party.
    d. police terror.

18. The three bureaucracies which Mills identified as being vital to controlling U.S. decision making were:

   a. military, religion, and government.
   b. government, industry, and military.
   c. industry, education, and military.
   d. government, industry, and education.

19. The state uses three primary types of coercion. Which of these is NOT one of the primary types?

   a. police power.
   b. mass media.
   c. taxation.
   d. maintain an armed force.

20. The age group LEAST likely to be registered to vote is:

   a. 35-44.
   b. 45-64.
   c. 65+
   d. 18-24.

21. Experts today who compare the political processes in the U.S. and the Soviet Union:

   a. describe the processes in the same terms.
   b. see greater and greater differences.
   c. see trends toward totalitarianism in both.
   d. see competition between bureaucracies in the U.S. but not in the Soviet Union.

22. What percent of those eligible to vote in local elections actually vote?

   a. 90 - 100%.
   b. 80 - 90%.
   c. 50 - 75%.
   d. 25% or less.

23. Studies show that voters differ from non-voters in that non-voters are MORE likely to be:

   a. less well educated.
   b. male.
   c. white.
   d. older.

24. The proportion of voters who call themselves independents is now approximately:

    a. 5 percent of all voters.
    b. 10 percent of all voters.
    c. 20 percent of all voters.
    d. 30 percent of all voters.

25. The state claims a monopoly on the legitimate use of:

    a. influence.
    b. coercion.
    c. media.
    d. charismatic authority.

26. A major school of thought today suggests that decision making in the Soviet Union represents:

    a. institutionalized pluralism.
    b. totalitarianism.
    c. communism.
    d. military junta.

27. Which is true about governments?

    a. most soviets have lacked the conditions for democracy.
    b. most people in most times have lived under democracies.
    c. authoritarian governments are very uniform in the extent to which they control peoples' lives.
    d. no authoritarian governments have governed through rational-legal authority.

28. Which of the following BEST describes the two major political parties in the U.S.?

    a. both are centrist.
    b. both are left wing.
    c. both are right wing.
    d. one is left wing and one is right wing.

29. A more varied group of people in the U.S. who have been seeking political offices in recent years but continue to lag behind others in their office holding are:

    a. women.
    b. blacks.
    c. Hispanics.
    d. nonelites.

30. According to your text, people with higher income are
_____ likely to vote and people with higher education are _____ likely to vote:

  a. more, more.
  b. more, less.
  c. less, more.
  d. less, less.

ESSAY QUESTIONS

1. Briefly outline the characteristics and activities of
    PAC's.

2. Discuss the factors that contribute to the perpetuation
    of the two party system.

3. Explain the lack of working class solidarity.

4. What are the consequences for low levels of political participation?

5. How critical is the abortion issue in politics?

Chapter 16
Economic Institutions

LEARNING OBJECTIVES

1. Discuss what is meant by an economic institution including the following terms: distribution, production, macroeconomic, and microeconomic levels.

2. Outline the major characteristics and lifestyle for pre-industrial, industrial, and post-industrial economic structures.

3. Differentiate between primary, secondary, and tertiary production.

4. Compare and contrast capitalism, socialism, and communism.

5. Demonstrate how America has a mixed economy.

6. Describe the elements of the dual economy including the industrial core, the size of units, interdependence, the competitive sector, and the segmented labor market.

7. Discuss the question "Are corporate capitalism and government too close?"

8. Note the benefits and problems attributed to multi-national corporations.

9. Who are the petit bourgeois and what role do they play in the American economy?

10. Describe the differences between professional, blue collar, white collar, and pink collar work.

11. Discuss the problems of employment and unemployment in today's economy.

12. Discuss the impact of unemployment on the individual.

13. Explain the nature and origins of alienation on the job.

14. Describe the conditions that produce work satisfaction and note the role played by intrinsic and extrinsic rewards.

15. Discuss the impact of automation on the economy.

CHAPTER OUTLINE

I. Economic Institutions

   A. Sociologists focus on the enduring pattern of norms, roles, and statuses at both the macroeconomic and microeconomic levels that make up the economic system.

   B. There are three types of economic institutions. They are:
       1. Pre-industrial economic structures are characterized by small settlements, small production units, the utilization of human and animal energy sources and a labor force engaged in extracting raw materials from the environment or primary production.
       2. The industrial economic structure is characterized by a reliance upon new sources of energy, large, bureaucratically organized work units and secondary production or the processing of raw materials.
       3. Post-industrial economic structures rest upon tertiary production or the production of services like government, education, medical care, repairs, etc.
           (a) The tertiary sector has grown rapidly and has replaced blue collar workers with white collar and pink collar workers.
           (b) Post-industrial society creates enormous potential for deliberate social change.

II. Modern Economic Systems

   A. Capitalism is the economic system in which most wealth is private property to be used by its owners to maximize their own gain.
       1. Individual self-seeking is a prime incentive for increasing productivity and the material standard of living.

(a) Capitalism is self-regulating as capital and labor seek to maximize their position in relation to changing supplies and demands in the marketplace.

(b) Capitalism maximizes production at the expense of distribution and does not provide for public goods.

B. Socialism is an economic structure in which productive tools are owned and managed by the workers and used for their collective good.

1. Socialism has advantages over capitalism in that societal resources can benefit as a whole. Central planning is possible and equitable distribution of goods and services can be assured.

2. The concept of "political economy" arises from the fact that any economic system is dependent on its political system.

3. Most western economies represent a mixture of both capitalism and socialism.

(a) Many services and key industries have been nationalized.

(b) The United States has done the least of western economies to create this mixed system. One exception being in human services, especially education, which is our oldest socialized industry.

III. The U.S. Economic System

A. The U.S. has a dual economy composed of an industrial core and a set of small competitive organizations.

1. The industrial core consists of a large pool of capital and a series of industrial giants.

(a) The size of each unit is quite large on the average with larger American corporations being among the largest in the world.

(b) The American corporate unit is tied to others through interlocking directorates where common membership on boards of directors ties many companies together.

(1) Size and interdependence have reduced some competition for markets, but competition over resources is still strong.

(c) In our political economy some fear that the interdependence between government and the economy is too strong.

(1) Government and the industrial core work together to the benefit of big business and to the detriment of peripheral business.

(2) The federal government has power over business while the local level of government is often powerless against business.

    (d) <u>Multi-nationals</u> are large corporations that
    operate internationally. Their vast power and
    resources have caused some worry because of
    their potential as political actors.
  2. The competitive sector consists mainly of small,
   family-owned businesses or partnerships. They are
   mainly the <u>petit bourgeois</u>.
   (a) These businesses are characterized by few
    employees, low levels of bureaucratization,
    particularism in employment, and economic
    uncertainty.
   (b) The self-employed are typically blue collar, do
    independent contracting, own franchises or
    beauty salons. While many are on the edge of
    economic disaster, the competitive sector
    contains many secure and profitable small
    businesses.
   (c) The dual economy features a <u>segmented labor
    market</u> in which hiring, advancement, and bene-
    fits disproportionately favor the industrial
    core over the competitive sector.

IV. Work in the United States

  A. Employment is characteristic of over two-thirds of the
   adult population in the labor force at any given time.
   1. The <u>labor force</u> consists of the <u>unemployed</u> and the
    <u>employed</u>.
  B. Minorities, especially blacks and Hispanics, are over
   represented among the unemployed.
   1. Employment determines ones status, income, and
    structures lives.
   2. Unemployment depends upon individuals and struc-
    tural factors.
    (a) Individual factors are education, race, and
     skill.
    (b) The structural factor is which sector of the
     economy one is employed in.
     (1) Blue collar workers and minorities are the
      most vulnerable.
     (2) Unemployment and layoffs are typical of the
      industrial core while quitting, being
      fired, and discrimination are found in the
      periphery.

  C. Occupations may be classified as professional, white
   collar, blue collar, or pink collar.
   1. <u>Professions</u> are occupations that demand specialized
    skills and creative freedom. They are character-
    ized by the production of unstandardized products,
    personality involvement, knowledge of specialized
    techniques, a sense of obligation, group identity,
    and significant service to society.

2. White <u>collar</u> workers work with their "head." <u>Blue</u> <u>collar</u> <u>workers</u> are employed in primary and second-ary industry and work with their "hands."
   (a) Blue collar workers have lower incomes, status, security, and suffer closer supervision and more routinized work.
   (b) Post-industrial economies use fewer blue collar workers, consequently problems lie ahead for the traditional working class.
   (c) Pink collar work is primarily in the service sector and features a nonexistent career ladder and minimum wage.
   (d) Employment in the future will be of two types: high education, high skill, or no skill.
       (1) The skilled blue collar worker is the most likely victim of this shift in occupations.

V. The Meaning of Work

A. Work is a means to a livelihood, a major structural determinant of our lives and has a direct effect upon self-esteem and identity.
   1. Work satisfaction may be <u>intrinsic</u> and arise from the process of work itself or it may be <u>extrinsic</u> in the form of tangible benefits like income and security. The learned professions are the most satisfied workers and auto assembly line workers the least satisfied.
   2. <u>Alienation</u> occurs when conformity to role expecta-tions estranges the individual from personal crea-tivity and judgement. Alienation can result from reducing work to simple, boring repetitive tasks, or binding people to regulations so as to rob them of personal judgement.
      (a) Professional workers are low on alienation while clerical and blue collar workers have higher alienation scores.
          (1) Alienation may be offset by adequate salaries and job security.
   3. <u>Self-direction</u> in ones work affects satisfaction, alienation, and our personalities.
      (a) Job complexity, degree of supervision, and degree of routinization are the components of self-direction.
          (1) Low routine, low supervision, and high complexity provide the most benefits.
          (2) High routine, high supervision, and low complexity create alienation.

VI.   Technology and the Future of Work

A.   When technology is introduced to the job <u>deskilling</u>
occurs, workers are displaced, and management gains
greater supervision over the worker.

B.   Labor opposes these practices and argues that labor
need not suffer with automation.
1.   Management obviously opposes labor's agenda.
2.   A radical critique of the situation argues for a
different system for the distribution of profit.
3.   The issue is not particularly new, the <u>Luddite</u>
movement in 1811 had similar concerns.

MATCHING

A. Anti-automation

B. White collar

C. Professionals

D. Tertiary production

E. Labor force

F. Petit bourgeois

G. Multi-nationals

H. Primary production

I. Blue collar

J. Capitalism

K. Socialism

L. Mixed economies

M. Alienation

N. Pink Collar

O. Secondary production

_____ 1. Maximize personal gain.

_____ 2. Luddites.

_____ 3. Work with ones hands.

_____ 4. Processing raw materials.

_____ 5. Work with ones head.

_____ 6. Extracting raw materials.

_____ 7. Freedom from supervision.

_____ 8. Production of services.

_____ 9. Small family owned businesses.

_____ 10. U.S. is the least advanced in the west.

CHAPTER 16

FILL IN THE BLANK QUESTIONS

1. In _____ economic structures, the children, the elderly, and the sick were the responsibility of the family.

2. The shift from _____ production to _____ production is characterized by growing surpluses.

3. The _____ _____ has grown very rapidly while those employed in _____ production has been reduced to nil and the portion employed in _____ production has halved.

4. _____ is an economic system that maximizes production at the expense of distribution and _____ is a system that stresses distribution at the expense of production.

5. An explicit goal of _____ is to eliminate unequal reward as the major incentive to labor.

6. The _____ are one of America's first socialized industries.

7. _____ is socialism grafted onto an authoritarian political system.

8. As a result of changes in the _____ of units and an increasing use of _____ in capitalism, the marketplace is no longer an efficient regulator of supply and demand.

9. A segmented labor market is one in which hiring, advancement, and benefits vary systematically between the _____ and the _____.

10. It is little wonder that _____ is associated with high levels of alcoholism, violence, and depression.

11. An important characteristic of _____ workers is a short or non-existent career ladder coupled with minimum wages.

12. The shift to a post-industrial society means more unemployment or worse unemployment for the traditional _____.

13. Marxists argue that being satisfied with a job that has no opportunity for individual talent and ability is _____ _____.

14. Two kinds of rewards are _____ which arise from the process of work and _____ which are more tangible benefits such as income and security.

15. The impact of computers and automation have been _____,
    _____ of the labor force, and greater
    _____ of the worker.

MULTIPLE CHOICE

1. An issue related to the production side of economic insti-
    tution is:

    a. scarcity or abundance.
    b. what proportion goes to workers versus the manager.
    c. who is responsible for the support of non-workers.
    d. how much of society's production is distributed on the
        basis of need rather than effort.

2. Which economic system focuses upon production and neglects
    distribution?

    a. capitalism.
    b. socialism.
    c. communism.
    d. totalitarianism.

3. A term used to show the close relationship between the econ-
    omy and the political system is:

    a. power elite.
    b. middle class.
    c. political economy.
    d. mixed economy.

4. The MOST important reward all professionals have shared is:

    a. high income.
    b. freedom from supervision.
    c. prestige.
    d. large amounts of time free for leisure.

5. The condition where workers have no control over the work
    process or products of their labor is called:

    a. unemployment.
    b. alienation.
    c. socialism.
    d. blue-collar work.

6. The dual economy of the U.S. is defined as the coexistence
    of which two elements:

    a. production and distribution.
    b. industrial core and the competitive sector.
    c. blue-collar industries and white-collar industries.
    d. capitalist industry and socialized services.

7. Sociologists interested in the economic institution focus
    upon which of the following:

    a. the federal reserve system.
    b. the causes of inflation, recession, and economic
        depression.
    c. the enduring pattern of norms, roles, and statuses that
        make up the economic system.
    d. the national debt.

8. Which of the following is a production activity stressed in
    an industrial economic structure?

    a. fishing.
    b. farming.
    c. foresting.
    d. steel production.

9. Those who do NOT have required credentials may successfully
    find employment in:

    a. the competitive sector.
    b. the industrial core.
    c. the professions.
    d. multinationals.

10. Which of the following is a socialized service in the U.S.?

    a. religion.
    b. agriculture.
    c. public schools.
    d. railroads.

11. According to your text, which of the following is thought to
    be a symptom or evidence of the increased interdependency in
    the dual economy of the U.S.?

    a. power elite.
    b. proletariat.
    c. increased size of enterprises.
    d. interlocking directorates.

12. Flight attendants who smile all day, even when they have a cold and their customers are rude, and then find that they cannot smile at their own family are suffering from:

    a. lack of extrinsic rewards.
    b. emotional abuse.
    c. alienation.
    d. false consciousness.

13. Which is NOT a condition associated with the shift from primary to secondary production:

    a. growing scarcity.
    b. larger work groups.
    c. increased education.
    d. political democracy.

14. Development experts would predict that this economic activity would increase in a post-industrial economy:

    a. primary production.
    b. secondary production.
    c. services.
    d. manufacturing.

15. Which of the following is NOT thought to be an advantage of socialism?

    a. societal resources can be used for the benefit of society as a whole.
    b. central planning.
    c. automatically makes adjustments in changing supplies and demands.
    d. produces equitable distribution.

16. Which of the following BEST describes the expected production in socialist countries compared to capitalist countries:

    a. production is higher in socialist countries.
    b. production is higher in capitalist countries.
    c. production is the same in socialist and capitalist countries.
    d. there is no relationship between the form of the economy and production.

17. Which of the following is MOST vulnerable to unemployment?

    a. adult women.
    b. young men.
    c. young women.
    d. minorities.

18. Marx's version of socialism has become the basis for which contemporary form of political economy:

    a. Christian socialism.
    b. Fabian socialism.
    c. democratic socialism.
    d. communism.

19. An example of an intrinsic reward from work is:

    a. pride felt in creativity.
    b. income.
    c. security.
    d. benefits.

20. This person believed that a democratic coalition of workers would form a temporary "dictatorship of the proletariat":

    a. Karl Marx.
    b. David Riesman.
    c. Che Guevera.
    d. C. Wright Mills.

21. Which U.S. corporation has a direct or indirect linkage with hundreds of other corporations?

    a. Polaroid.
    b. General Motors.
    c. Gulf Oil.
    d. Alcoa.

22. This country has done the LEAST among major Western powers in creating a mixed economy:

    a. France.
    b. United States.
    c. Great Britain.
    d. West Germany.

23. All of the following are true about multi-national corporations EXCEPT:

    a. they are mostly European in origin.
    b. they owe no allegiance to any particular country.
    c. they dwarf many national governments in size.
    d. they must also be seen as political actors.

24. At any given time, about _____ percent of the adult population of the U.S. is in the labor force.

    a. 50.
    b. 67.
    c. 80.
    d. 95.

25. Pre-industrial economic structures are characterized by all of the following EXCEPT:

    a. small production units.
    b. reliance upon human and animal power.
    c. bureaucratically organized work units.
    d. emphasis on primary production.

26. An undesirable transformation associated with industrialization is:

    a. long life.
    b. greater education.
    c. population growth.
    d. reduction of intolerance.

27. Post-industrial development rests on which stage of productivity:

    a. primary.
    b. tertiary.
    c. secondary.
    d. a combination of primary and tertiary.

28. Opportunities during the 1980s to 1990s are expected to decline for:

    a. paralegals.
    b. medical assistants.
    c. stenographers.
    d. nurses.

29. The competitive sector of the American economy is largely
    made up of:

    a. small businesses.
    b. large businesses.
    c. home offices of multi-national corporations.
    d. the self-employed.

30. Which of the following kinds of people are likely to be
    attracted to work in the competitive sector?

    a. the well educated.
    b. those with good work records.
    c. those who want to work part time.
    d. those who want security.

ESSAY QUESTIONS

1. What is your view? Are corporate capitalism and government
    too close?

2. Briefly describe the benefits and problems arising from the
    existence of multi-national corporations.

3. Summarize the intrinsic and extrinsic rewards of blue collar work.

4. Summarize the intrinsic and extrinsic rewards of white collar work.

5. What problems have accompanied our shift to tertiary production?

Chapter 17
Religion

LEARNING OBJECTIVES

1. Define what is meant by the concept of religion and note the aspects of religion that interest sociologists.

2. Carefully outline Durkheim's and Weber's approach to religion.

3. Explain how conflict theory interprets religion's role in society.

4. Spell out Weber's main argument in the Protestant Ethic and the Spirit of Capitalism.

5. Use the concept of tension between religion and society to differentiate between the church-like religions (ecclesiae and denominations) and the sect-like religions (established sects, sects and cults).

6. Discuss the structure and functions of church-like and sect-like religions using the Amish and the People's Temple as examples.

7. Explain the difference between a cult and a sect.

8. Recount the role played by history in the patterns of religious participation in America.

9. Summarize the correlates of religiosity and commitment.

10. Identify the consequences of religiosity and religious affiliations.

11. Discuss the current practice of electronic religion and its
    impact on the contemporary religious scene.

12. Outline the changes in American religious behavior over the
    last two decades paying special attention to fundamentalism
    and civil religion.

13. Describe how the religious institution can have an impact
    on other institutions in society.

CHAPTER OUTLINE

  I.   The Scientific Study of Religion

     A. Religion is a system of beliefs and practices related
         to sacred things that unites believers into a moral
         community.

     B. Sociologists treat religion as a set of values and
         examine the ways in which culture, society, and class
         relationships affect religion and the ways in which
         religion affects individuals and social structure.

 II.   Why Religion?

     A. Durkheim identified three universal aspects of religion
         called the elementary forms of religion.
         1. The elementary forms of religion include a distinc-
            tion between the sacred and the profane.
            (a) The process of transferring an idea or event
                from the sacred to the profane is called
                secularization.
         2. Another universal aspect of religion is a set of
            beliefs, myths, and creeds about the supernatural.
         3. The third universal aspect is the expression
            through ritual of the things that are held sacred.
         4. Durkheim believed that religion was functional for
            individuals and for society as a whole.
            (a) Religion offers the individual support, conso-
                lation, and reconciliation.
            (b) The major function of religion for society is
                that religion gives values and norms credence
                making them sacred. Religion gives tradition
                a moral imperative.

     B. To Weber, the essence of religion is a search for know-
         ledge about the unknown that may challenge the status
         quo as well as support it.
         1. Weber saw a major source of religion as lying in
            the charisma of extraordinary individuals.

2. The <u>Protestant</u> <u>Ethic</u> and the Spirit of Capitalism thesis asserts that the Protestant Reformation paved the way for bourgeois capitalism.
   (a) The moral values that came to embody Protestantism became the values of early capitalism.

C. Conflict theory as interpreted by Marx saw religion as a delusion deliberately fostered by the elite to distract workers from their state of oppression.

III. The Tension Between Religion and Society

A. Each religion is confronted with the tendency to compromise with the world and the tendency to reject the world. The resolution of this dilemma affects the form and structure of the religion.
   1. <u>Churches</u> are religious organizations that have become institutionalized. They have endured for generations and are supported by societies norms and values, and have become an active part of of society.
      (a) <u>Ecclesia</u> are church-like religious organizations that automatically includes every member of society.
      (b) <u>Denominations</u> are church-like religious organizations that have accommodated to society and to other religions.
      (c) Ecclesiae and denominations tend to be formal bureaucratic structures with hierarchical positions, specialization, and official creeds. Leadership is by professionals who received formal training at specialized schools.
   2. <u>Sects</u> are religious groups that reject the social environment in which they exist.
      (a) A <u>cult</u> is a sect-like religious organization that is independent of the religious traditions of society. They challenge established religions.
         (1) Cults experience a high degree of tension with the environment and arise in times of rapid social change.
      (b) Sects typically seek to preserve their spiritual purity by remaining apart from the world.
         (1) Sects view themselves as restoring true faith and preserving religious tradition by cleansing the church of its secular associations.
      (c) An <u>established</u> <u>sect</u> is a sect that has adapted to the institutional environment.
         (1) In general, sect members prefer to withdraw from the world while established sect members attempt to influence the world.

            (d) All sects and cults are opposed to some basic societal institution and the appeal of the sect-like religions is focused upon those who are left out of or estranged from society: the poor, alienated, or handicapped.
               (1) Leaders have no formal training and the services are informal.
               (2) Sects and cults are like primary groups: small, informal, and loyal.
               (3) Close control exerted over members enhances identity and fosters cohesion.

IV. Religion in the United States

    A. America was not always a religious nation.
        1. Many of the founding fathers were <u>Deists</u>, not Christians and did not accept the Bible as the word of God.
        2. The growing religious pluralism reflected the patterns of immigration with membership in the three major religions being as much a statement about status and ethnicity as about ones creed.

    B. <u>Civil religion</u> is the set of institutionalized rituals, beliefs, and symbols sacred to the American nation.
        1. For many Americans civil religion and regular religion are inseparable.

    C. Religiosity or ones degree of religious commitment is an important American characteristic with the majority of Americans defining religion as being very important to their lives.
        1. Older people and women are among the most religious with younger people and males being less involved.
        2. High status individuals predominate among the church-like religions while those of lower status seek the sect-like religions.
        3. Adult religious involvement is strongly associated with community involvement and conventional values.
            (a) The young and the liberal participate less.

    D. Increasingly religious fervor is a more important influence on behavior than religious affiliation.
        1. High religious involvement makes people more satisfied, happier, and more conservative.
        2. Those with no religious affiliation are the most liberal and the least happy.

V. Current Religious Trends in the United States

    A. Religion is a dynamic and changing structure in the United States and it is currently undergoing two important and contradictory changes.

1. While church attendance and general identification with religion remain high, the proportion who say religion is very important to their own lives has dropped significantly. Along with a modest decline in church attendance, there is a decrease in the proportion of people believing that the Bible is the actual word of God.

2. <u>Fundamentalism</u> is a movement to restore original religious principles. Fundamentalism has been growing.
   (a) Fundamentalism occurs in all religions and the common aim is to bring the church back into tension with society.
   (b) The growth of fundamentalism is attributed to the fact that it does a better job of meeting the functions of religion for individuals.
       (1) It provides its members with common activities, a group identity, and a sense of community.

3. The new Christian Right is a loose fundamentalist coalition that believes American government and social institutions must operate according to Christian principles.
   (a) There is a Christian obligation to be political active.
   (b) This is a political rather than a religious movement and has attracted more publicity than power.

B. Electronic religion allows people to enjoy religious participation without leaving home.
   1. People using media religion are older, female, poorer, poorly educated, Protestant, and usually come from the southern and mid-western regions.
   2. Televangelism has created national controversy over the money raised.
      (a) Critics argue the money raised is for the evangelist and not for their religious activities.
          (1) Recent scandals lend support to these views.

CHAPTER 17

MATCHING

A. Weber

B. Ecclesia

C. Established sect

D. Durkheim

E. Amish

F. Sect

G. Profane

H. Secularization

I. Denomination

J. Political movement

K. Ritual

L. Sacred

M. Diests

N. Cult

O. Marx

_____ 1. Things held in
          awe or respect.

_____ 2. Religion is a
          delusion deliber-
          ately fostered by
          the elite.

_____ 3. Religious group
          independent of the
          religious tradi-
          tions of society.

_____ 4. Founding fathers.

_____ 5. The most institu-
          tionalized of all
          religious
          structures.

_____ 6. Things known and
          familiar.

_____ 7. Religious groups
          that have accommo-
          dated to society.

_____ 8. Religion gives
          tradition a moral
          imperative.

_____ 9. A desire to spread
          the word and make
          converts.

_____ 10. Peculiar people.

FILL IN THE BLANK QUESTIONS

1. According to Durkheim, all religions share a distinction between the _____ and the _____, a set of _____ and a set of _____.

2. Weber's major contribution was the notion that religion could be a source of _____ in society.

3. In the Protestant ethic, _____ was an unintended consequence of behavior that was directed by religious motives.

4. _____ differed from _____ in that he saw religious support for tradition in a negative light.

5. _____ are religious organizations that are the most institutionalized while _____ are religious organizations that reject the social environment in which they live.

6. In _____ religions, congregations often function more as audiences than as active participants.

7. The _____ represents the successful compromisers and the _____ represents the virtuous outsiders.

8. In today's sociological research on religion, it is religious _____ rather than religious _____ that is important.

9. Higher-status people are more often members of _____ religions whereas lower-status people are more often members of _____ and _____.

10. People who have high religious involvement are significantly more _____ than are people who are not religiously involved.

11. _____ _____ provides a sacred context for understanding the nation's history and current responsibilities.

12. _____ is a grass roots conservative movement that began at the turn of the century.

13. In the past 30 years there has been a modest _____ in the proportion of people belonging to and attending church and the proportion finding religion to be very important to their own lives has _____ substantially.

14. The _____ _____ _____ is best under-
    stood as a political rather than a religious movement.

15. Controversy arises largely from the use of television to
    _____ _____.

MULTIPLE CHOICE

1. The system of beliefs and practices related to sacred things
   that unites believers into a moral community is called:

   a. Marxism.
   b. religion.
   c. Church.
   d. fundamentalism.

2. The process of transferring things, ideas, or events from
   the sacred to the profane is called:

   a. religion.
   b. science.
   c. secularization.
   d. religiosity.

3. Which is NOT a practice or emphasis of American civil
   religion?

   a. The Pledge of Allegiance.
   b. Regular attendance at a church.
   c. Worshipful attitude toward liberty.
   d. Rituals for folding and displaying the flag.

4. Fundamentalism is a grass roots conservative movement in the
   U.S. Which of these statements is NOT true about
   fundamentalism?

   a. It is found almost entirely in Protestant churches.
   b. The aim is to bring the church back to its tension with
      society.
   c. It began as a countermovement to liberal trends within
      religion.
   d. It favors a requirement that the Genesis story be taught
      along with or instead of evolutionary theory.

5. The New Christian Right is BEST understood as a:

   a. religious movement.
   b. rebirth of the Protestant Ethic.
   c. political movement.
   d. body of homogeneous conviction.

6. Which type of religious organization is MOST likely to compromise with society's norms and values?

   a. civil religions.
   b. churches.
   c. cults.
   d. sects.

7. Which statement is NOT true about the place of religion in society?

   a. Religion is important only in capitalistic societies.
   b. Religion helps people face personal dilemmas.
   c. Religion is an explanation for incomprehensive events.
   d. Religion provides a familiar and comforting context even when rituals fail to solve immediate problems.

8. What do these historical figures have in common that is important for a sociological explanation of their success -- Christ, Muhammed, Joseph Smith, and Jim Jones?

   a. All were men.
   b. All were upper-middle class.
   c. All had charisma.
   d. All were religious.

9. When John states that, "He doesn't really enjoy his work, that he was put here on earth to work, and that it is a way of serving God" he is in Weber's analysis responding to:

   a. a "calling."
   b. predestination.
   c. rationalism as a means to salvation.
   d. the profane.

10. This Sect developed from Protestant reformers who moved to Pennsylvania in 1927:

   a. Old Order Amish.
   b. Baptists.
   c. Mormons.
   d. Christian Scientists.

11. Which of the following is sometimes referred to as "the church of the disinherited":

    a. ecclesia.
    b. denominations.
    c. civil religions.
    d. sects.

12. Which of the following would NOT be considered a sect in modern America:

    a. Amish.
    b. Jehovah's Witnesses.
    c. Jews.
    d. Quakers.

13. Which question correctly illustrates the sociological perspective on religion?

    a. Does God exist?
    b. Are these religious values good?
    c. What are the origins of religious values and what are their consequences?
    d. Which is the best religion?

14. Which of the following is NOT included as one of Durkheim's three fundamental elements in all religion:

    a. charismatic figures.
    b. a distinction between the sacred and profane.
    c. a set of beliefs.
    d. a set of rituals.

15. Marx, unlike Durkheim or Weber, saw religion:

    a. as a supporter of tradition.
    b. as a delusion deliberately fostered by the elite.
    c. from a strict value-free position.
    d. as an endorser of inequality.

16. From the functional perspective, the worship of God is a barely disguised worship of:

    a. man.
    b. nature.
    c. society.
    d. the unknown.

17. Televangelists are LEAST likely to reach and appeal to people who are:

    a. well educated.
    b. Protestant.
    c. female.
    d. older.

18. A universal tension between religion and society exists primarily because religions tend to:

    a. attribute supernatural powers to events in everyday life.
    b. develop belief systems that cannot be refuted scientifically.
    c. reject the world but must also make compromises with the world.
    d. grant ultimate authority to religious leaders rather than political leaders.

19. The Jonestown "cult" headed by Jim Jones was different from other sects with links to Christianity in that:

    a. it was a religion of the disinherited.
    b. Jones abandoned the Bible and the Bible's God.
    c. its membership formed a strong primary group.
    d. rigid adherence to norms reminded the members of their common situation.

20. Approximately what percent of adults interviewed in the U.S. say that they believe in God?

    a. 10%.
    b. 20%.
    c. 50%.
    d. 94%.

21. The approximate percent of the U.S. population that belonged to a church in 1800 is?

    a. 95% or more.
    b. between 50 and 75%.
    c. about 25%.
    d. less than 10%.

22. Which of the following is a characteristic of Americans who are LEAST likely to attend a church or synagogue on a regular basis?

    a. 50 or older.
    b. Protestant.
    c. male.
    d. Midwesterners.

23. The religious group with the MOST members in the U.S. is:

    a. Catholic.
    b. Jewish.
    c. Protestant.
    d. other.

24. Which early sociologist put forth the idea that religion, by searching for knowledge about the unknown, challenges the status quo?

    a. Durkheim.
    b. Weber.
    c. Marx.
    d. Comte.

25. Which is a characteristic of sects but not of ecclesia or denominations?

    a. emphasis upon a hierarchy of positions.
    b. informal.
    c. specialization.
    d. official creeds.

26. The correct ordering of religions from MOST to LEAST tensions with society is:

    a. sects, cults, churches, established sects.
    b. churches, cults, sects, established sects.
    c. cults, churches, established sects, sects.
    d. cults, sects, established sects, churches.

27. If current trends continue, religion in the 1990s will be characterized by:

    a. a continued growth of fundamental churches.
    b. a large decrease in church membership.
    c. the rejection of the Old Testament.
    d. the government's outlawing of civil religion.

28. These people report GREATER attachment to religion than do other Americans:

    a. Easterners and Westerners.
    b. older people and women.
    c. males and better educated people
    d. young adults.

29. Persons who are more religious differ from less religious persons in that MORE religious persons report being:

    a. less happy.
    b. more conservative.
    c. likely to use marijuana.
    d. more likely to be delinquent.

30. The elementary forms of religion identified by Durkheim included all of the following EXCEPT a:

    a. set of beliefs.
    b. distinction between the sacred and the profane.
    c. belief in God.
    d. set of rituals.

ESSAY QUESTIONS

1. Discuss the text's definition of religion and note the aspects of religion of interest to sociologists.

2. Briefly summarize the current practice of electronic religion and its impact on the current religious scene.

3. Under what conditions do cults and sects flourish and why.

4. Discuss the changes in American religious behavior over the last two decades.

5. Describe the consequences of religiosity and religious affiliation for the individual.

Chapter 18
Secondary Institutions: Sport, Science, and Medicine

LEARNING OBJECTIVES

1. Recount the process of institutional development through the creation of secondary institutions.

2. Outline the development of modern leisure pursuits.

3. Explain the difference between sport and leisure and note the functions and types of sport.

4. Discuss the relationship between sport and the athlete regarding the values learned in sport competition.

5. Describe the issues raised regarding sport by conflict theorists.

6. Define what is meant by the phrase the sociology of knowledge and list the ideal norms of science.

7. Explain how the real practice of science falls short of the ideal norms.

8. Discuss the organization of science and the transformation from little science to big science.

9. Differentiate between the following terms: health, illness, deviance, and the sick role.

10. Explain how medicine may be considered a profession.

11. Contrast functional and conflict explanations of the income and prestige of physicians.

12. Describe the Chinese rural medical systems.

13. Discuss why we do not have equality in health care delivery in the U.S.

14. Explain the problems in defining AIDS as an illness and the social consequences that follow.

CHAPTER OUTLINE

I. Institutional Development

   A. Within the 20th Century, science, medicine, sport, etc., emerged as new institutions and may be regarded as secondary institutions.
      1. They are secondary in the timing of their development and in their importance for understanding human societies.

II. Leisure and the Institutionalization of Sport

   A. Leisure constitutes all the voluntary activities that people undertake to fill their free time.
      1. Americans spend less time at work than in previous decades but actually have somewhat fewer leisure hours available to them.
      2. Leisure activities are immensely varied with television viewing being a major activity. Increasingly, indoor and outdoor recreation activities are catching on.

   B. Competitive physical activities that base winning and losing on a set of structured rules are sports. Sports are characterized by a specific set of rules as well as a common set of values and norms.
      1. Three kinds of sports are playful sport, organized sport, and corporate sport.
         (a) Playful sport features flexible rules and a goal of having fun.
         (b) Organized sport is a formally run sport that provides pleasure for fans and participants alike.
         (c) Corporate sport is a money-making operation where participating in the sport is a job.

   C. Functionalists argue that sports contribute to the maintenance of society through reinforcing the norms of competition, teamwork, and obedience.

1. Sport competition teaches the importance of giving your best and winning. Teamwork teaches the individual to put the group interests above the individual and stresses loyalty and cooperation. Sport teaches obedience and reinforces the need for an authority structure.
    (a) Sport is like civil religion; it teaches and reinforces societal values through ceremonial rituals.
    (b) Identification with a team can create a sense of community and enhance social integration.
2. Basically, sport has a conservative influence and in all societies it functions to teach the young discipline while providing a channel for hostility and aggression.

D. Many believe that sport builds "character into the athlete".
    1. Evidence shows that successful athletes' self-concept and identity are positively influenced.
        (a) Values espoused in athletic training emphasize mental and physical toughness as well as the ability to take punishment.
    2. At best it can be said that no evidence exists that athletic participation actually damages character.

E. Conflict theorists contend that sport contributes to sexism, militarism, and exploits the athletes while serving as a mechanism to support current inequalities.
    1. Sport may support sexism by taking male and female differences in performance and magnifying them into major differences in worth and ability which are then used to rationalize the inferior status of women.
        (a) Sexism in sport is reflected in the unequal opportunities afforded to male and female athletes.
    2. Sport may promote racism by giving false direction to the aspirations of minority athletes so that they value sport more than values like educational achievement.
        (a) Discrimination exists in sports with few black or minority coaches and executives, especially in corporate sports.
    3. Conflict theory asserts that sport exploits the athlete by encouraging them to risk long term health problems from injury. Long term financial gains go predominantly to the owners, coaches, and sporting industries.
        (a) College athletes are five times more likely to leave college without a degree than are other students.

4. Sporting events may contribute to the maintenance
    of inequality by developing a false consciousness
    among the followers of sport and thus distracting
    them from the realities of inequality.

III. Science: An Institutionalized Way of Knowing

A. The sociology of knowledge is concerned with the
    development and change of criteria for authorizing
    knowledge. In most areas of life, modern societies
    give preference to science as a way of knowing; in
    fact, most Americans have revised their religious
    knowledge to make it consistent with scientifically
    authorized knowledge.

B. Merton contends that the goal of science is the exten-
    sion of certified knowledge. Five norms are utilized:
    communalism, universalism, disinterest, organized
    skepticism, and emotional neutrality.

C. The practice of real or actual scientific research
    falls far short of the ideal norms. Criticisms center
    upon the fact that the norms of science may not be
    completely institutionalized and that many violations
    occur. Others argue that the ideals are faulty and
    and science serves capitalist society.
    1. The primary mechanism for uncovering fraud is
        replication or repeating empirical studies again
        and again to make sure that different observers
        get similar results.
        (a) Replication results in identifying core
            knowledge.
    2. The practice of science can never be truly free
        from the influence of the culture in which it
        is practiced.

D. Science possesses many of the characteristics of a
    profession with most scientists remaining loyal to
    their profession rather than their employer. Scien-
    tists loyal to their employing institutions are re-
    ferred to as "locals" and those loyal to their pro-
    fession are called "cosmopolitans."

E. The increasing use of scientific terms and massive
    resources has marked a shift from little science to
    big science.

IV. Health and the Institution of Medicine

A. In the 20th-century, illness came to be defined solely
    in terms of physical causes. These changes coincided
    with the emergence of the modern profession of
    medicine.

B. The <u>sick</u> <u>role</u> consists of the rights and obligations
    that accompany the social label sick.
    1. Although there are biological and chemical indi-
        cators of illness, calling a behavior an illness
        is basically a process of social labeling.

C. <u>Illness</u> is the state of mind and body that prevents
    a person from fulfilling his or her usual social roles.
    A person who cannot fulfill the usual obligations is
    referred to as sick.
    1. Many people labeled as deviant because they cannot
        fulfill normal roles are now being defined as sick.
        (a) Alcoholics, gamblers, and child abusers may be
            so labeled.

D. The professionalization of physicians has paralleled
    the institutionalization of medicine.
    1. Professionals are characterized by: specialized
        knowledge, a sense of obligation to ones field,
        service to society, a strong feeling of identity
        with others in ones field, high personal involve-
        ment in ones work, and an unstandardized product.
        (a) The pressure of learning medicine forces doc-
            tors to depersonalize their patients and GROP.
        (b) Practicing physicians quickly leave these
            practices behind and practice more humane
            medicine that incorporates biological, psycho-
            logical, and social factors into patient care.
    2. There are several explanations why physicians enjoy
        high status and incomes.
        (a) Functionalists follow Davis and Moore, arguing
            that high rewards (income and status) must be
            offered to motivate the few capable to do the
            work.
        (b) Conflict theorists are not so forgiving.
            Instead, physicians' use of power in their
            self-interest explains their status and income.

E. Three general problems face the U.S. system of health
    care delivery.
    1. A decreasing supply of general practitioners has
        led to a condition of overspecialization where the
        number of medical specialists has mushroomed.
    2. Overspecialization means that specialists flock to
        major urban centers where specialized facilities
        are available for them to practice medicine.

MATCHING

A. Sport

B. Functionalist view

C. Overurbanization

D. Competition

E. Sick role

F. CUDOS

G. Leisure

H. Conflict view

I. Professionalism

J. Teamwork

K. Institution

L. Communalism

M. Disinterest

N. Replication

O. Organized skepticism

_____ 1. Importance of giving ones best effort.

_____ 2. A major problem of U. S. medicine.

_____ 3. Four norms of science.

_____ 4. Teaches and re-inforces societal values.

_____ 5. Scientists must freely share new knowledge.

_____ 6. Putting the group above the individual.

_____ 7. Sport is sexist and exploitive.

_____ 8. All new knowledge claims must be critically examined.

_____ 9. Primary mechanism for uncovering fraud.

_____ 10. Sport contributes to individual and societal integration.

FILL IN THE BLANK QUESTIONS

1. Studies agree that _____ has replaced many
   of the past leisure activities.

2. To some, criticism of sport is criticism of the
   _____.

3. Functional and conflict theorists agree that sport
   _____ traditional American values.

4. Character building in sport ignores _____,
   _____, or _____.

5. The long term gains in sport go to _____, _____,
   and _____ rather than to the _____
   themselves.

6. Most Americans revised their _____ knowledge to
   make it consistent with _____ authorized
   knowledge.

7. What a society accepts or rejects as knowledge is directly
   related to its _____ _____ and
   _____ _____.

8. The first loyalty of a scientist is to their _____
   rather than to their _____.

9. Approximately half of the nations poor are not covered by
   _____.

10. Since World War II we have made the shift from _____
    science to _____ science.

11. To the extent that AIDS results from individual choices,
    many people feel that AIDS victims are not entitled to the
    _____ _____.

12. To a significant extent, _____ is relative
    rather than absolute; it depends upon the social situation.

13. The _____ of physicians has paralleled the
    _____ of medicine.

14. The three types of sports are _____ sport,
    _____ sport, and _____
    sport.

15. China has accepted Western medical _____ but
    rejected the _____ of medicine.

16. The prevailing mode of health care in the U.S. is on a
_____ basis.

MULTIPLE CHOICE

1. An enduring social structure built around a relatively distinct and socially important set of positions that provide
   solutions to basic human problems is called:

   a. a group.
   b. an organization.
   c. an institution.
   d. a set.

2. "Secondary" as used in the term secondary institution means
   that:

   a. these institutions developed after the primary
      institutions.
   b. they are not responsive to change.
   c. they do not adapt to new countries.
   d. they are static and do not change.

3. All of the voluntary activity that people undertake to fill
   their free time after they have finished their required work
   is called:

   a. education.
   b. religion.
   c. education.
   d. leisure.

4. This specialty field is concerned with the development and
   change of criteria for authorizing knowledge.

   a. science.
   b. law.
   c. sociology of knowledge.
   d. history.

5. Marxist sociologists trace the acceptance of new knowledge
   to:

   a. religious dogma.
   b. political ideologies.
   c. economic relationships.
   d. dominant values and social structures in society.

6. The sick role is linked conceptually to which previously defined process?

    a. social control.
    b. labeling.
    c. cohesion.
    d. self-fulfilling prophecy.

7. Which of the following is a secondary institution?

    a. family.
    b. education.
    c. medicine.
    d. economy.

8. An ideology reinforced by the practice within sports of segregating men and women:

    a. democracy.
    b. sexism.
    c. competition.
    d. patriotism.

9. The conflict perspective on sport suggests that this group is LEAST likely to benefit in terms of long-term gains from sport:

    a. coaches.
    b. athletes.
    c. team owners.
    d. advertisers.

10. Each of the following are ideal norms of science EXCEPT:

    a. communalism.
    b. conformity.
    c. universalism.
    d. disinterest.

11. The primary mechanism responsible for uncovering error and fraud in science is known as:

    a. government grants.
    b. statistics.
    c. team research.
    d. replication.

12. Conflict theorists argue that sport contributes to the maintenance of inequality between men and women by:

    a. supporting masculine sex-types traits such as competitiveness and aggression.
    b. emphasizing teamwork and authoritarianism.
    c. magnifying the importance of relatively unimportant physical abilities (like throwing, running).
    d. encouraging physical inactivity and inability among women.

13. The major function of institutions is to:

    a. promote change in society.
    b. help people fill idle time.
    c. produce continuity in society.
    d. promote democracy.

14. One area of recreation that is governed by distinct norms is:

    a. reading.
    b. sports.
    c. photography.
    d. camping.

15. Conflict sociologists point out that a negative value which may inadvertently be learned through sports is:

    a. the perpetuation of inequality and authoritarian relationships.
    b. obedience.
    c. teamwork.
    d. competition.

16. Which of the following is NOT included as a right or obligation of the sick role? A sick person is:

    a. exempt from normal social roles.
    b. not responsible for his/her condition.
    c. expected to seek competent help.
    d. not expected to try to get better.

17. According to your text, the MOST political of diseases
    because of labeling is:

    a.   mental illness.
    b.   AIDS.
    c.   alcoholism.
    d.   obesity.

18. An individual who argues that physician's high incomes are
    a just reflection of their long years of training and
    unique talents is likely to come from which theoretical
    perspective:

    a.   structural-functionalism.
    b.   conflict theory.
    c.   modernization theory.
    d.   evolutionary theory.

19. According to studies done in the 1970's, Americans have at
    least some leisure each day. How much leisure does the
    typical American have each day?

    a.   30 minutes.
    b.   one hour.
    c.   none.
    d.   four hours or more.

20. Over the last 50 years American workers have experienced
    each of the following EXCEPT:

    a.   A sustained fall in the average work week.
    b.   An increase in vacation time.
    c.   A decrease in the number of years spent in the labor
         force.
    d.   Much more leisure time.

21. Which is true about the impact of television on the leisure
    activities of Americans?

    a.   The variety of leisure activities has been sharply
         reduced.
    b.   Television has replaced many of the activities that
         people engaged in 30 or 40 years ago.
    c.   Decreasing proportions of people fill their free time
         with indoor and outdoor recreation.
    d.   Participation in organized activities has increased but
         the participation in other activities has decreased.

22. Which factor is largely responsible for the increased parti-
     cipation of girls in athletics since 1970?

     a. better coaching.
     b. Title IX legislation.
     c. better training techniques.
     d. mass media influence.

23. Physicians are the most powerful and richly rewarded members
     of the medical work force. About what percent of the
     medical work force are physicians?

     a. about 10%.
     b. about 1%.
     c. about 25%.
     d. about 50%.

24. The scholar whose work is most important in establishing
     the sociology of science is:

     a. Robert Merton.
     b. Richard Spencer.
     c. Talcott Parsons.
     d. Newton.

25. Each of the following are included as norms for sport
     EXCEPT:

     a. win at all costs.
     b. be a cheerful loser.
     c. be a gracious winner.
     d. play fair.

26. Third World countries that hope to copy China's present
     health care system should emphasize:

     a. delivering health care to urban population.
     b. heavy reliance upon full-time professionals.
     c. high status for health-care workers.
     d. preventive medicine.

27. It has been proposed by some that sports build character.
     The conclusion drawn in your text concerning the relation-
     ship between sport participation and character is:

     a. It is largely an untestable hypothesis.
     b. Strong evidence exists to confirm the hypothesis.
     c. Data show that this is true for males only.
     d. The hypothesis is true for young people only.

28. According to Talcott Parsons, there are rights, duties, and obligations associated with the sick role. The "rights" part includes:

    a. being exempt from usual obligations.
    b. trying to get better.
    c. seeking competent help.
    d. not being responsible for being sick.

29. Critics of the medical profession tend to emphasize which of the following characteristics?

    a. the use of power to promote self-interest.
    b. possession of specialized knowledge.
    c. a sense of obligation to one's field.
    d. their service to society.

30. In most areas of life, modern societies give preference to:

    a. authority as a way of knowing.
    b. science as a way of knowing.
    c. religion as a way of knowing.
    d. economics as a way of knowing.

ESSAY QUESTIONS

1. Discuss the emergence of secondary institutions.

2. Explain how real science falls short of the ideal norms of science.

3. Account for the prestige and income of physicians.

4. Why does the U.S. lack equality in the distribution of health care?

5. What kind of character does sport build?

Chapter 19
Population

LEARNING OBJECTIVES

1. Define the following: crude birthrate, crude deathrate,
    natural growth rate, fertility, mortality, life expectancy,
    and demography.

2. Fully describe the process called the demographic
    transition.

3. Compare the West (Europe and America) to the emerging
    nations of the world regarding the operation of the
    demographic transition.

4. Recount how the bubonic plague altered economic relation-
    ships in feudal society.

5. Discuss the effects of social structure on fertility and on
    mortality, then discuss the effects of fertility and mortal-
    ity on social structure.

6. Briefly describe the relationship between population and
    social structure for Kenya, Europe, and China.

7. Differentiate between pronatalism and antinatalism and note
    the circumstances contributing to each.

8. Explain the vicious circle formed by the interaction of
    population and poverty.

9. Outline the three approaches to the problem of population
    and poverty.

10. Discuss the problem posed by momentum and differentiate between zero population growth and replacement level fertility.

11. Describe current patterns of fertility and mortality in the U.S.

12. Identify the problem posed by immigration in America and note the particular problem posed by Hispanic immigration.

CHAPTER OUTLINE

I. The Demographic Transition

A. Students of demography calculate the world population in 1984 as 5.0 billion and growing rapidly. Since 1950 the world population has doubled leaving millions in poverty. Malnutrition and undereducation abound while the world economic system strains toward bankruptcy.
    1. Three measures of population are important in understanding demographic changes. They are the crude birthrate, crude deathrate, and the natural growth rate.

B. For most of history, especially the pre-industrial era, fertility (childbearing) was barely able to keep up mortality (death), life expectancy was low, and the population grew little or not at all.
    1. A birthrate of 50 per 1,000 means a lifetime of childbearing for the average woman and precludes any participation in social structures outside the family.
    2. A mortality rate equally high would mean that a high proportion of the population dies in infancy and death is a frequent visitor to the household.

C. The demographic transition is the process of reducing birthrates and deathrates set in motion by the industrial revolution. During the transition, fertility exceeds mortality and population growth occurs.

D. In the nations of the West, improvements in nutrition were the first major cause of the decline in mortality. A second major cause centered upon a general increase in the standards of living.

E. In the non-West, death and birthrates remained at pre-industrial levels until World War II brought medicine and public health engineering. The tumbling of deathrates was accompanied by continued high birthrates resulting in a population explosion.

II. Fertility, Mortality, and Social Structure

   A. The effects of social structure is reflected in the
       fact that the level of fertility in a society is
       strongly related to the roles of women. When the
       family is the source of security, income, social
       interaction, and even salvation, fertility is high.

   B. Fertility also affects the role of women in that the
       greater the number of children, the less likely she
       is to have any involvement outside the family.
       1. Fertility influences age structure. A high
           fertility rate produces a young population.
       2. Mortality also influences family structure and
           composition. A high mortality rate most likely
           produces a fractured family of stepmothers, half-
           sisters and stepbrothers.

III. Population and Social Structure: Three Examples

   A. Kenya is a society with traditional social structures
       that encourage high fertility.
       1. Kenyan society has several pronatalist, or socially
           structured, pressures for childbearing.
       2. High population growth has diverted a large share
           of the national budget from development to meeting
           immediate needs.

   B. European fertility is too low and Europe as a whole
       will begin losing population over the next few
       generations.
       1. There are fears of "population suicide", an age
           structure with too many old people and labor force
           shortages.
       2. Factors influencing fertility include: changed
           gender roles, reduced importance of the family, low
           marriage rates, and increased dependence upon
           government support programs.
       3. Pronatalist policies are being used as incentives
           to encourage fertility. These include paid
           maternity leaves and cheap day care.

   C. China, with a population of one billion, has an aggres-
       sive and effective antinatalist policy of structured
       disincentives for childbearing.
       1. Low fertility will offset the effects of periodic
           food shortages and free more women to enter the
           work force, reduce education costs, and free more
           funds for development.
       2. A woman's esteem, security, and income depend on
           the state and community. Her self-interest lies
           in her work, not in having children.
       3. In 1986 the birthrate rose slightly reflecting a
           relaxation of policies.

          (a) Enforcing the antinatalist policy was difficult and fear of an older age structure led to a more flexible policy of having two children spaced 8-10 years apart.

IV. The Population Problem: Dilemmas and Approaches

    A. Poverty has an indirect effect on population growth. Poverty precludes the economic development that led to a change in traditional values in the west and reduced fertility. Poverty supports the maintenance of traditional childbearing values.

    B. High fertility and poverty form a vicious circle in the less developed world. A number of other consequences of this situation are intense pressures on the environment and political instability.

    C. There are three basic approaches to the problem. They are family planning, economic development, and manipulation of incentives. The most successful programs utilize all these approaches.

    D. World fertility has steadily declined since 1970 but the high fertility nations have a population of children or future parents that is much larger than the current generation of parents. This situation is referred to as momentum.

        1. Zero population growth means that the number of births is the same as the number of deaths and results in no population growth.

        2. Replacement level fertility requires that each woman have approximately two children, a replacement for herself and her husband. This insures that each generation will remain the same size.

V. Population in the United States

    A. While our problems are not of the magnitude of some nations, fertility, mortality, and migration still influence social structure.

    B. Fertility trends are toward the two-child family with an increasing number of families stopping at one child or remaining childless.

        1. U.S. social policy is strongly antinatalist.

    C. Mortality declined spectacularly during this century. As the mortality rates level off, race and class differences are declining.

    D. Migration is a major factor in American population growth with nearly one-third of our growth coming from immigration instead of natural increase.

1. Most immigrants come legally or illegally from
    Mexico and Latin America.
2. To stop illegal immigration means closing our
    borders and deporting the illegal aliens. This
    is quite difficult to do without offending our own
    self-image, alienating Mexico, and harassing legal
    Hispanic residents.

MATCHING

A.   Demographic transition

B.   Bubonic plague

C.   Childbearing

D.   Pronatalist pressures

E.   Death

F.   Demography

G.   Planned Parenthood

H.   Role of women

I.   Crude birthrate

J.   Withdrawal

K.   Nutrition

L.   Anglos

M.   Dependency ratio

N.   Antinatalist

O.   Hispanics

_____ 1. Studies of
           population.

_____ 2. Fertility.

_____ 3. One measure of
           society's age
           structure.

_____ 4. China.

_____ 5. Primary cause
           of mortality
           declines in
           the west.

_____ 6. Basis for
           the fertility
           decline in
           Europe.

_____ 7. Kenya.

_____ 8. Mortality.

_____ 9. Factor
           affecting the
           fertility level
           in society.

_____ 10. Majority of
            illegal
            immigrants.

FILL IN THE BLANK QUESTIONS

1. Almost all the world population growth in the next few decades will be in the _____ developed nations.

2. The major cause of the decline of fertility in the West was in response to changed _____ and _____ triggered by the whole transformation of life.

3. The second most important factor influencing mortality is an increase in the _____ _____ _____.

4. The higher the fertility, the _____ the population.

5. Historical data indicates that three generational families constituted a _____ percentage of all families.

6. In Kenya a decision to have a child is rational on the _____ level and ultimately irrational on the _____ level.

7. In contemporary China, a woman's esteem, security, and income depend upon the _____ and _____.

8. The major reasons for declining fertility in Europe are changed _____ _____ and the reduced importance of the _____.

9. In Europe, it is increasingly evident that people believe that one child provides a reasonable balance of _____ and _____.

10. Twenty-one percent of the next generation will start life in a _____ home.

11. Over the last 200 years, U.S. fertility has _____.

12. The spectacular gains in life expectancy in America this century are attributable to control of _____.

13. Population size and composition are jointly determined by _____, _____, and _____.

14. The main attraction that draws illegal immigrants from Mexico and Central America is _____ _____ and _____ _____ labor.

15. It is estimated that by 2020 or 2030 the U.S. will reach _____ _____ _____.

MULTIPLE CHOICE

1. The transformation of population since the Industrial
    Revolution is called:

    a. demography.
    b. natural growth rate.
    c. fertility.
    d. demographic transition.

2. This measure of population is obtained by dividing the
    number of births per year by the total population and
    multiplying by 1000:

    a. crude birth rate.
    b. crude death rate.
    c. fertility.
    d. natural growth rate.

3. Zero population growth (ZPG) means that:

    a. births equal deaths.
    b. no births are allowed.
    c. each woman is encouraged to have two children.
    d. the number of deaths are greater than the number of
        births.

4. By 1980, the three top causes of death in the U.S. were:

    a. pneumonia, heart diseases, and cancer.
    b. heart diseases, cancer, and stroke.
    c. diarrhea, cancer, and stroke.
    d. pneumonia, tuberculosis, and heart diseases.

5. Immigrants are those who move from one country to another.
    Which people were favored by immigration policies in the
    U.S. prior to 1965?

    a. Hispanics.
    b. Asians.
    c. Africans.
    d. Western and Northern Europeans.

6. We refer to the forces that encourage and reward child-bearing as:

   a. positive reinforcements.
   b. fertility rewards.
   c. pronatalism.
   d. maternity incentives.

7. A crude birth rate of 50 per 1000 population essentially means that there are really about 153 potential mothers. Each woman will bear a child approximately:

   a. every year.
   b. every other year.
   c. every third year.
   d. every 19 years.

8. A crude death rate of 50 per 1000 population means that:

   a. the society has many older people.
   b. the average life expectancy is about 75 years.
   c. many people die in infancy.
   d. one is old at 35.

9. According to your text, a major factor contributing to the first significant cause of mortality decline in the West was:

   a. Better medicine.
   b. Improvements in nutrition.
   c. A general increase in the standard of living.
   d. Changes in hygiene.

10. A dependency ratio of 1.0 means that:

    a. there are ten producers for each dependent.
    b. there is one producer for each dependent.
    c. there are ten dependents for each producer.
    d. there is one dependent for every two producers.

11. Kenya has the highest crude birth rate in the world at this time (52) and a crude death rate of 12. This means that its natural growth rate is:

    a. 64.0.
    b. 4.0.
    c. 12.0.
    d. 40.0.

12. What percent of illegal immigrants to this country are estimated to be from Mexico and Latin America?

    a. 50 percent.
    b. 75 percent.
    c. 90 percent.
    d. 99 percent.

13. A number of hypotheses have developed about the decline in the death rate, the decline in fertility, and the development of industrialization. What is considered to be the main and direct cause of the fertility reduction in the West?

    a. Reduced mortality.
    b. Greater industrialization.
    c. Changed values and aspirations.
    d. Government intervention.

14. It has been strongly suggested that meaningful reductions in the birth rate are not possible without modern contraceptives. Which of these methods was primarily responsible for the decline in fertility in Europe?

    a. Coitus interruptus.
    b. Condoms.
    c. Diaphragms.
    d. Delaying the age of marriage.

15. Many have wondered if the demographic transition in the non-West would mirror that in the West. A major cause of the fertility decline in the West was:

    a. Better contraceptives.
    b. Urbanization.
    c. New technology.
    d. The role of the family and women.

16. What is the relationship between high fertility and poverty in the developing countries today?

    a. High fertility causes poverty.
    b. Poverty causes high fertility.
    c. There is no simple cause and effect relationship between fertility and poverty.
    d. There is no relationship between fertility and poverty.

17. It is very important to be able to predict the number of babies that women will have. The long-term decline in fertility in the U.S. is due mainly to:

    a. rising costs of having children.
    b. increased alternatives for women.
    c. spread of contraceptive knowledge.
    d. planning.

18. The first major cause of declines in mortality in the West was:

    a. modern medicine.
    b. improvements in hygiene.
    c. vaccinations.
    d. improvements in nutrition.

19. The present world population is about 5 billion. By the time this generation of college students reaches retirement age, the world population will be about:

    a. 1 billion.
    b. 9 billion.
    c. 20 billion.
    d. 30 billion.

20. For the world as a whole, the crude birthrate and crude deathrate in 1987 were approximately:

    a. 28 and 10.
    b. 10 and 10.
    c. 10 and 20.
    d. 20 and 20.

21. A population increase of 1.8 percent per year doesn't seem like very much. If the population of the world does grow at this rate, it would double every:

    a. 100 years.
    b. 500 years.
    c. 5 years.
    d. 39 years.

22. These people became the scapegoat and received blame for the
     plague that swept the world during the 14th century:

     a. religious leaders.
     b. Jews.
     c. blacks.
     d. academics and scientists.

23. What is the "good news" and the "bad news" with regard to
     current population trends in the world?

     a. fertility is declining but the momentum is still bad.
     b. fertility is declining most among nations that have
         made the least steps toward development.
     c. fertility is still increasing at alarming rates but may
         soon begin to decline.
     d. fertility is still high but the death rates will soon
         fall dramatically.

24. A very low fertility society takes on an age structure
     that looks like:

     a. a pyramid.
     b. a square.
     c. a rectangle.
     d. an inverted pyramid.

25. The natural growth rate for the world's population in 1984
     continues to alarm some people. The highest rate is found
     in:

     a. Europe.
     b. North America.
     c. Africa.
     d. Asia.

26. Which statement about life expectancy in the U.S. during the
     past 40 years is true?

     a. life expectancy for whites but not for blacks has
         increased.
     b. life expectancy for white males but not for black males
         has increased.
     c. the gain in life expectancy has been greatest for white
         males.
     d. females continue to live longer than males, and the gap
         has increased.

27. The demographic transition in the non-West began when the crude death rate fell in a very dramatic fashion. About when did this occur?

    a. 1750.
    b. 1850.
    c. 1900.
    d. 1940.

28. What is the official population policy today in the Soviet Bloc and in China?

    a. Pronatalism for both.
    b. Antinatalism for both.
    c. Pronatalism for Soviet Bloc and antinatalism for China.
    d. Pronatalism for China and antinatalism for Soviet Bloc.

29. Which strategies have been used in successful programs like China's?

    a. Family planning.
    b. Economic development.
    c. Manipulations of incentives.
    d. Family planning, economic development, and manipulation of incentives.

30. The momentum of the age structure has to do with:

    a. which generation is winning the battle between the generations.
    b. the ratio of children to their parents.
    c. the proportion of the population that is elderly.
    d. how fast the population is growing.

ESSAY QUESTIONS

1. Describe the effect of the bubonic plague on economic relationships in Feudal society.

2. Explain the vicious circle formed by the interaction of poverty and population.

3. Account for the long term fertility decline in the U.S. population.

4. Discuss the relationship between fertility and social structure in Europe.

5. Describe the relationship between declining fertility and momentum in the U.S.

Chapter 20
Urban
Living

LEARNING OBJECTIVES

1.   Recount the factors associated with the development of the
     pre-industrial, industrial, and late-industrial city.

2.   Use the concentric zone, sectoral, and multiple nuclei
     theories to depict the patterns of urban growth.

3.   Discuss how changes in communication and transportation
     have influenced the shape of the city.

4.   Differentiate between metropolitan and nonmetropolitan.

5.   Contrast western urban centers with third world cities.

6.   Describe how Tonnies, Durkheim, and Weber characterized
     urbanization.

7.   Compare Wirth's "Urbanism as a Way of Life" with the
     compositional and subcultural views.

8.   Discuss the consequences of urban living on the personal
     integration of family, friends and neighbors, and upon
     life satisfaction.

9.   Explain what is meant by the term suburbanism and note its
     role in metropolitan decline, nonmetropolitan resurgence,
     and the move to the sun belt.

10. Describe how rural and urban areas differ by reference to
     the stereotypes of each.

11. Describe the impact on the city of poverty, racial segregation, and a declining tax base.

12. Contrast the past World War II suburban life styles to the suburbs of today.

13. What is urban revitalization and what problems arise when it occurs?

CHAPTER OUTLINE

I. Urban Growth and Change

    A. Urban growth began in earnest in the last century and has resulted in over one-half of the U.S. populations and one-quarter of the world population being urban.

    B. The pre-industrial city is dominated by primary production with the emerging cities being largely trading and administrative centers.
        1. The pre-industrial city was quite small with a concentration of life into crowded, teeming squares. Segregation was not between business and family but between kinds of businesses.
        2. The city was a dominant force in the development of art and culture while also being a crowded, filthy, and dangerous place.

    C. The industrial city was a result of industrial production in urban factories that occurred in the 19th century.
        1. The density of these cities occurred as cities grew around urban factories where the majority still walked to work. There was a dense crowding of working class housing around the factories.
        2. A lack of transportation and communication facilities led to the development of the central business district that became the hub of the city.
        3. Spatial analysis of early urban growth indicated that cities grew in a series of expanding rings or concentric zones.
        4. The sectoral pattern used a similar approach but stressed the role played by the radial highways and railroad tracks in directing urban growth toward the edge of the city.

    D. The late-industrial city was shaped by the greater ease of transportation and communication, the change of tertiary production, and the rise of single unit housing.
        1. The contemporary central city is dominated by white collar industries, services, and retail trade.

(a) The shift of tertiary production has eliminated the industries that shaped the development of the 20th century U.S. city.

(b) Modern telecommunications allow for even greater geographic dispersion of activities.

2. Modern cities are most likely to be characterized by the <u>multiple nuclei</u> model.

(a) Cities arising after 1950 easily adapt to this model while older cities suffer major declines in the C.B.D.

(1) These older cities face the vexing issues of urban revitalization.

(b) Government programs aiding home ownership and urban highway systems facilitated this growth pattern.

E. A <u>metropolitan area</u> is a county that has a city of 50,000 or more in it plus any neighboring counties that are significantly linked, economically, or socially with the core county.

1. A <u>nonmetropolitan area</u> is a county that has no major city in it and is not closely tied to a county that does have such a city.

2. Three-fourths of Americans live in metropolitan areas, with most living in suburban rings.

(a) Most recent metropolitan growth has occurred in the Sunbelt while the Northeast and the Midwest have lost population.

(1) Most nonmetropolitan residents live in the Midwest or the South.

3. Progressive urbanization occurred in the U.S. until the decade of 1970.

(a) Urbanization has returned as the dominant pattern in the 1980's with the most rapid growth occurring in the South and the West.

F. Third world cities are predominantly trade and administrative centers which are growing at staggering rates as rural residents migrate to find greater economic opportunities.

II. Urban Life in the United States

A. <u>Urbanization</u> is the process of population concentration and is distinct from the unique mode of life developed in cities called <u>urbanism</u>.

B. Western theoretical views of urban life are strongly anti-urban with classic and contemporary theorists believing that the quality of life in the cities is significantly worse.

1. Early writers developed analytical typologies of urban and rural differences.

        (a) <u>Tonnies</u> use the terms <u>gemeinschaft</u> and <u>gesell-</u>
<u>schaft</u> to differentiate between rural primary
group ties and urban secondary relationships.

        (b) <u>Weber</u> saw a parallel shift from tradition to
rationalism.

        (c) <u>Durkheim</u> saw the social cohesion of rural
society arising from the similarity of the
residents while urban solidarity was based more
upon a high division of labor and interdependence.

2. <u>Wirth's</u> "Urbanism as a Way of Life" was the classic
negative statement about the consequences of urban
living. Wirth argued that the size, heterogeneity,
and density of urban life led to a breakdown of
norms and morality.

3. Compositional theorists see the city as a mosaic of
small worlds that are manageable and knowable for
the individual.

4. The subcultural view argues that the size of the
urban center allows for the formation of a critical
mass of people who share an uncommon set of norms.

C. Evidence on the personal integration of family and
friends in urban settings indicates they are no more
lonely, alienated, or estranged from their family and
friends than others.

1. A <u>neighborhood</u> is a geographically bounded set of
streets that has a common sense of identity and
some basis of shared ties.

        (a) The neighborhood is a weak group because urban
dwellers have been freed from the necessity
of liking the people they live next to.

        (b) Urban people do have intimates but they are
unlikely to live in the same neighborhood
with them.

2. Urban living offers the availability of quality
services, entertainment, culture, etc. These
constitute important incentives to many who prefer to live in urban centers.

        (a) Noise, crowding, fear of crime, and expensive
living act to deter many.

        (b) Most people prefer to live close to a large
city, not in one.

3. Urban poverty has increased sharply in the last two
decades with the influx of rural minorities.

        (a) Most non-white minorities are migrating to
urban centers while most urban whites prefer
suburban living.

           (1) The affected cities are called "doughnut
cities".

        (b) Declining tax bases that occur with migration
to the suburbs have resulted in higher taxes,
increased user fees, and fewer government
services.

4. Research on crowding shows that urban dwellers are no less crowded than rural residents and there is no evidence that high urban densities lead to pathological behavior.
5. Most of today's rural and urban differences are more stereotypic than real.

III. The Other Americans

A. Most Americans do not live in the massive urban centers of New York or San Francisco. They live in suburbs and small towns.

B. Suburbs are changing from bedroom communities to retail shopping centers and major manufacturing centers.
   1. Suburbia is becoming more crowded and less dominated by families with young children.
      (a) Suburban life styles now include singles, childless married couples, and the elderly.
         (1) Townhouses, duplexes, and apartments are often typical.
         (2) Older suburbs continue to deteriorate and renters are more frequent than before.
   2. Open discrimination, racial steering, and intimidation insure that blacks still live in racially segregated housing, even if it is a mostly black suburb.
   3. Suburban living increasingly brings with it problems of high housing costs, weak local governments, transportation, crowding, and crime.
      (a) These problems arise with increasing demands for housing and more crowded living conditions.

C. The nonmetropolitan population of the U.S. continues to grow.
   1. The young leave for urban employment while the elderly remain behind.
   2. Community involvement, affordable housing, open space, and low crime rates attract people to nonmetropolitan living.
      (a) Small town residents enjoy less crime, more conformity, and greater social control.
         (1) Lifestyle options are often limited due to a lack of a critical mass of nonconformers.
   3. The city is still the major source of innovation and change but modern transportation and telecommunication have greatly reduced rural-urban differences.

MATCHING

A. Late industrial city

B. Subcultural view

C. Multiple nuclei

D. Neighborhood

E. CBD

F. Defensible space

G. Automobile

H. Gemeinschaft

I. Urban revitalization

J. Sectoral pattern

K. Gesellschaft

L. Suburban segregation

M. Trade and administrative centers

N. Pre-industrial city

O. Compositional model

P. Wirth

_____ 1. Classic statement of the negative consequences of urban life.

_____ 2. Area of highest land values.

_____ 3. Eliminated needed housing for the working poor.

_____ 4. Discrimination on the part of realtors.

_____ 5. Urban sprawl.

_____ 6. The diminishing role of the central business district.

_____ 7. Rural associations dominated by primary group ties.

_____ 8. Patterns of urban transportation.

_____ 9. Critical mass.

_____ 10. Characteristics of third world cities.

FILL IN THE BLANK QUESTIONS

1. Urban growth and development is largely a story of the _____ century.

2. In pre-industrial cities, living conditions were so poor that the _____ could not keep up with the _____.

3. The industrial city was a product of a _____ economy and a relatively _____ labor force.

4. The major growth in single-family living occurred immediately after _____ _____ _____ and was subsidized largely by the _____ _____.

5. Durkeim, Tonnies, and Weber believed that the quality of human social life was significantly worse in the _____.

6. Compositional theorists envision the city as a mosaic of small worlds that are _____ and _____.

7. Compositional theory argues that deviants, etc., are _____ _____ the cities rather than _____ _____ them.

8. There is no evidence that urban people are disproportionately _____, _____, or _____ from family and friends.

9. Urban people do have intimates and they are _____ to live in the same neighborhood.

10. Neighbors are not strangers and there are instances in which being _____ is more important than being _____ _____.

11. There is no evidence that high urban densities lead to human _____.

12. For the most part urban revitalization is aimed at _____ neighborhoods.

13. By the year 2000, _____ _____ will be the largest city in the world.

14. Rather than being a natural cycle of aging, urban decay is the result of _____ _____ _____ decisions.

15. Most people who _____ in the suburbs _____ in the suburbs.

MULTIPLE CHOICE

1. Which is a characteristic of the industrial but not the pre-industrial city?

    a. a central business district.
    b. largely trading and administrative centers.
    c. most smaller than 300,000.
    d. segregation based upon kinds of business.

2. The industrial city, in contrast to the preindustrial and late-industrial city:

    a. was safer with less crime.
    b. had much more advanced transportation systems.
    c. saw much more crowding.
    d. had yet to develop a central business district (CBD).

3. A metropolitan area in the U.S. is a county of at least:

    a. 100,000 population.
    b. 50,000 population.
    c. 10,000 population.
    d. 20,000 population.

4. Which term was coined by Frederick Tonnies to mean dominated by primary group ties?

    a. primary group.
    b. gemeinschaft.
    c. gesellschaft.
    d. rural.

5. A geographically bounded set of streets that has a common sense of identity and some basis of shared ties is a:

    a. township.
    b. neighborhood.
    c. city.
    d. community.

6. Urbanism refers to:

   a. living in cities with more than 50,000 people.
   b. the concentration of a population in an area where the density is greater than 1000 persons per square mile.
   c. the process where urban areas join together to form a megalopolis.
   d. a distinctively urban mode of life that is developed in the cities but not confined there.

7. Spatial analysis of early industrial cities suggest that they approximated a series of rings or concentric zones. Zone 1 was the:

   a. low class residential district.
   b. central business district.
   c. wholesale and light manufacturing district.
   d. medium class residential district.

8. Mexico City has been cited in the text as the most dramatic example of third-world urbanization. Which of these statements is true about Mexico City?

   a. it is expected to be the largest city in the world by the year 2000.
   b. most of its growth is due to migration to the city.
   c. there is almost no substandard housing.
   d. it has a very adequate level of public services.

9. Which is NOT a characteristic of urban life as seen by Louis Wirth:

   a. greater conformity.
   b. cold and calculating personal styles.
   c. heightened awareness of subcultures.
   d. more crime.

10. Some stereotyping of urban and rural life does occur. Research does show that some differences are real. For example, urban people are LESS likely to:

    a. oppose labor unions.
    b. help a stranger in trouble.
    c. be opposed to abortions.
    d. disapprove of legalizing marijuana.

11. While many would like to move to the suburbs, some who do
    live there find it very inconvenient. A major inconveni-
    ence factor is the lack of:

    a. good schools.
    b. adequate fire and police protection.
    c. public transportation.
    d. desirable housing.

12. The idea that cities provide opportunities for a critical
    mass--a relatively large number of people sharing some
    relatively uncommon set of norms or values--is central
    to which perspective:

    a. subcultural view.
    b. functional view.
    c. urban determinism.
    d. compositional model.

13. The industrial city was a product of a manufacturing economy
    and relatively immobile labor force. It has been suggested
    that one element has been the "chief architect" of American
    Cities since 1950. This has been:

    a. the growth in single-family homes.
    b. greater ease of communication.
    c. greater consolidation of production units.
    d. the automobile.

14. Urban theory suggests that new cities are shaped more like
    a multiple nuclei than concentric zones or sectors. Which
    is NOT a characteristic of these new cities in contrast to
    older industrial cities?

    a. smaller.
    b. less dominated by the CBD.
    c. vertical growth diminished.
    d. huge, climate-controlled, pedestrian-safe suburban
        malls.

15. This sociologist is given credit for developing the classic
    statement of the negative consequences of urban life for the
    individual and for social order:

    a. Louis Wirth.
    b. Frederick Tonnies.
    c. Max Weber.
    d. Emile Durkheim.

16. Emile Durkheim thought that social cohesion in urban centers would be provided by:

    a. similarity (mechanical solidarity).
    b. a shift from traditionalism to rationalism.
    c. an increase in gemeinschaft.
    d. the division of labor (organic solidarity).

17. In his influential book <u>Urbanism</u> <u>as</u> <u>a</u> <u>Way</u> <u>of</u> <u>Life</u>, Louis Wirth proposed that a breakdown of the normative and moral fabric would be caused by:

    a. size.
    b. size and homogeneity.
    c. size, heterogeneity, and density.
    d. homogeneity and density.

18. Mexico City is projected to become the largest city in the world by the year 2000 with an expected population of approximately:

    a. 50 million.
    b. 23 million.
    c. 12 million.
    d. 32 million.

19. How does the urban population of the U.S. compare with that of the world?

    a. the U.S. is more urban than the rest of the world.
    b. the U.S. is less urban than the rest of the world.
    c. the U.S. and the rest of the world are equally urban.
    d. most of the U.S. population and most of the world's population live in cities of 100,000 or more.

20. Because of this problem, all areas of the industrial city were densely packed:

    a. poor planning.
    b. corrupt politicians.
    c. inadequate transportation.
    d. the desire to know one's neighbor.

21. Considerable research has been conducted to determine the actual affects of urban living on personal integration. The research indicates that urban living:

    a. narrows the kin group while expanding the number of non-kin intimates.
    b. significantly reduces the number of intimate ties.
    c. makes people feel more lonely.
    d. makes people less likely to develop a hard shell against non-intimates.

22. The composition of many U.S. cities is changing. Included among those who are LEAST likely to stay in the central cities are:

    a. blacks.
    b. white middle class.
    c. elderly.
    d. poor whites.

23. Since 1980, most of the population growth in the U.S. has been in the:

    a. West.
    b. South or West.
    c. East.
    d. North.

24. An important characteristic of the industrial cities of the 19th century was that:

    a. production was based primarily in rural areas.
    b. improved transportation reduced the problems of density and crowding.
    c. there was a tremendous expansion of single-family housing.
    d. cities were built around manufacturing plants and factories.

25. Preindustrial cities can be compared to rural villages of the same period. Which is NOT a characteristic of pre-industrial cities?

    a. a major force for the development of art, culture, and technology.
    b. a crowded, filthy, and dangerous place.
    c. lower death rates than rural areas.
    d. dense housing favored the spread of epidemics.

26. Which is NOT an advantage of city life:

    a. less expensive housing.
    b. medical services.
    c. entertainment.
    d. culture.

27. A characteristic of cities in the third world that is NOT shared by cities in the developed world is:

    a. few are industrial centers.
    b. growth rates are slower.
    c. more attractive to the working-class because of job opportunities.
    d. better planning and more adequate services.

28. What is the distinction, if any, between urbanization and urbanism?

    a. both refer to population concentration.
    b. both refer to a way of life.
    c. the former refers to concentration and the latter to a way of life.
    d. the former refers to a way of life and the latter to population concentration.

29. A popular conception of urban life held by persons in the Western world:

    a. sophisticated and aware.
    b. less iniquity and vice.
    c. little corruption of youth.
    d. a good place to rear a family.

30. Which of the following is a chief characteristic of suburbia:

    a. high density housing.
    b. a well developed public transportation system.
    c. greater convenience and access to shopping and city services.
    d. single-family dwelling.

CHAPTER 20

ESSAY QUESTIONS

1. Discuss how the quality of life in pre-industrial and industrial cities differed from today's urban centers.

2. Why are rural-urban differences declining?

3. Discuss the process of urban revitalization, who wins, and who looses?

4. Explain how changes in transportation and communication have altered patterns of urban growth.

5. Note the impact of urban living on the personal integration of family, friends, and neighbors.

Chapter 21
Collective Behavior and Social Movements

11. Describe the gay rights movements.

CHAPTER OUTLINE

I. <u>Collective behavior</u> is nonroutine action by an emotionally aroused gathering of people who face an ambiguous situation.

   A. A <u>crowd</u> is a gathering of people who are reacting to a nonroutine event.

   B. Theories of crowd behavior include contagion theory, convergence theory, and the emergent norm theory.

      1. <u>Contagion theory</u> stresses crowd situations that lead to the development of unanimous and intense feelings and behaviors that are at odds with the usual predispositions of the individual participants. It explains only one type of crowd behavior: the escalating response.

      2. <u>Convergence theory</u> contends that the cause, or triggering event, for crowd action selectively draws people who share a common set of pre-dispositions.

         (a) The convergence of many like-minded people provides the critical mass for their predis-positions to be put into action.

         (b) The major criticism against convergence theory is that it ignores the heterogeneity of most crowds.

      3. <u>Emergent-norm</u> theory suggests that each crowd is governed by norms developed and validated by group processes within the crowd. That is, the crowd develops a shared conviction that their behavior is appropriate to the situation.

         (a) The process is similar to the one used by which we negotiate encounters.

            (1) The crowd improvises an answer to the ques-tion "what is going on here?"

            (2) The crowd frames the encounter and decides upon appropriate action.

            (3) The crowd will act with unity as the members maintain the appearance of group conformity.

      4. Emergent norm theory enjoys great support because of its ability to explain a variety of crowd behaviors despite apparent differences especially in different historical and cultural contexts.

      5. Collective behavior theories can lend insight into such diverse occurrences as the 1983 Bedford gang rape, the 1967 Newark race riot, or the tearing down of goal posts after a football game.

II. A <u>social</u> <u>movement</u> is an ongoing, goal-directed effort to
     change social institutions from the outside.

   A.   <u>Relative</u> <u>deprivation</u> <u>theory</u> sees social movements
        arising when social change causes people to redefine
        their deprivation as illegitimate and fixable. It is
        also known as <u>breakdown</u> <u>theory</u>.
        1. Deprivation is not absolute; instead, one is
            deprived relative to some other group or
            circumstance. Deprivation only leads to social
            movements when it is defined as illegitimate.
        2. Criticisms point out that the theory fails to
            specify the conditions under which relative
            deprivation will lead to social movements.
            (a) Empirical evidence fails to clearly support
                the notion that deprivation leads to action.

   B.   <u>Resource</u> <u>mobilization</u> <u>theory</u> suggests that social move-
        ments develop when organized groups are competing for
        scarce resources.
        1. Organization is thus the key to creating a social
            movement.
            (a) Social movements are rational attempts to
                change the distribution of societal resources.
                (1) The emphasis on organization leads some to
                    call this <u>solidarity</u> <u>theory</u>.
        2. A major shortcoming is to overlook the role played
            by anger and spontaneity as triggers for social
            movements.

   C.   An integration of relative deprivation and resource
        mobilization theories allows for an emphasis on the
        emotional and spontaneous triggering event as well as
        the organization needed to sustain a social movement.

   D.   A social movement entails many diverse organizations,
        each pursuing the same general goal. These social
        movement organizations (<u>SMO</u>) may be divergent and also
        competitors.
        1. Diversity is usually seen as being functional to
            the overall social movement.
            (a) <u>Indigenous</u> SMO's are characterized by volunteer
                staffing while <u>professional</u> SMO's have a paid
                staff.
            (b) Indigenous organizations maintain a sense of
                urgency and generate publicity while profes-
                sional organizations solicit support from a
                <u>conscience</u> <u>constituency</u>.

   E.   <u>Mobilization</u> is the process by which a unit gains
        significantly in the control of assets it previously
        did not control.

1. <u>Micro-mobilization</u> is the recruitment of individuals. It usually entails a process of frame alignment.
   (a) The tactics of frame alignment are <u>frame bridging</u>, <u>frame application</u>, <u>frame extension</u>, and <u>frame transformation</u>.
2. <u>Bloc Mobilization</u> is the recruitment of other organizations to the social movement.

F. There are a number of success factors associated with social movements.
   1. The demands of the movement must be consistent with the broader values of society.
   2. The movement has the support of influential third parties or demonstrates its demands benefit other groups as well.
   3. The movement's demands are concrete and focused.
   4. The movement can exert pressure on those responsible without harming third parties.
   5. The movement adopts techniques the authorities are unfamiliar with.
   6. Neutral third parties interested in restoring harmony are present.
   7. The movement's demands are negotiable.
   8. The movement's demands are reasonable in that they do not demand a fundamental redistribution of income and power.
   9. The movement seeks to veto proposed policies rather than to implement new ones.
   10. The movement is large enough to organize for conflict, but is not perceived as a serious threat to the dominant group.

G. <u>Counter movements</u> seek to resist or reverse the change advocated by a social movement; they are defenders of the status quo.

III. Social Movements are related to collective behavior in that instances of collective behavior keep the issues before the public and help maintain a sense of grievance.

IV. The mass media contributes to nonroutine collective behavior by publicizing events, demonstrating techniques, and providing rationales.

A. The mass media can also be vital to social movements by portraying dramatic events and providing authoritative sources.
   1. SMO's can also plan events so that they coincide with news cycles (timing) and fit into established news nets.

MATCHING

A. Contagion theory

B. Spectator crowd

C. Resource mobilization theory

D. Collective actions

E. Micro-mobilization

F. Relative deprivation theory

G. Frame alignment

H. Gay rights

I. Countermovement

J. Social movement

K. Emergent norm theory

L. Volunteers

M. Crowd

N. Bloc mobilization

O. Convergence theory

_____ 1. Crowds are moved to extremes and irrational be-havior through a vicious cycle of exchange.

_____ 2. Seeks to maintain the status quo.

_____ 3. Actions prompted by nonroutine events.

_____ 4. A process by which SMO's recruit other organizations.

_____ 5. Another name for breakdown theory.

_____ 6. An attempt to ex-plain quiet as well as rowdy crowds.

_____ 7. Deliberate, or-ganized attempts to change social institutions.

_____ 8. Another name for solidarity theory.

_____ 9. The New Bedford gang rape.

_____ 10. Indigenous SMO.

FILL IN THE BLANK QUESTIONS

1. _____ theory attempts to explain only one kind of crowd behavior: the escalating response.

2. According to _____ theory, there is no process within crowds: nothing new develops.

3. The _____ _____ theory of crowd behavior is broader than either contagion or convergence theory.

4. The New Bedford gang rape was best explained by reference to _____ _____ theory.

5. According to mobilization theory, one should _____ _____ and _____ _____ to sabotage a social movement.

6. Bridging, amplification, extension, and transformation are all tactics associated with _____ _____.

7. The mass media contributes to non-routine collective action by _____ _____, _____ _____, and _____ _____.

8. According to _____ _____ theory, the key to social movements is expectations.

9. According to _____ _____ theory, solidarity rather than disorganization is the key to the formation of social movements.

10. _____ _____ are almost always right wing in orientation.

11. _____ theory is particularly appropriate for understanding countermovements.

12. _____ _____ is a vital mechanism through which resource poor organizations can generate public debate over their grievance.

13. The American Psychological Association voted in 1974 to declare that _____ is not a sickness.

14. One result of the interdependence between social movements and the media is the development of _____ _____.

15. In the U.S. social movements on the _____ have traditionally been viewed as more threatening than those on the _____.

MULTIPLE CHOICE

1. Which of the following is a characteristic of social movements?

    a. spontaneous.
    b. broad based.
    c. short term.
    d. confined to a particular place and time.

2. Collective behavior actions are episodes that are prompted by an ambiguous situation. Which of these should NOT be included as examples of collective actions?

    a. temporary crowds.
    b. the gay rights movement.
    c. minor riots.
    d. disorganized protests.

3. A kind of crowd in which groups of people attack each other is known as a:

    a. riot.
    b. mob.
    c. spectator crowd.
    d. social movement.

4. An organized attempt to change social institutions which is carried on outside of legitimate channels is a:

    a. mob.
    b. riot.
    c. social movement.
    d. rumor.

5. A relatively large number of people drawn to a common location by some nonroutine event is called a(n):

    a. organization.
    b. public.
    c. crowd.
    d. social movement.

6. A movement which seeks to resist or reverse changes advocated by other groups is called a:

    a. reform social movement.
    b. countermovement.
    c. reactionary social movement.
    d. revolutionary social movement.

7. Collective behavior is:

    a. a rare event in our society.
    b. part of the conventional social structure of our society.
    c. well defined and goal directed.
    d. nonroutine activity.

8. The 1983 rape incident in the tavern in New Bedford is cited in the text as an example of:

    a. a spectator crowd.
    b. panic.
    c. a mob.
    d. rampage "riot".

9. Each of the following are examples of a social movement effort EXCEPT:

    a. the effort by XYZ University to reduce racism.
    b. gay rights.
    c. antinuclear.
    d. antiabortion.

10. The process by which a social movement gains significantly in the control of assets it previously did not control is associated with:

    a. contagion theory.
    b. micro-mobilization theory.
    c. resource mobilization theory.
    d. breakdown theory.

11. Many men and women in the U.S. participate in the current gay rights movement. The major schism within this movement is between:

    a. men and women.
    b. whites and blacks.
    c. lower-class and middle-class people.
    d. charismatic leaders and rank-and-file members.

12. Emergent norm theory argues that crowd behavior results from:

    a. circular stimulation.
    b. a critical mass of like-minded individuals.
    c. ideas developed and validated by the crowd.
    d. rising social movements.

13. Contagion theory of crowds emphasizes:

    a. extreme and irrational behavior caused by a vicious cycle of exchanges.
    b. selective factors that draw people together who share common norms.
    c. the convergence of like-minded people.
    d. that crowds are governed by norms that emerge from within the crowd.

14. Each of the following apply to convergence theory EXCEPT:

    a. it attempts to explain only rowdy crowds.
    b. it shows concern for triggering events.
    c. it ignores process within crowds.
    d. it focuses on the like-mindedness of persons in the crowd.

15. Which is true about emergent norm theory?

    a. it has its roots in group conformity.
    b. it ignores or downplays the importance of inter-personal exchange processes.
    c. it completely ignores the role of contagion.
    d. it is narrower than either contagion or convergence theory.

16. Mobilization theory of social movements stresses:

    a. the role of social disorganization.
    b. discontent.
    c. structural strain.
    d. competing interests of organized groups.

17. In mobilization theory, the coincidence of organized groups and one other element is thought to lead to social movements. What is this OTHER element?

   a. resources.
   b. strain.
   c. rumors.
   d. triggering events.

18. According to relative deprivation theory, social movements arise when:

   a. poverty and injustice develop.
   b. people experience an intolerable gap between their rewards and what they expect.
   c. ongoing efforts have fallen short of goals.
   d. organized groups develop internal solidarity.

19. Recently, the male homosexual movement has been galvanized by:

   a. police brutality.
   b. AIDS.
   c. more frequent discrimination.
   d. action by the American Psychological Association.

20. The triggering event in the 1967 Newark race riot was:

   a. an assault on a white youth.
   b. arson in a white neighborhood.
   c. the rape of a white woman.
   d. the police arresting a black cab driver.

21. Which of the following is NOT a tactic of frame alignment in mobilization?

   a. frame bridging.
   b. frame amplification.
   c. frame destruction.
   d. frame extension.

22. Of the 10,000 members of the Ku Klux Klan in 1976, how many were paid FBI informants?

   a. 2,000.
   b. 100.
   c. 1,000.
   d. 500.

23. Counter social movements often develop when it begins to look like a controversial social movement mobilizes sufficiently to make it look at least possible that its goals will be realized. Most of the COUNTER social movements to the gay movement in the U.S. today come from:

    a. the mental health profession.
    b. the academic community.
    c. corporate leadership.
    d. the Christian Right.

24. The great expansion of the birth control movement in England in the 1870s was due to:

    a. overcrowding and increased demand.
    b. mobilization of existing groups in its support.
    c. massive free publicity.
    d. legalization of mobilization strategies.

25. If you wanted to sabotage a social movement, theory suggests that you should:

    a. "stonewall" the issue and do nothing.
    b. encourage mobilization.
    c. reduce solidarity.
    d. eliminate poverty and injustice.

26. Which theory explains how the black community in Newark first defined the riot as a protest and later as a white attack:

    a. emergent-norm theory.
    b. convergence theory.
    c. contagion theory.
    d. mobilization theory.

27. Research shows that the MOST effective social movements share these two characteristics:

    a. conservative ties, homogeneity.
    b. overlapping ties, little publicity.
    c. heterogeneity, overlapping ties.
    d. homogeneity, overlapping ties.

28. Poverty and injustice are nearly universal phenomena in that they seem present in nearly all societies and in all time. What is true about the role of poverty and injustice in social movements?

    a. They almost always lead to social movements.
    b. They lead to social movements only if the triggering events are quite severe.
    c. Poverty and injustice must be very deep before they lead to social movements.
    d. The poverty and injustice must be defined as illegitimate.

29. Generalizing from relative deprivation theory, which condition is LEAST likely to result in relative deprivation?

    a. level of living increases faster than expectations.
    b. level of living drops relative to expectations.
    c. both level of living and expectations are improving but expectations rise faster.
    d. expectations rise faster than level of living.

30. Your text concludes that the wide variety of SMOs that exist within many social movements may be:

    a. functional for the success of the movement.
    b. more common among the least successful movements.
    c. more common among revolutionary than reform social movements.
    d. dysfunctional for the success of the movement.

ESSAY QUESTIONS

1. Discuss how a social movement differs from a crowd.

2. Use convergence theory and emergent norm theory to analyze the New Bedford gang rape.

3. Describe the factors associated with social movement success.

4. Discuss the role played by the mass media in collective actions.

Chapter 22
Social Change: An International Perspective

LEARNING OBJECTIVES

1. Describe what is meant by the term ecosystem.

2. Describe the interrelationship between population, social organization, the physical environment, and technology, science, and knowledge (POET) as they influence social change.

3. What is development and how evenly has it occurred throughout the world.

4. Outline modernization theory and note how it may be seen as being ethnocentric.

5. Describe the basic assumptions of world system theory and differentiate between core societies, peripheral societies, the first world, the second world, and the third world.

6. Carefully describe the development strategies of China, Nicaragua, the U.S.S.R., and the U.S.A.

7. Differentiate between "going" MAD and NUT(s).

CHAPTER OUTLINE

I. POET: a Model of the Ecosystem

  A. The <u>ecosystem</u> consists of the interrelationships within
      a complex natural and social environment.

  B. Societal change often influences both natural and
      social environments. The interdependence of four
      factors critical to understanding social change is
      summarized in the <u>POET</u> model. The four factors are
      <u>population</u>, <u>social organization</u>, <u>physical environment</u>,
      and <u>technology</u>.
      1. Changes in the concentration, distribution, or
          growth of the population can be the cause and con-
          sequences of other changes in the ecosystem.
      2. Changes in social organization can have a profound
          effect on the environment, population, and tech-
          nology of an ecosystem.
      3. When the environment changes, cultural adaptations
          to the environment must change also.
      4. Technology is an important source of change but the
          acceptance of new technology depends on the broader
          sociocultural and physical environment.

II. Developmental Frameworks

  A. <u>Development</u> refers to the process of increasing the
      productivity and standard of living of a society.
      1. There are massive disparities between the Western
          nations and the less developed nations.
          (a) Two theories explain these discrepancies.

  B. <u>Modernization theory</u> is a functionalist theory of
      development based upon Western experiences. It assumes
      that developing nations can follow the Western path to
      wealth through industrialization.
      1. Critics point out that the fortuitous circumstances
          of Western development are not present for non-
          industrialized nations of today's world.

  C. <u>World system theory</u> is a Marxist analysis of the rela-
      tionship between developing and developed countries,
      and suggests that the economic dominance of core socie-
      ties will prevent the progress of peripheral societies.
      1. <u>Core societies</u> are rich and powerful nations that
          are economically diversified and relatively free of
          outside control.
      2. Peripheral societies are poor and weak, with highly
          specialized economies over which they have little
          control.
      3. The economic relationship becomes one of perpetual
          economic colonialism.

4. A major insight of world system theory is that
   individual economies cannot be understood in
   isolation.
   (a) Worldwide economic activity is regulated only
       by market forces like supply and demand.
       (1) Western capitalist nations and multi-
           national corporations continue their 200
           year domination of the world economic
           system.

D. Countries are classified on the basis of their position
   in a world system of inequality.
   1. The <u>first world</u> consists of the core of major
      capitalist nations who dominate the world system.
   2. The <u>second world</u> consists of the European communist
      countries, their allies, and dependents.
   3. The <u>third world</u> consists of the less developed
      nations on the periphery of the world capitalist
      system.

E. The cold war is a political and economic battle between
   the first and second worlds over the world capitalist
   system.
   1. An ongoing struggle is occurring over the dominance
      of the third world nations.

III. Three Case Studies

A. China was consistently isolated from the Western economic influences by national policies, wars, and
   revolution.
   1. The communist victory in 1949 has produced a
      ruling communist party and an authoritarian
      government.
   2. In efforts to enhance development, equality, and
      to solidify power important reforms were utilized.
      They are the <u>Great Leap Forward</u>, the <u>Great Prole-
      tarian Revolution</u>, and the <u>Four Modernizations</u>.
      (a) These revolutionary reforms are moving China
          toward the direction of free enterprise and
          economic development.

B. Nicaragua spent most of this century under U.S. domination, both economic, and military.
   1. The Sandinista forces overthrew the U.S. backed
      military dictatorship of Somoza and established a
      less repressive and more participatory government.
   2. Development strategies center upon independence
      from foreign investment and establishing secondary
      industries.
      (a) Land reforms are being implemented.
   3. Development has slowed as the U.S. and the Soviet
      block contend for control of the country.

    C.   The Soviet Union dominates the second world.

        1.   As a communist nation, it seeks to become a modern, efficient egalitarian society through the collective ownership of the means of production.

            (a) The government is highly authoritarian.

        2.   Economic development lags far behind the West and the Soviet Union is not a serious threat to the world capitalist system.

            (a) Their military policies do exert a strong international influence, especially in the third world nations.

    D.   The U.S. emerged as the dominant capitalist nation through its participation in World War II.

        1.   The internationalization of our economy has led to a reduced manufacturing output and a smaller share of the world market.

        2.   Other core nations have increased their competitive edge and our dominance has weakened.

MATCHING

A.   POET

B.   First world

C.   Second world

D.   Third world

E.   MAD

F.   Predictions

G.   Diffusion

H.   HSI

I.   Development

J.   Core societies

K.   Conflict functionalism

L.   Technology

M.   World system theory

N.   Modernization theory

O.   Peripheral Societies

_____ 1. The tools used to solve problems.

_____ 2. Development is a natural, evolutionary process.

_____ 3. Sees the international economic system through Marxist eyes.

_____ 4. United States and Western Europe.

_____ 5. Dominant strategy of both super powers.

_____ 6. The Soviet Bloc Nations.

_____ 7. The connectedness of environments and institutions.

_____ 8. Increasing productivity and living standards.

_____ 9. Criteria used to assess human suffering.

_____ 10. Coffee plantations of Brazil and Uganda.

FILL IN THE BLANK QUESTIONS

1. The effectiveness of _____ requires massive arsenals on both sides and a willingness to engage in _____ behavior.

2. The _____ strategy is based upon the idea that a winnable nuclear war is impossible.

3. More than two-thirds of the world's population live in countries with extreme or high measures of _____ _____.

4. The interrelationships within a complex natural and social environment is called the _____.

5. In the future we can expect that _____, as well as new forms of education, government, and economy will demand a readjustment of our social and physical environments.

6. _____ is an important source of change, but it is seldom an independent source of change.

7. The process of increasing the productivity and standard of living of a society is called _____.

8. _____ theory sees development as a natural evolutionary process.

9. On a global basis _____ operates with less restraint than it does within any single nation.

10. _____ _____ _____ theory is a conflict analysis of the economic relationships between developed and undeveloped countries.

11. The _____ world includes the U.S., the _____ world includes the U.S.S.R. and the _____ world includes the undeveloped nations.

12. The _____ _____ are aimed at ridding society of low productivity associated with the "iron rice bowl" system.

13. In _____ agrarian land reform has emphasized cooperatives, state farms, and small plots for individual farmers.

14. Nicaragua aims to develop _____ industries that will manufacture raw materials into _____ goods.

15. The _____ _____ has a bureaucratic, authoritarian government, backed by a strong military and police force which functions to repress individual freedoms.

MULTIPLE CHOICE

1. The E in POET stands for:

    a. Energy.
    b. Ego.
    c. Environment.
    d. Ecosystem.

2. _____ includes the tools that are used to solve problems.

    a. population.
    b. physical environment.
    c. development.
    d. technology.

3. NOT included as a facet of development:

    a. productivity.
    b. life expectancy.
    c. education.
    d. military power.

4. _____ societies dominate the world system.

    a. Peripheral.
    b. European.
    c. Third world.
    d. Core.

5. This has replaced the "iron rice bowl" system in China:

    a. wooden bowl system.
    b. system of private land ownership.
    c. individual responsibility system.
    d. system of equality for all.

6. In world system theory, core societies are:

    a. members of the United Nations.
    b. rich and powerful nations that are economically diversified and free of outside control.
    c. poor and weak nations that have highly specialized economies over which they have little control.
    d. attempting to modernize by following the path of Western industrialization.

7. Included in the First World:

    a. U.S., Japan, Western Europe.
    b. U.S., Japan, China.
    c. Japan, China, Russia.
    d. U.S., China, Japan.

8. Countries that would like to duplicate China's "four modern-izations" would emphasize:

    a. agriculture, science, industry, defense.
    b. religion, education, science, defense.
    c. large families, science, education, defense.
    d. social services, sciences, sports, education.

9. Which of the following is NOT a Third World country?

    a. West Germany.
    b. China.
    c. Zambia.
    d. Nicaragua.

10. If a political candidate in a developing country calls for a "Great Leap Forward" comparable to the one in China, he/she seeks:

    a. better athletic programs.
    b. decentralized planning.
    c. war with the weakest neighbor.
    d. more exports.

11. The Soviet Union states that it is for "liberation" of Third World countries. This means they are for:

    a. liberation from capitalism.
    b. political democracy.
    c. equality for all countries.
    d. a stronger United Nations.

12. What percent of the world's population lives in countries
     ranked as high or extreme on the human suffering index?

     a. 20 percent.
     b. 44 percent.
     c. 67 percent.
     d. 85 percent.

13. The major cause of social change according to Marx was:

     a. the economy.
     b. government.
     c. education.
     d. the family.

14. The primary reason that less-developed countries have not
     followed the developed countries footsteps to modernization
     is because:

     a. they face a different ecosystem.
     b. they were initially too backward.
     c. of corrupt governments.
     d. they have inadequate motivation.

15. The prevailing ideology that supports the world systems
     division of labor is:

     a. socialism.
     b. communism.
     c. capitalism.
     d. modernization.

16. Which is NOT an element of modernization theory?

     a. simple to complex societies.
     b. development as a natural unfolding of evolutionary
         process.
     c. exploitation by industrial core.
     d. structural-functional theory.

17. The chief actors in the world system's free market economy
     are:

     a. the educated elite.
     b. military leaders.
     c. small business managers.
     d. nation-states.

18. The assumption that developing nations can follow the Western path to wealth through industrialization is basic to:

    a. world system theory.
    b. conflict theory.
    c. third world development theory.
    d. modernization theory.

19. The percent of world energy used and percent of gross world product produced by the Second World is:

    a. 50 percent.
    b. 80 percent.
    c. 65 percent.
    d. 25 percent.

20. The estimated population of China, the largest Third World country, is:

    a. one billion.
    b. fifty million.
    c. five hundred million.
    d. ten billion.

21. Soldiers from this country occupied Nicaragua from 1912 to 1933:

    a. Germany.
    b. U.S.
    c. France.
    d. Spain.

22. Nicaragua's development plan calls for:

    a. aid to the contras.
    b. increased exports of raw materials.
    c. development of secondary industries.
    d. an embargo on U.S. goods and services.

23. The largest country in the First or Second Worlds is:

    a. Russia.
    b. China.
    c. Canada.
    d. U.S.

24. According to your text, all of the following are reasons why the less developed nations have NOT followed the Western path to modernization EXCEPT:

    a. they are latecomers to the world market.
    b. they don't have the right cultural values.
    c. they face a different ecosystem.
    d. they have greater population pressure.

25. A sociologist with a POET perspective would expect increased mechanization of agriculture to affect:

    a. population, organization, and environment.
    b. population and environment.
    c. environment only.
    d. organization only.

26. In the past, without much considering the consequences, we have been able to rather easily change the environment. Evidence now suggests that:

    a. further changes are impossible.
    b. our advanced technology frees us from environmental considerations.
    c. there are limitations to the physical environment.
    d. the environment has been irreparably damaged.

27. Which of the following are associated with development?

    a. longer life, better diet, better education.
    b. higher morals, better diet, longer life.
    c. democracy, better education, better housing.
    d. fewer consumer goods, traditional gender roles.

28. A negative effect of dependence on economies of Third World countries is that dependence:

    a. stimulates the production of manufactured goods.
    b. produces a small, local elite.
    c. expands the middle class.
    d. stimulates local investment of surplus capital.

29. The HSI is positively correlated with:

    a. life expectancy.
    b. GNP per capita.
    c. percentage of labor force in agriculture.
    d. cars per capita.

30. According to your text, China currently has a _____
    economic system and a(n) _____ political
    system.

    a. capitalist/authoritarian.
    b. capitalist/democratic.
    c. socialist/authoritarian.
    d. socialist/democratic.

ESSAY QUESTIONS

1. Discuss how an ecosystem functions.

2. Explain the meaning behind the acronym POET.

3. Describe the relationship between population and social
    change.

4.   How might modernization theory be seen as ethnocentric?

5.   Describe the basic assumption of world system theory.

CHAPTER 1

MATCHING

1.	H	p. 16		5.	J	p. 20		8.	L	p. 15
2.	G	p. 14		6.	C	p. 10		9.	E	p. 13
3.	I	p. 19		7.	F	p. 20		10.	A	p. 8
4.	D	p. 11								

FILL IN THE BLANK

1. Positivism p. 8
2. thesis, antithesis, synthesis p. 10
3. Verstehen sociology p. 12
4. manifest p. 21
5. disorganization, poverty p. 8
6. poverty, alienation p. 9
7. Weber, Marx's p. 12
8. University of Chicago, Albion Small p. 13
9. definition of the situation p. 14
10. Stability, harmony p. 16
11. functions, dysfunctions p. 17
12. macro, micro p. 24
13. symbolic interaction p. 21
14. sociological imagination p. 5
15. critical, systematic p. 7

MULTIPLE CHOICE

1.	a,	4		16.	c,	16
2.	c,	5		17.	d,	12
3.	b,	8		18.	c,	16
4.	d,	9		19.	a,	8
5.	a,	6		20.	d,	13
6.	a,	13		21.	a,	13
7.	b,	4		22.	c,	25
8.	d,	5		23.	b,	8
9.	a,	11		24.	d,	12
10.	b,	14		25.	a,	5
11.	a,	14		26.	d,	25
12.	a,	16		27.	b,	7
13.	a,	20		28.	a,	7
14.	b,	19		29.	a,	12
15.	a,	18		30.	b,	11

ANSWER KEY

CHAPTER 2

MATCHING

1.	H	p. 31	5.	B	p. 36		8.	K	p. 53
2.	G	p. 33	6.	N	p. 37		9.	F	p. 32
3.	O	p. 37	7.	M	p. 37		10.	I	p. 38
4.	A	p. 38							

FILL IN THE BLANK

1. common sense p. 30
2. replication p. 40
3. description, explanation p. 30
4. data, theory p. 32
5. probability p. 34
6. incidence, trends, differentials p. 37
7. Interviewing, participating, observing p. 39
8. participant observation p. 39
9. sporadic, episodic p. 46
10. manly flaws p. 48
11. lone, known p. 51
12. experiment p. 37
13. operational definition p. 33
14. Incidence p. 37
15. decreased p. 44

MULTIPLE CHOICE

1.	a,	30		16.	d,	39
2.	a,	35		17.	d,	41
3.	c,	33		18.	a,	30
4.	b,	33		19.	c,	30
5.	d,	38		20.	d,	36
6.	c,	37		21.	b,	45
7.	a,	32		22.	c,	46
8.	c,	33		23.	a,	51
9.	c,	33		24.	a,	39
10.	c,	45		25.	c,	32
11.	c,	42		26.	a,	39
12.	a,	37		27.	c,	37
13.	a,	34		28.	c,	38
14.	c,	36		29.	b,	42
15.	b,	38		30.	b,	43

CHAPTER 3

MATCHING

1.	K	p. 59	5.	N	p. 78	8.	E	p. 79
2.	M	p. 65	6.	A	p. 60	9.	L	p. 62
3.	G	p. 61	7.	H	p. 70	10.	F	p. 70
4.	J	p. 73						

FILL IN THE BLANK

1. culture   p. 73
2. linguistic relativity hypothesis   p. 60
3. dominant cultural theme   p. 80
4. sanctions   p. 64
5. symbol   p. 60
6. mores   p. 62
7. material culture   p. 59
8. language   p. 73
9. countercultures, subcultures   pp. 69-70
10. Sociobiology   p. 72
11. ethnocentric   p. 76
12. self fulfillment   p. 68

MULTIPLE CHOICE

1.	a,	59	16.	b,	73
2.	c,	62	17.	c,	76
3.	b,	64	18.	a,	75
4.	c,	73	19.	a,	66
5.	d,	75	20.	d,	70
6.	b,	60	21.	a,	80
7.	c,	62	22.	a,	81
8.	b,	64	23.	b,	74
9.	d,	70	24.	c,	81
10.	a,	76	25.	d,	64
11.	a,	69	26.	c,	64
12.	b,	69	27.	b,	68
13.	a,	61	28.	a,	64
14.	a,	78	29.	b,	76
15.	d,	70	30.	c,	64

ANSWER KEY

CHAPTER 4

MATCHING

1.	F p. 96	5.	I p. 86	8.	H p. 102
2.	D p. 91	6.	L p. 91	9.	N p. 88
3.	G p. 90	7.	J p. 98	10.	O p. 99
4.	K p. 93				

FILL IN THE BLANK

1. consumers, producers pp. 104-105
2. competition, conflict p. 87
3. agriculture p. 100
4. structured social interaction p. 86
5. stable social structures p. 105
6. norm of reciprocity p. 86
7. role strain p. 91
8. basic human problems p. 93
9. Cooperation p. 87
10. interdependence p. 98
11. social structure p. 106
12. surplus p. 99

MULTIPLE CHOICE

1.	a, 94	16.	d, 93
2.	d, 89	17.	c, 99
3.	c, 90	18.	a, 96
4.	c, 93	19.	a, 103
5.	b, 99	20.	d, 94
6.	d, 91	21.	c, 97
7.	b, 86	22.	b, 100
8.	a, 91	23.	a, 101
9.	d, 87	24.	c, 103
10.	c, 88	25.	b, 87
11.	c, 90	26.	d, 95
12.	b, 93	27.	c, 88
13.	c, 101	28.	d, 88
14.	a, 96	29.	b, 94
15.	b, 99	30.	c, 98

CHAPTER 5

MATCHING I

1.	E	p. 120	5.	I	p. 124	8.	C	p. 114
2.	K	pp. 113-14	6.	D	p. 117	9.	B	p. 225
3.	G	p. 116	7.	N	p. 110	10.	M	p. 117
4.	H	p. 114						

MATCHING II

1.	E	p. 126	5.	O	p. 118	8.	A	p. 125
2.	J	pp. 123-24	6.	G	p. 128	9.	K	p. 118
3.	B	p. 123	7.	C	p. 123	10.	H	p. 125
4.	M	p. 128						

FILL IN THE BLANK

1. secondary groups p. 117
2. bureaucracy p. 125
3. size p. 111
4. efficiency p. 126
5. voluntary associations p. 120
6. interaction, turnover p. 113
7. social structure, dependency p. 110
8. exclusion p. 113
9. behavior, perceptions and values p. 111
10. expressive activity p. 117
11. social cohesion p. 112
12. all channel network p. 112

MULTIPLE CHOICE

1.	b,	113	16.	d,	117
2.	a,	114	17.	a,	124
3.	b,	118	18.	b,	124
4.	a,	123	19.	d,	112
5.	c,	127	20.	c,	116
6.	c,	117	21.	b,	118
7.	b,	110	22.	a,	121
8.	b,	114	23.	b,	122
9.	b,	114	24.	d,	117
10.	a,	123	25.	b,	110
11.	a,	118	26.	c,	114
12.	c,	118	27.	d,	116
13.	c,	120	28.	a,	117
14.	c,	123	29.	d,	124
15.	c,	124	30.	d,	113

ANSWER KEY

CHAPTER 6

MATCHING I

1.	C	p. 149	5.	J	p. 137	8.	F	p. 146
2.	D	p. 154	6.	I	p. 140	9.	B	p. 140
3.	G	pp. 139-40	7.	E	p. 138	10.	H	p. 153
4.	A	p. 140						

MATCHING II

1.	C	p. 148	5.	M	p. 141	8.	G	p. 136
2.	E	p. 140	6.	K	p. 136	9.	H	pp. 139-40
3.	L	p. 141	7.	N	p. 143	10.	D	p. 149
4.	A	p. 144						

FILL IN THE BLANK

1. Identity salience hierarchy p. 143
2. structural p. 141
3. personality, socialization p. 136
4. significant others p. 140
5. developmental p. 146
6. personality, role p. 147
7. generalized other p. 141
8. interaction p. 139
9. role identities p. 141
10. Anticipatory socialization p. 148
11. motivations, socially desirable p. 136
12. socialization p. 136

MULTIPLE CHOICE

1.	b,	138	16.	b,	141
2.	c,	136	17.	d,	148
3.	d,	139	18.	c,	141
4.	a,	147	19.	b,	138
5.	a,	150	20.	a,	139
6.	d,	136	21.	b,	149
7.	a,	136	22.	d,	140
8.	a,	139	23.	a,	154
9.	a,	143	24.	c,	154
10.	d,	148	25.	c,	138
11.	a,	142	26.	c,	141
12.	a,	141	27.	a,	144
13.	a,	137	28.	d,	142
14.	d,	139	29.	b,	148
15.	c,	146	30.	a,	149

CHAPTER 7

MATCHING

1.	D	p. 167
2.	I	p. 174
3.	A	p. 175
4.	L	p. 171

5.	C	p. 174
6.	F	p. 175
7.	K	p. 166

8.	G	p. 174
9.	J	p. 162
10.	N	p. 174

FILL IN THE BLANK

1. social status p. 162
2. dialectic p. 164
3. Thick description p. 164
4. keying p. 167
5. Altercasting p. 168
6. nonverbal cues p. 169
7. shared relevance p. 173
8. break experiments p. 173
9. accounts and disclaimers pp. 174–75
10. withdrawing, pass, denying p. 176

MULTIPLE CHOICE

1.	d,	161
2.	c,	164
3.	a,	166
4.	a,	173
5.	d,	174
6.	b,	164
7.	a,	163
8.	a,	168
9.	a,	169
10.	b,	170
11.	a,	174
12.	c,	168
13.	b,	162
14.	c,	163
15.	b,	169

16.	c,	171
17.	d,	172
18.	b,	160
19.	d,	160
20.	d,	169
21.	a,	176
22.	b,	178
23.	d,	179
24.	d,	182
25.	a,	161
26.	a,	175
27.	b,	176
28.	d,	165
29.	c,	182
30.	c,	171

ANSWER KEY

CHAPTER 8

MATCHING I

1.	G	p. 198	5.	D	p. 197	8.	C	p. 201
2.	L	p. 204	6.	H	p. 201	9.	O	p. 206
3.	B	p. 196	7.	E	p. 197	10.	J	p. 201
4.	K	p. 204						

MATCHING II

1.	G	p. 208	5.	J	p. 208	8.	L	p. 204
2.	N	p. 205	6.	F	p. 207	9.	E	p. 193
3.	A	p. 208	7.	M	p. 208	10.	C	p. 208

FILL IN THE BLANK

1. formal, informal p. 186
2. internalize p. 186
3. nonconformity, deviance p. 187
4. ritualism p. 189
5. differential association, deviance, deviance, conformity
       p. 191
6. control theory p. 191
7. so label p. 192
8. primary deviance p. 192
9. secondary deviance p. 192
10. male, young, minority group members p. 199
11. Lower, middle p. 201
12. alien p. 188
13. deviance p. 189
14. primary deviance p. 193
15. Less p. 194

MULTIPLE CHOICE

1.	a,	186	16.	c,	191
2.	c,	187	17.	c,	191
3.	a,	187	18.	b,	192
4.	c,	192	19.	a,	196
5.	b,	193	20.	d,	197
6.	c,	191	21.	c,	206
7.	b,	186	22.	a,	208
8.	a,	189	23.	a,	206
9.	d,	193	24.	d,	198
10.	a,	196	25.	a,	192
11.	c,	204	26.	d,	198
12.	c,	207	27.	d,	194
13.	a,	189	28.	c,	196
14.	b,	189	29.	b,	199
15.	b,	194	30.	d,	203

CHAPTER 9

MATCHING

1. N p. 216	5. O p. 226	9. G p. 239
2. A p. 217	6. J p. 219	10. L p. 217
3. F p. 217	7. D p. 233	11. I p. 241
4. B p. 218	8. M p. 234	12. C p. 222

FILL IN THE BLANK

1. caste, class pp. 216-17
2. class pp. 216-17
3. False consciousness, class consciousness p. 218
4. class, status, power p. 218
5. rewards, incentives p. 219
6. Structural-functional p. 222
7. Conflict p. 222
8. inequality p. 223
9. inequality, productivity p. 223
10. real income, public services p. 228
11. occupational, individual p. 229
12. indirect inheritance model p. 230
13. achievement motivation, intelligence p. 232
14. Ideology p. 233
15. working class p. 236

MULTIPLE CHOICE

1. c, 216	16. b, 223
2. a, 220	17. c, 243
3. b, 229	18. a, 223
4. d, 230	19. a, 227
5. a, 240	20. d, 226
6. c, 239	21. c, 227
7. d, 225	22. a, 228
8. a, 227	23. b, 235
9. b, 233	24. c, 238
10. d, 238	25. c, 231
11. d, 240	26. a, 218
12. a, 219	27. a, 230
13. a, 217	28. b, 236
14. c, 219	29. b, 236
15. c, 222	30. b, 234

ANSWER KEY

CHAPTER 10

MATCHING I

1.	M	p. 258		5.	L	p. 252		8.	O	p. 252
2.	F	p. 248		6.	K	p. 248		9.	H	p. 253
3.	G	p. 273		7.	J	p. 259		10.	A	p. 256
4.	B	p. 254								

MATCHING II

1.	F	p. 259		5.	K	p. 260		8.	A	p. 264
2.	G	p. 259		6.	D	p. 269		9.	O	p. 267
3.	E	p. 265		7.	B	p. 268		10.	H	p. 264
4.	M	p. 255								

FILL IN THE BLANK

1. social p. 248
2. majority, minority p. 251
3. acculturation p. 252
4. social distance p. 253
5. Prejudice, discrimination p. 256
6. authoritarianism, scapegoating p. 254
7. institutionalized racism p. 257
8. involuntary, earliest p. 260
9. underclass p. 264
10. Jews p. 267
11. unacculturated and unassimilated p. 270
12. blacks p. 273

MULTIPLE CHOICE

1.	b,	248		16.	b,	258
2.	a,	252		17.	b,	254
3.	d,	252		18.	b,	249
4.	b,	256		19.	a,	253
5.	d,	258		20.	b,	257
6.	b,	257		21.	b,	257
7.	d,	253		22.	d,	273
8.	c,	249		23.	c,	260
9.	a,	251		24.	b,	262
10.	c,	252		25.	d,	249
11.	b,	257		26.	b,	259
12.	c,	254		27.	a,	262
13.	b,	253		28.	c,	264
14.	c,	254		29.	b,	267
15.	a,	253		30.	d,	258

CHAPTER 11

MATCHING

1. E   p. 297
2. I   p. 278
3. L   p. 278
4. H   p. 280

5. B   p. 295
6. K   p. 278
7. C   p. 295

8. A   p. 283
9. F   p. 292
10. D   p. 296

FILL IN THE BLANK

1. 35   p. 281
2. childless   p. 281
3. 30, 5   pp. 283-84
4. Men, women   p. 285
5. women, men   p. 291
6. 59   p. 288
7. sex typed   p. 293
8. male   p. 293
9. support, prove   p. 301
10. androgeny   p. 287
11. Pornography   p. 302
12. nurturance, sharing, intuition   p. 297

MULTIPLE CHOICE

1. b,   278
2. d,   278
3. b,   278
4. a,   295
5. b,   294
6. d,   295
7. a,   287
8. a,   280
9. b,   287
10. d,   291
11. a,   296
12. d,   280
13. b,   295
14. a,   293
15. d,   287

16. c,   293
17. b,   296
18. b,   296
19. d,   280
20. a,   282
21. d,   290
22. d,   292
23. c,   284
24. b,   288
25. d,   292
26. b,   287
27. a,   278
28. b,   280
29. a,   283
30. b,   283

ANSWER KEY

CHAPTER 12

MATCHING

1.	F	p. 318		5.	B	p. 311		8.	H	p. 323
2.	J	p. 307		6.	A	p. 307		9.	I	p. 314
3.	M	p. 309		7.	L	p. 310		10.	O	p. 326
4.	C	p. 324								

FILL IN THE BLANK

1. social structure   p. 306
2. cohort   p. 307
3. four   p. 308
4. job, spouse, children   p. 310
5. roleless, absence   p. 311-12
6. health   p. 312
7. youth   p. 313
8. image, demeanor, argot   p. 314
9. 16   p. 316
10. bfoq   p. 318
11. female, minority   p. 319
12. children, elderly   p. 322
13. 8   p. 327
14. mortality cross over   p. 327
15. putting out, militia   p. 315

MULTIPLE CHOICE

1.	b,	307		16.	d,	325
2.	a,	308		17.	b,	323
3.	d,	309		18.	a,	324
4.	a,	311		19.	d,	306
5.	d,	314		20.	d,	308
6.	a,	326		21.	b,	312
7.	d,	306		22.	b,	313
8.	a,	306		23.	a,	314
9.	d,	307		24.	a,	321
10.	d,	321		25.	a,	307
11.	a,	326		26.	c,	310
12.	c,	310		27.	b,	308
13.	a,	318		28.	a,	312
14.	a,	321		29.	c,	313
15.	c,	324		30.	d,	316

CHAPTER 13

MATCHING

1.	I	p. 344	5.	E	p. 349	8.	K	p. 349
2.	F	p. 336	6.	A	p. 336	9.	H	p. 345
3.	G	p. 350	7.	N	p. 343	10.	C	p. 352
4.	L	p. 338						

FILL IN THE BLANK

1. family, kin group   p. 335
2. Marriage   p. 335
3. stepparenting   p. 352
4. personal freedom, economic security   p. 341
5. unmarried   p. 341
6. divorce   p. 341
7. men, women   p. 342
8. cohabitation   p. 346
9. women   p. 348
10. sex   p. 349
11. duty, powerlessness, bargaining tool   p. 350
12. Parenthood   p. 351
13. Higher status   p. 354
14. leave home, release, renewal   p. 352
15. age at marriage   p. 353
16. eventually   p. 341

MULTIPLE CHOICE

1.	a,	335	16.	a,	352
2.	d,	335	17.	c,	345
3.	b,	336	18.	b,	339
4.	c,	336	19.	a,	334
5.	d,	338	20.	b,	335
6.	a,	344	21.	b,	342
7.	d,	336	22.	d,	340
8.	b,	336	23.	b,	341
9.	a,	344	24.	a,	343
10.	b,	345	25.	a,	337
11.	a,	348	26.	c,	338
12.	c,	345	27.	c,	338
13.	b,	344	28.	a,	342
14.	b,	343	29.	a,	346
15.	b,	349	30.	a,	352

ANSWER KEY

CHAPTER 14

MATCHING

1.	O	p. 369		5.	H	p. 365		8.	M	p. 365
2.	D	p. 367		6.	I	p. 377		9.	F	p. 370
3.	C	p. 374		7.	B	p. 363		10.	L	p. 369
4.	A	p. 370								

FILL IN THE BLANK

1. elite, mass, bureaucratization   p. 362
2. moral, religious   p. 362
3. local control, standardization   p. 366
4. inequality   p. 370
5. hidden curriculum   p. 369
6. high ability, low ability   p. 375
7. mental ability, cultural deprivation   p. 373
8. cultural capital   p. 374
9. female, male   p. 378
10. high school   p. 378
11. tolerant, prejudiced, more   p. 382
12. conventional religious preference, partying, liberalism
        p. 382
13. excellence, dropout   p. 383
14. teacher expectations   p. 384
15. workers, citizens   p. 364

MULTIPLE CHOICE

1.	b,	362		16.	b,	370
2.	a,	365		17.	a,	370
3.	b,	367		18.	a,	380
4.	d,	375		19.	b,	363
5.	c,	371		20.	a,	364
6.	b,	374		21.	b,	363
7.	c,	362		22.	d,	370
8.	c,	370		23.	c,	383
9.	b,	370		24.	c,	380
10.	a,	369		25.	d,	365
11.	d,	380		26.	a,	375
12.	d,	380		27.	a,	366
13.	b,	369		28.	a,	373
14.	d,	369		29.	b,	384
15.	c,	367		30.	c,	377

CHAPTER 15

MATCHING

1. E p. 401
2. F p. 388
3. I p. 395
4. C p. 389

5. M p. 399
6. K p. 388
7. A p. 409

8. O p. 390
9. B p. 399
10. N p. 403

FILL IN THE BLANK

1. Power, coercion p. 388
2. rational-legal authority p. 389
3. Authority p. 390
4. jurisdiction, coercion p. 391
5. police power, taxation, armed force pp. 392-93
6. democracies p. 393
7. authoritarianism p. 394
8. winner take all rule p. 396
9. power elite p. 401
10. conflict/dialectic p. 403
11. social class p. 407
12. age p. 408
13. white, professional p. 409
14. independent p. 397
15. social choice p. 409

MULTIPLE CHOICE

1. c, 388
2. c, 388
3. b, 388
4. b, 396
5. b, 401
6. d, 399
7. b, 389
8. a, 390
9. d, 391
10. a, 401
11. d, 402
12. a, 394
13. a, 393
14. c, 399
15. c, 404

16. a, 404
17. b, 402
18. b, 401
19. b, 392
20. d, 408
21. a, 402
22. d, 406
23. a, 408
24. d, 397
25. b, 391
26. a, 403
27. a, 394
28. a, 397
29. d, 409
30. a, 406

CHAPTER 16

MATCHING

1. J p. 419
2. A p. 435
3. I p. 429
4. O p. 418

5. B p. 429
6. H p. 417
7. C p. 429

8. D p. 418
9. F pp. 425-26
10. L p. 422

FILL IN THE BLANK

1. preindustrial p. 416
2. primary, secondary p. 418
3. tertiary sector, primary, secondary p. 418
4. Capitalism, socialism pp. 419-20
5. socialism p. 420
6. public schools p. 422
7. Communism p. 421
8. size, interlocking directorates p. 423
9. industrial core, periphery p. 427
10. unemployment p. 428
11. pink collar p. 429
12. working class p. 431
13. false consciousness p. 433
14. intrinsic, extrinsic p. 432
15. deskilling, displacement, supervision p. 436

MULTIPLE CHOICE

1. a, 416
2. a, 419
3. c, 421
4. b, 429
5. b, 432
6. b, 422
7. c, 416
8. d, 418
9. a, 427
10. c, 422
11. d, 423
12. c, 433
13. a, 418
14. c, 418
15. c, 419

16. b, 421
17. d, 438
18. d, 421
19. a, 432
20. a, 421
21. b, 423
22. b, 422
23. a, 425
24. b, 427
25. c, 418
26. c, 418
27. b, 418
28. c, 430
29. a, 425
30. c, 427

CHAPTER 17

MATCHING

1. L   p. 444
2. O   p. 447
3. N   p. 450
4. M   p. 458

5. B   p. 449
6. G   p. 444
7. I   p. 450

8. D   p. 445
9. C   p. 452
10. E   p. 453

FILL IN THE BLANK

1. sacred, profane, beliefs, rituals   p. 444
2. change   p. 446
3. wealth   p. 447
4. Marx, Durkheim   p. 449
5. Ecclesiae, sects   p. 449
6. church-like   p. 450
7. church, sect   pp. 448-49
8. fervor, affiliation   p. 462
9. church-like, sects, cults   p. 461
10. conservative   p. 462
11. Civil religion   p. 460
12. Fundamentalism   p. 463
13. decrease, dropped   pp. 462-63
14. New Christian Right   p. 465
15. raise money   p. 466

MULTIPLE CHOICE

1. b,   442
2. c,   444
3. b,   458
4. a,   463
5. c,   465
6. b,   448
7. a,   442
8. c,   446
9. a,   446
10. a,   453
11. d,   452
12. c,   453
13. c,   442
14. a,   444
15. b,   447

16. c,   445
17. a,   466
18. c,   448
19. b,   457
20. d,   457
21. d,   458
22. c,   461
23. c,   458
24. b,   446
25. b,   450
26. d,   450
27. a,   462
28. b,   460
29. b,   462
30. c,   444

ANSWER KEY

CHAPTER 18

MATCHING

1.	D	p. 477	5.	L	p. 483	8.	O	p. 484
2.	C	p. 494	6.	J	p. 477	9.	N	p. 485
3.	F	p. 483	7.	H	p. 479	10.	B	p. 477
4.	A	p. 476						

FILL IN THE BLANK

1. television p. 475
2. United States p. 476
3. reinforces p. 482
4. integrity, honesty, empathy p. 478
5. owners, coaches, advertisers, athletes p. 481
6. religious, scientific p. 483
7. dominant values and social structures p. 483
8. profession, employer p. 487
9. medicaid p. 494
10. little, big p. 487
11. sick role p. 495
12. illness p. 490
13. professionalization, institutionalization p. 491
14. playful, organized, corporate pp. 475-76
15. knowledge, institution p. 492
16. fee for service p. 494

MULTIPLE CHOICE

1.	c,	474	16.	d,	489
2.	a,	474	17.	b,	495
3.	d,	475	18.	a,	491
4.	c,	483	19.	d,	474
5.	c,	483	20.	d,	474
6.	b,	490	21.	b,	475
7.	c,	474	22.	b,	480
8.	b,	479	23.	a,	491
9.	b,	480	24.	a,	483
10.	b,	484	25.	a,	477
11.	d,	485	26.	d,	492
12.	c,	479	27.	a,	478
13.	c,	474	28.	a,	489
14.	b,	475	29.	a,	493
15.	a,	481	30.	b,	483

CHAPTER 19

MATCHING

1. F   p. 505
2. C   p. 504
3. M   p. 510
4. N   p. 516

5. K   p. 505
6. J   p. 508
7. D   pp. 511-13

8. E   p. 504
9. H   p. 504
10. O   p. 524

FILL IN THE BLANK

1. less   p. 503
2. values, aspirations   p. 506
3. standard of living   p. 505
4. younger   pp. 509-10
5. small   p. 511
6. individual, societal   p. 513
7. state, community   p. 517
8. gender roles, family   p. 515
9. costs, rewards   p. 515
10. fatherless   p. 522
11. fallen   p. 522
12. infectious diseases   p. 522
13. fertility, mortality, migration   p. 522
14. low wage, low skill   p. 526
15. zero population growth   p. 524

MULTIPLE CHOICE

1. d,   502
2. a,   503
3. a,   520
4. b,   522
5. d,   524
6. c,   511
7. c,   504
8. c,   505
9. b,   505
10. b,   510
11. b,   503
12. c,   524
13. c,   506
14. a,   508
15. d,   508

16. c,   517
17. d,   506
18. d,   505
19. b,   502
20. a,   503
21. d,   503
22. b,   507
23. a,   519
24. d,   514
25. c,   503
26. d,   523
27. d,   508
28. c,   516
29. d,   519
30. b,   520

CHAPTER 20

MATCHING

1. P p. 540
2. E p. 532
3. I p. 551
4. L p. 548

5. C p. 535
6. A p. 533
7. H p. 539

8. J p. 533
9. B p. 541
10. M p. 537

FILL IN THE BLANK

1. last p. 530
2. birthrate, deathrate p. 531
3. manufacturing, immobile p. 533
4. World War II, federal government p. 534
5. cities p. 539
6. manageable, knowable p. 541
7. attracted to, created by p. 541
8. lonely, alienated, estranged p. 542
9. unlikely p. 543
10. nearby, emotionally close p. 543
11. pathologies p. 545
12. disintegrated p. 551
13. Mexico City p. 538
14. political and economic p. 550
15. live, work p. 547

MULTIPLE CHOICE

1. a, 531
2. c, 531
3. b, 535
4. b, 539
5. b, 542
6. d, 539
7. b, 538
8. a, 538
9. a, 540
10. b, 545
11. c, 548
12. a, 541
13. d, 534
14. a, 535
15. a, 540

16. d, 539
17. c, 540
18. d, 538
19. a, 537
20. c, 538
21. a, 542
22. b, 546
23. b, 536
24. d, 532
25. c, 531
26. a, 544
27. a, 537
28. c, 539
29. a, 549
30. d, 546

CHAPTER 21

MATCHING

1. A p. 557
2. I p. 570
3. M p. 556
4. N p. 566

5. F p. 565
6. O p. 558
7. J p. 556

8. C p. 566
9. B p. 561
10. L p. 568

FILL IN THE BLANK

1. contagion p. 557
2. convergence p. 558
3. emergent norm p. 559
4. emergent norm p. 561
5. limit mobilization, reduce solidarity p. 578
6. frame alignment pp. 568-69
7. publicizing events, demonstrating techniques, providing rationales p. 576
8. relative deprivation p. 564
9. resource mobilization p. 566
10. Counter movements p. 570
11. Mobilization p. 570
12. Media coverage p. 576
13. homosexuality p. 575
14. media stars p. 577
15. left, right p. 578

MULTIPLE CHOICE

1. b, 556
2. b, 556
3. a, 561
4. c, 556
5. c, 556
6. b, 570
7. d, 556
8. a, 560
9. a, 556
10. c, 565
11. a, 573
12. c, 558
13. a, 557
14. a, 558
15. a, 558

16. d, 565
17. a, 565
18. b, 564
19. b, 575
20. d, 561
21. c, 568
22. a, 578
23. d, 575
24. c, 574
25. c, 578
26. a, 563
27. d, 565
28. d, 564
29. a, 565
30. a, 567

ANSWER KEY

CHAPTER 22

MATCHING

1. L p. 585	5. E p. 603	8. I p. 585
2. N p. 585	6. C p. 590	9. H p. 588
3. M p. 587	7. A p. 585	10. O p. 590
4. B p. 590		

FILL IN THE BLANK

1. MAD, MAD p. 603
2. MAD p. 603
3. human suffering p. 588
4. ecosystem p. 582
5. ideologies p. 583
6. Technology p. 584
7. development p. 585
8. Modernization p. 585
9. capitalism p. 587
10. World system p. 587
11. first, second, third pp. 590-91
12. four modernizations p. 594
13. Nicaragua p. 596
14. secondary, export p. 597
15. Soviet Union p. 598

MULTIPLE CHOICE

1. c, 582	16. c, 585
2. d, 584	17. d, 587
3. d, 585	18. d, 585
4. d, 587	19. d, 590
5. c, 594	20. a, 592
6. b, 587	21. b, 595
7. a, 590	22. c, 597
8. a, 594	23. a, 597
9. a, 590	24. b, 586
10. b, 592	25. a, 582
11. a, 602	26. c, 584
12. c, 588	27. a, 585
13. a, 583	28. b, 590
14. a, 586	29. c, 598
15. c, 587	30. c, 592